The Percu. Guide to Injury Treatment and Prevention

The Percussionists' Guide to Injury Treatment and Prevention

The Answer Guide for Drummers in Pain

Dr. Darin "Dutch" Workman

Routledge
Taylor & Francis Group
New York   London

Routledge is an imprint of the
Taylor & Francis Group, an informa business

Routledge
Taylor & Francis Group
270 Madison Avenue
New York, NY 10016

Routledge
Taylor & Francis Group
2 Park Square
Milton Park, Abingdon
Oxon OX14 4RN

© 2006 by Taylor and Francis Group, LLC
Routledge is an imprint of Taylor & Francis Group, an Informa business

Printed in the United States of America on acid-free paper
10 9 8 7 6 5 4 3 2 1

International Standard Book Number-10: 0-415-97685-5 (Softcover) 0-415-97684-7 (Hardcover)
International Standard Book Number-13: 978-0-415-97685-5 (Softcover) 978-0-415-97684-8 (Hardcover)

Visit the Taylor & Francis Web site at
http://www.taylorandfrancis.com

and the Routledge Web site at
http://www.routledge-ny.com

CONTENTS

Contents

LIST OF INJURIES

FOOT AND ANKLE

KNEE

HIP AND PELVIS

LOWER BACK AND ABDOMEN

ACKNOWLEDGMENTS

I would like to thank all of those without whose help this work would not be possible. The top of the list is my wife, Christine, for all of her honest opinions, endless help in writing and creating, and straightforward advice. Next are our children Stephen, Monica, Andrea, Tara, and Drew for their patience and enthusiasm to have me follow my passion.

I would also like to extend my sincere appreciation to the following for their support, counsel, and advice on this project: SABIAN cymbals; Drum Workshop drums and hardware; Vic Firth sticks; Ronald Killian, DPM; Camille Goff, MD; David Cunningham, Ph.D. (professor, Audiology Division, Department of Surgery, University of Louisville School of Medicine); Toni Hauser; my office staff; Ray Dillard; Joe Porcaro; Ralph Humphrey; Percussive Arts Society; Rick Mattingly; Ortho-McNeil Pharmaceutical, Inc.; Anatomical Chart Company; Lippincott Williams & Wilkins; Lake Houston YMCA; Rex and Karen Wilcken; Cheryl Castle (proofing many, many times); Rose Workman; and Chet Duboe.

Most important, thank you to the many musicians around the world who have conversed with me about playing-related injuries. You are the ones who shaped the book, and you are the ones for whom I wrote it. I hope that the information enables you to continue expressing your inner self musically for many years to come.

I would also like to express my appreciation to the many who took a personal interest in this book by reading the early copies and giving their endorsement (listed in alphabetical order):

Alex Acuna
John Beck
John Beck Jr.
Louis Belleson
Remo Belli
Joe Bergamini
John Best

Gary Cook
Chet Duboe
Dom Famularo
Vic Firth
Mark Ford
Robert Friedman
Camille Goff, MD

Acknowledgments

Terri Haley
Mike Harris, MD
Ralph Humphrey
David Jenson, DPM
Bruno Kalani
Ronald Killian, DPM
Don Lombardi
Matt Marucci
Brian Mason

Rick Mattingly
John McKinney
Sean Paddock
Joe Porcaro
Emil Richards
Frank Shaffer
Blake Wilckens
Jay A. Workman, DC

All photos were exposed by Christine M. Workman and Dr. Darin Workman at Kingwood Photographers Studio. Many thanks to Ernest Loera "Ochoa" for his kind help. Dr. Workman's biography photograph was taken by Allen Hauser.

All illustrations are by Dr. Darin W. Workman unless otherwise indicated.

INTRODUCTION

As music has evolved, the demands on the drummer/percussionist have increased. Today's player must have increasingly more speed, power, control, and endurance to accurately express the music. Because of this, injuries to the musician have become more common. With just one use, the player will find that this book will pay for itself in money saved from lost gigs, injury, doctors' visits, or pain medication.

In my years of treating drumming/percussion injuries, I have discovered that by the time the patient comes to me for treatment, the injury has been there so long that it is extremely difficult (if not impossible) to fully cure.

In almost every case, if the musician had done some very simple things, such as preventative (or early) care, the injury would never have become a serious issue.

This book is designed to help in that early prevention and treatment. *It is not a substitute for the clinical diagnosis and care a doctor can give you*, but it should help you treat the injury in its early stages before it becomes a large problem. Every injury in this book is accompanied by a section that explains when to seek a doctor's advice and suggests what kind of doctor to see. Allied health care practitioners are also mentioned.

There are many injured musicians who have contacted me in recent years seeking help. Those whom I was able to work with the way I needed to got better. Unfortunately, many times, if I can't work with them, I can't heal them.

If the suggestions given in this book don't get you results within a few weeks, or in the time mentioned for that particular injury, see your personal physician (medical doctor, doctor of osteopathy, doctor of chiropractic, etc.) immediately for an examination. Thinking that an injury or illness will just magically go away if you ignore it is dangerous. Chances are, your injury is something that can be cured easily if it is dealt with early on.

It has been said that an ounce of prevention is worth a pound of cure. This book is aimed at those who already suffer from an injury and need help. For musicians who don't like to see doctors, this will give you some self-help ideas. I cannot guarantee that following the guidelines will heal you, but I can assure you that these guidelines will get you going in the right direction.

Our hope is to help drummers become more savvy and intelligent about dealing with injuries. I hope that through my book, the new generation of drummers/percussionists can become more highly educated in all things having to do with the instruments they play—including their bodies (the most important instruments of all).

CHAPTER 1

THE PURPOSE AND PROPER USE OF THIS BOOK

The Percussionists' Guide to Injury Treatment and Prevention discusses injuries that come about as a result of improper ergonomics (positions, postures, and movements that are most efficient for the body) and biomechanics (ways the body is designed to move) during drumming. It begins by explaining basic human anatomy and biomechanics. The next step discusses basic concepts on how injury occurs (a very important concept in using the remainder of the book). All of this knowledge prepares the reader for the practical use of the remainder of the text. Many photographs and illustrations are used to help the reader understand the text.

This knowledge will enable the drummer/percussionist to achieve a higher level of music making through efficient movement, injury prevention, and healing.

HOW TO USE THIS BOOK

The bulk of this book deals with identifying and resolving injury. It is designed to be easy to use and understand. Here's how to use it:

1. Read the first three chapters first to better understand basic body and injury concepts.
2. Look in the Contents for the area of your body that hurts (wrist, knee, lower back, etc.) and turn to that section.
3. Read the symptoms and signs at the top of each page until you find the one that best describes what you are feeling.
4. The rest of the page will describe the injury, its cause, and how to help and prevent it.
5. Definitions of unfamiliar terms can be found in the Glossary at the end of the book.

The injuries in this book follow the basic outline shown below. I have explained in parentheses what each of the headings means so you can better understand how to treat them.

REGIONAL ANATOMY (ILLUSTRATIONS)

This section is found at the *beginning of each chapter* to teach you the general information on that area of the body and to get you in the right neighborhood.

INJURY OUTLINE

SIGNS AND SYMPTOMS

This section is found at the beginning of each injury section and lists the aches, pains, and anything else one may feel because of this particular ailment. If you are feeling these symptoms, this may be your injury. Keep in mind that more than one injury may have these symptoms. The more symptoms in this category that you have, the more sure you can be that you are on the right page.

NAME OF INJURY

This section gives the common name or street name of the injury. Technical names may be in parentheses.

DESCRIPTION

This section tells you what is wrong with the body for this injury.

CAUSE

This section tells you what most commonly causes this injury to occur.

TREATMENT

Immediate Relief

This section describes the first thing you should do to relieve the *immediate pain*. You will most likely need to do something more (found later) to *heal the injury*.

PREVENTION

Technique

If you hurt while you play, or shortly thereafter, chances are that something in your playing is causing your problem. If this is the case, you should pay close attention to the suggestions in this section, because they can help you remove the cause of the injury.

Stretches

This section tells you which stretches will help rid yourself of the injury—if any. Most of the stretches are found at the end of that chapter and are referenced only there. *Look them up and do them*.

Exercises

This section is for injuries that exercises can help and prevent. Most of the exercises are listed in Appendix B. The exercises are very important: *Look them up and do them.*

IF NO RELIEF

This section gives further suggestions about what to do if you follow these guidelines and your condition doesn't improve.

PROGNOSIS

This section explains how bad the injury that you might have is and the chances of full or partial recovery.

OTHER POSSIBILITIES

This section lists other injury possibilities in case this injury is not the right one.

DIGGING A LITTLE DEEPER

This area suggests sections in Appendix C that offer interesting facts about the injury.

RELATED AREAS

This section is found at the *end of each chapter*. Sometimes injuries to one area of the body may be caused by problems in another area. So, if you don't find your symptoms in a particular chapter, look in the chapter concerning one of those related areas.

This book should give drummers of any level the ability to deal with most injuries they encounter. More important, it will arm them with the knowledge to avoid further occurrences.

CHAPTER 2

BASIC ANATOMY PRINCIPLES

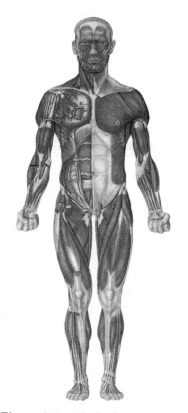

Figure 2.1 The body in "anatomical position." This is the position we use when we describe parts of the body (Anatomical Chart Company, Lippincott Williams & Wilkins 2003).

To understand injuries and their prevention, one must first learn some basic parts of the body and their functions. The following is just a basic description of the body and its functions so the reader can understand the injury portion of this book more thoroughly.

THE BODY ... IN GENERAL

When scientists refer to the body, or any part of it, they describe it in anatomical position. This position looks like the illustration in Figure 2.1. We refer to anatomical position because there is a definite front and back, top and bottom, and lateral and medial view. This is universal, meaning that everyone in the world uses the same position when describing the anatomical position. If you use this description, any level of scientist will understand you.

Below are the basic relative directions of the body:

Anterior: the front of the body, including the face, chest, palms of the hands, and tops of the feet

Posterior: the back of the body, including the back of the hands and the soles of the feet

Lateral: to the side of the center of the body—right or left

Medial: toward the midline or center of the body

Cephalad: toward the head

Caudad: toward the tail end (or tailbone in humans)

RELATIVE TERMS

Superior to: above something else (e.g., the head is superior to the chest)

Inferior to: below something else (e.g., the chest is inferior to the head)

Proximal to: close to the midline, or closer to the midline than another object (e.g., the elbow is more proximal to the shoulder than the wrist is)

Distal to: distant from the midline or in relation to something else (e.g., the wrist is more distal to the shoulder than the elbow is)

HOW THE BODY MOVES

Below we discuss how the muscles, ligaments, tendons, and vessels work together to give the body function and movement.

MUSCLES

There are many different types of muscles, but the one we are most concerned with is skeletal muscle. Its name comes from the fact that it moves the skeleton (bones). In short, muscles cause the parts of the body to move.

Skeletal muscles are all basically constructed the same way. They are designed in straight lines. They contain hundreds of threadlike strands separated into bundles. These strands slide in relation to each other to shorten (contract) and lengthen (relax) the muscle belly.

Muscles do their work by shortening. They can only pull, not push. In our door analogy (see Figure 2.2), the door represents a bone, the hinges represent a joint, and the people represent the muscles. If they cooperate, things run smoothly; if they pull against each other, it wears both of them out and nothing gets accomplished (except maybe breaking the door or the people, or both).

In Figure 2.3, notice that both the bicep and the tricep muscles attach in ways that pull the arm in opposite directions (like the door). The bicep pulls the arm into flexion, and the tricep must relax and lengthen so as not

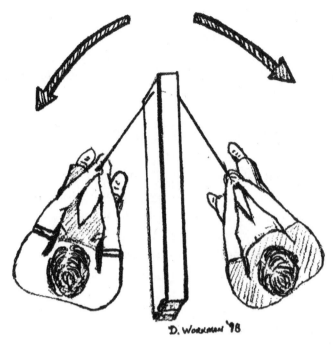

Figure 2.2 Two men pulling opposite each other to move a door is similar to two muscles pulling to move a joint such as in Figure 2.3.

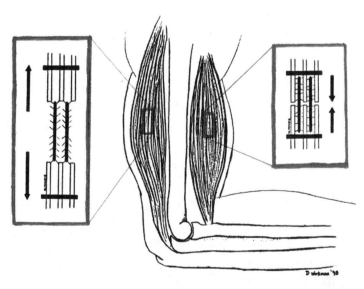

Figure 2.3 This demonstrates the upper arm with the bicep pulling (agonist) and the tricep relaxing (antagonist) to allow the forearm movement (much like the two men pulling the door in Figure 2.2). On each side of the arm is a magnification of the fibers of each muscle. Note how they slide on each other to lengthen and shorten.

to fight (or oppose the movement of) the bicep. If the tricep refuses to relax, it resists the arm movement. This makes the bicep work harder.

The opposite is true if the tricep is attempting to pull the arm straight (extension). The tricep is the one pulling and the bicep must relax to allow the movement.

The muscle that does the pulling is called the agonist, and the one that must relax and allow the pull is the antagonist.

The antagonist also has an important role of slowing the limb down at the end of the motion. It is to the joint what the brakes are to a car.

For example, the bicep brings the hand toward the shoulder, and when the motion is almost done, the tricep tightens to slow the arm down. If this does not take place, the bicep will pull too far, forcing the ligaments to stop the motion. This damages the ligaments, causing instability to the joint and making it more susceptible to injury (not to mention that you would hit yourself in the face).

OPPOSING MUSCLE PULL

Together, the agonist and the antagonist control the motion of the joint. Both play important roles. When the antagonist is tight and inflexible (from injury or a hard workout), it tends to fight the motion of the agonist. This battle of the muscles is what I call "opposing muscle pull." The greater the opposing muscle pull, the more energy that is needed to accomplish a movement. This not only is inefficient but also increases the pressure on the joint, the ligaments, the tendons, and the muscles. This causes misuse of the joint and increased wear and tear to the area.

Opposing muscle pull is like pushing the gas pedal and brake pedal at the same time when driving a car. It adds more wear to the joint, leading to premature aging and injury. The ramifications of this problem are felt after years of misuse—when it's often too late to reverse the process.

TENDONS

Tendons are the fibers that attach the muscle belly to the bone. Let me attempt to illustrate the concept: If you took a ball of hamburger and dropped it on a sheet of plastic wrap, then rolled up the wrap and pulled it tight at the ends, you would have an oblong-shaped piece of hamburger wrapped up. When the hamburger shortened, it would pull the ends closer together, and when it stretched, it would allow the ends to lengthen. Muscles and tendons relate the same way, although the process is much more complicated. If you take this example of hamburger (being one strand of muscle) and put thousands of them together, you would have a section of muscle (see Figure 2.4).

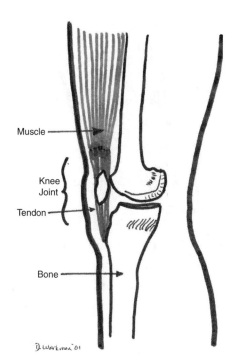

Muscle

Knee
Joint

Tendon

Bone

Knee
Joint

Knee Joint
Ligaments

Figure 2.4   Relationship of the bone, tendon, and muscle in the knee.

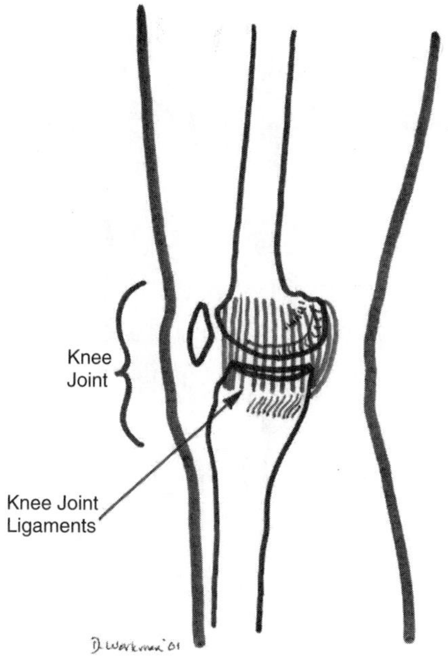

Figure 2.5   This illustrates the position of the ligaments and how they support the knee joint.

BONES

The bones of the body function as a frame. They hold up the body and allow it to move when the bones move in relation to each other.

LIGAMENTS

Ligaments bind the bones together at the joints. They surround the joint, securing it and giving it maximum stability while allowing it proper and full movement. They do not stretch as easily as muscles. If the joint is a synovial joint (containing synovial fluid, a lubricant), the ligaments help it contain the fluid (see Figure 2.5).

NERVES

Nerves make up the communication system of the body. All parts of the body communicate with the brain in some way. That communication comes through the nerves. They resemble telephone lines in that they branch out to every area, gather information on its status to the brain, and then transmit orders back on how that area is to operate. This happens in fractions of a second at any given time. Without this communication, a part of the body cannot operate properly. Nerves are very sensitive to any stimulation,

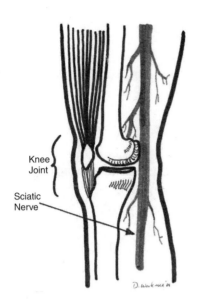

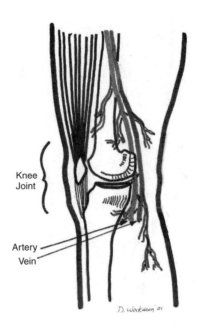

Figure 2.6   The nerve and its relation to the muscles, tendons, and ligaments.

Figure 2.7   The vessels (artery in gray, and vein in black) and their relation to the body. They bring blood to and from various areas.

including pressure, temperature, vibration, position change, and so on (see Figure 2.6).

VESSELS

Nutrition is necessary for the body to function. The amount of activity the body performs dictates how much nutrition it uses (this is known as metabolism). Some bodies naturally burn more energy than others—metabolism varies with each individual. In addition, any given movement can use a varying amount of energy depending on how efficiently it is done.

For nutritional supplies to get to the areas that need them (active areas), a type of road system exists. This is called the vascular system (arteries and veins). These roads go throughout the entire body, taking fresh supplies to areas and bringing the exhausted supplies away from the areas (to be taken out of the body). Blood is the vehicle that transports supplies out to and waste back from the body areas. The roads it travels on are the vessels. Blood takes supplies out through the arteries and brings the waste back through the veins. The waste is dumped, and the blood is then filled with supplies once again and the process repeats (see Figure 2.7).

Vascularity (ability to supply blood) increases to the most active areas in a person's body. In runners, the legs are highly active; in drummers, the arms and legs are very active. Therefore, those areas will be very vascular.

Arteries have thicker walls and typically are located deeper in the body or limbs. They are designed to take loaded blood to areas needing nutrition. Because this is a very important task, their structure and location are such that they are protected from being cut or compressed easily. Their walls are thick because of the high pressure of blood flowing through them, and this also protects them from decreased flow due to compression, thus providing more efficient and uninterrupted blood flow.

Veins are vessels that bring exhausted blood back to be refilled with nutrients. They have much thinner walls because they are under much less pressure than arteries. They are larger in diameter and run closer to the surface of the skin than do the arteries. It is more important to get blood to an area than to take it out. Therefore, even though they flow side by side in most cases, the vessels taking supplies to areas in need are stronger than those bringing the trash back.

This system of muscles, tendons, bones, ligaments, and vessels are a small but integral part of giving the body function. They are also the focus of the majority of injuries a drummer/percussionist encounters. By understanding how they work, you can begin to understand how injury occurs and what to do to reverse it.

Chapter 3 discusses this very thing: the process of how injury occurs.

CHAPTER 3

HOW INJURY OCCURS

The body was made to move. The less resistance it encounters while moving, the less energy it needs to operate. Moving without resistance is called *functioning efficiently.*

Resistance to any degree causes unnecessary wear and tear to that same degree. Wear and tear leads to injury.

One example of resistance is the friction caused by rubbing one tissue against another. Do an experiment: Rub the palms of your hands together lightly. Do you feel the warmth? This demonstrates light friction or resistance. Now push your hands together harder while rubbing. Notice how the friction and heat increases the harder you push or the faster you go. If you continue, the skin will wear away or blister (an injury).

This teaches us a couple of things. First, friction leads to injury. Second, the body can handle friction for a time, but the greater the friction, the less time the body can handle it before injury occurs. Third, if we are listening to our body, we will understand when we need to decrease the friction or the time in order to prevent injury. Pain is the more obvious of the body's communications.

Friction and resistance are not the only forces that can damage the body's tissues. Pulling, pressure, temperature, and chemicals are just a few others that we discuss in the injury chapters that follow.

When we allow the body to move naturally, it will do so without resistance and injury. However, when we force unnatural (*inefficient*) movements, it produces strain to the muscles, ligaments, and tendons (soft tissue). Unnatural movements (those that take them out of their designed movement patterns) cause heat and irritation to the area. This results in breakdown of the components to one degree or another: injury.

A common cause of breakdown in the body is when you force it to do something it is not capable of doing at that time. If you are patient and consistent, the body can *adapt* to almost any task. Given time, it can work its way to almost any level of playing. This is a concept that is visible in all aspects of life (saving money, driving long trips, running, building a fire, learning in school, etc.).

If you give the body time to adapt, it will be able to do most anything required of it without damage. There is really no limit to what the body can do if treated right. However, we usually become impatient in our playing and force our bodies to do too much, to do it too soon, or both; then we complain when our bodies break down.

LISTENING TO YOUR BODY

When something goes wrong, your body has ways of telling you. The sign that we most commonly notice is *pain*. Unfortunately, most of us see this as the only sign, when in fact that is one of the last signs just before total breakdown. By the time you feel pain, you have missed the many signs before it that were telling you something was wrong. Some of these signs include awkwardness, stiffness, shaking, grinding, and so on.

To illustrate how our bodies tell us something is wrong, I would like to compare injury to a fire. If we are perceptive, we can hear the fire, smell the smoke, and even feel the heat. However, most of the time our minds are so preoccupied with other things that we do not recognize the signs until the fire alarm sounds.

Pain is our body's fire alarm to warn us that problems exist. By the time an alarm sounds, the damage is progressing fast and becoming more difficult to stop. We can choose to ignore the alarm (ignore pain), or even turn it off (pain relievers, etc.), but that doesn't mean the fire will go out.

If you pay close attention to your body, the early signs that something is wrong become more obvious. A few of them are stiffness, uneasy feelings, or lack of fluidity as we play.

There are many books and classes that teach you how to listen to the subtle and not-so-subtle signs the body gives. A few of these options include, but are not limited to, yoga, martial arts, Alexander Technique, meditation, and so forth. Finding success in these techniques of understanding your body will take time and effort. Your years of bad habits will need to be changed to decrease the noise that prevents you from hearing what is truly happening within.

To reach its full potential, music must be an expression of your innermost feelings. You cannot express what you are not at that time feeling within yourself. The most effective musicians understand what they are feeling and have an incredible ability to express it so that others can feel and understand.

With all of this ability to feel and express, we as musicians should at the least be able to understand the feelings our own bodies are trying to communicate to us.

PREPARING THE BODY FOR ACTIVITY

This leads me into the next concept that is very important to athletes and performers of all kinds. And because the drummer/percussionist is one of the most active of all performers, and definitely the most active of musicians, this should be important to you.

Warming up and stretching are an integral part of our ability to perform at peak. It allows the body to prepare for activity, and is one of *the most effective things you can do to prevent injury.*

I believe that warming up the body for performance is a concept, not simply a series of movements. My definition of warming up includes gradually increasing the body's activity and circulation, then stretching the muscles to allow them their maximal performance. A warm-up is as individual as the person doing it. Listen to what your body is telling you as you go through the process. More crucial than the positions you use in warming up is the attitude with which you perform them. Here are some ideas that should save you time, pain, and frustration in the days to come.

WARMING UP

Many of us get up in the morning moving rather slowly. As our circulation increases, we become more alert and move more quickly and easily. Gradually, we reach a normal operating energy level. Warming up to perform follows the same pattern, but at a greater intensity. The more intense the performance, the higher level of warm-up needed.

When you begin the warm-up, it is wise to walk or jog or do jumping jacks for a short time to alert the body that it should start moving blood toward the muscles. In this way, we work the stiffness out. As you feel the muscles and joints loosen up, gradually increase the speed and range of movement.

Be careful not to push the process. Instead, allow the body the necessary time to adapt comfortably to the increased intensity before moving to a higher level. Also consider your breathing. It should increase in speed and volume, but not enough to create an oxygen debt, leading to an out-of-breath feeling.

As a rule, you are on the right track when you perspire slightly (not dripping). You may want to gauge your warm-up by noting a feeling of warmth beginning deep within the muscles. Overall, you should feel primed, alert, and ready to perform. In the beginning, it may take a little time and effort to start recognizing when your body is fully primed. Expect a few days when warm-ups aren't so good, but learn from those experiences. With practice, you will learn when your body is properly warmed up.

STRETCHING

Once you feel that warmth in the muscles, begin some stretches. To help you understand stretching, I have provided a few facts. First, muscles consist of thousands of fibers lined up in a bundle. They are designed to shorten. They do not push—they only pull. This pulling motion causes bones to move on each other at the joints.

Second, for these fibers to function at optimal efficiency, they need to be kept flexible and must be given proper nutrition. When you begin a warm-up jog, your circulation increases, supplying nutrition to and loosening the muscles.

Mentally, it may help to compare muscle fibers to strands of spaghetti—brittle until warm and moist. This image may help illustrate the fact that as we get colder, we become less flexible and more apt to break (or be injured). Conversely, the warmer we get, the more flexible we become. It is obviously best to stretch something when it is soft and flexible, rather than brittle and cold. The body responds in this way as well.

I am not going to take the time to discuss various stretching positions at this point. At the end of each chapter, there is a section demonstrating the various stretching positions for that body area. As you look up an injury, you will be referred to the stretches needed (if there are any) to help alleviate that particular ailment.

When stretching, remember these important points:

1. Don't let stretching become a painful process (if it is, you are doing it too hard or too quickly).
2. Stretch slowly, carefully, and relaxedly.
3. Don't bounce or jerk.
4. Spend more time stretching tight or painful areas to allow the body to stretch fully (without pulling harder on the muscle).

Note that the *intensity* of your warm-up should be similar to the level of intensity you will be performing at. If you plan to play long or very intensely, you should warm up more thoroughly than you would if you were doing a short, light performance.

Manual stretching gives the muscle flexibility within its normal range, creating a safety buffer against injury. As you stretch, allow the muscles to lengthen; do not force them. If you force a muscle to lengthen, natural reflex causes it to resist. Thus, instead of stretching, you have one muscle battling another, and nothing productive happens.

It is also important to mention that you can overdo it on both the warm-up and the stretching. If you warm up too much, you will be out of breath and sweaty and will use up energy needed for the performance.

The muscles should be loose enough to allow the joint to move its full range without resistant pull from those muscles, but it is equally important to have some tone (tightness). This provides control of the movement and protection for the joint. The muscles play an important part in supporting and protecting the joint from going too far and injuring itself. A certain amount of tone is optimal in protecting the joints—be sure not to stretch that tone until it becomes ineffective. If you do, the joint and its supports become more susceptible to injury.

COOLING DOWN

A commonly overlooked part of taking care of the body is the cooldown. Have you ever had a great workout, only to suffer soreness and pain the next day? What causes that? How do you prevent it?

When muscles operate for prolonged periods of time at a higher intensity than they are used to, they build up *lactic acid*. Lactic acid is what is left after the muscle uses the energy—it is much like the exhaust after a car engine uses fuel. If you do a long aggressive performance, it is important to cool down. Keeping the muscles moving and loose encourages circulation, which flushes lactic acid out of the muscles and to the areas that take it out of the body.

A cooldown should be just like the warm-up, only in reverse. Gradually let off the gas pedal and allow the body to adapt to slower speeds. Lightly stretch and play at a pace slow enough to avoid perspiring. Do some mild stretches as you cool down to avoid tightness a few hours down the road. You will know when you are cooled down, because your heart rate will return to normal, your sweat will dry up, and you will feel colder deep within the body.

Much too often, once we have gotten what we want from our body, we leave it as is. There is a phrase about horses that says, "Rode hard and put up wet." This is a way to abuse a horse—put it directly in the stall while it is still hot and sweaty. People too must be sure not to push themselves hard and then just stop. After significant activity, you must cool down the body, allowing the blood to replenish the muscles with supplies and cool them down, pulling excess blood out of them. It is bad to leave the muscle pumped up with blood and lactic acid. Allow the body to flush itself out with a good cooldown.

BREAKDOWN OF THE BODY

Breakdown of the body can happen for many reasons, and your body will break down with age, even though you may take exceptional care of it. With this in mind, I now mention some of the most common reasons for premature breakdown of the drummer/percussionist.

Parts of the body get misused by increasing the intensity or duration of their use too quickly for them to adapt to the change in load.

In the case of muscles, tendons, and ligaments, when some *damage* occurs, the body responds by tightening the muscles around the area to protect it from further injuring itself. *Swelling* begins immediately (the larger the injury, the quicker and greater the swelling), bringing in materials to re-build the damaged area and taking out the damaged materials to dispose of them.

Often, the swelling is so great while the new materials are being brought in that it presses on the veins and slows the trash from being taken out. Thus the area becomes engorged. Anti-inflammatories, ice, rest, elevation (gravity), and compression are some very effective ways of decreasing the swelling and pressure to the area. This in turn improves traffic flow to the area and accelerates the healing process.

As you ignore the initial signs, and things begin to break down, your body begins to lose its lines of defense, and a snowball effect occurs until the problem cannot be ignored anymore. In many cases, that is when play-ing becomes impossible, and the situation becomes an emergency.

To avoid further pain, the body begins to change the way it moves while playing, using less efficient techniques, which causes additional injuries. This is most commonly called *compensation.* Look at your technique close-ly in the mirror, or by video, some time when you have some problems. If you are looking closely enough, you will see changes and unnatural move-ments in your playing. They are subtle at first—noticed by a trained eye only, but as time goes on, they become strikingly more obvious.

As an example, if you have a blister on your toe, you will most likely walk differently than usual to accommodate and reduce the pain of the blister. By walking differently, you put undue stress on other areas of the body, and they soon begin to hurt.

If a muscle flexes and stays in that contracted state for a time, it can become fatigued and lock in *spasm.* After weeks and months, the spasm becomes *chronic*—unable to relax itself.

This process is much like concrete hardening. When it is new, you can mold it the way you want, but as time passes, you lose that option. So the longer you have the problem without correcting it, the more difficult any correction becomes and the less apt you are to resolve it completely.

In addition, materials are shipped in to form a patch known as *scar tissue*. This will not make the area of the injury exactly as new, but it will act very similar to the original materials. Most of us have cut or scraped ourselves and healed with a residual scar. Even though it looks similar to skin, the scar is obvious to the naked eye. This is the pattern of healing followed throughout the body.

During the scarring process, movement and stresses will condition the scar material to respond to the loads put on it. It is well known in the health community that bone and soft tissue (muscle, ligament, and tendon)—normal or abnormal—develop to withstand the forces and motions they usually deal with. The tissues that deal with forces to that body part become best developed.

A WORD OF WARNING AND ADVICE

Stop the injury early, or it will get worse and cause other injuries. Addressing it early not only saves you time and pain but also enables you to play better and avoid the long road back to recovery. That road gets longer when many injuries (not just one) must heal to resume proper playing.

Many times, performers avoid addressing the problem because they think "maybe it will go away on its own" or they fear that their position in the group or performance will be jeopardized. I have heard many cases where no doctor was consulted because the musician feared that he would be told not to play for some period of time.

Many times, the doctor takes a performer out of activity because he or she doesn't have enough expertise in performing injuries to know a better alternative, and complete rest is the safest way he or she knows to treat such injuries. Unfortunately, it may not be the safest or the most effective way to treat the injury.

Most injuries that are caught early and treated by a doctor experienced in performing injuries can be treated without interruption in playing. However, when enough time has gone by to cause deeper damage, the journey back becomes longer and more difficult. Address and treat all injuries immediately, before they become serious issues.

THE MOST COMMON TYPES OF INJURY

Because most drummer/percussionist injuries deal with soft tissue, we will discuss the most common soft tissues involved.

MUSCLE INJURIES

Muscles are usually the first soft tissue to be injured, and, because of their nature and circulation, are also the quickest to heal. They will usually heal four to six weeks after the injury. As described previously, muscles usually respond to fatigue (overuse) or injury by going into spasm, causing a splinting effect to protect the damaged area from further damage. In doing that, they compromise the blood flow to the injured area (slowing the healing process).

TENDON INJURIES

Irritation to an area leads to muscles tightening involuntarily (spasm) to protect the area. However, muscle spasm puts stress on the tendons that attach the muscle to the bone. This irritates the tendon. In addition, the muscle will lose its elasticity to some degree, causing the tendon to be pulled instead, resulting in greater injury to the tendon. Muscles are more elastic than tendons and ligaments, and they have greater circulation (allowing for quicker healing). This constant pressure and force on the tendon is a common cause of tendonitis. Tendons typically take around twelve weeks to heal.

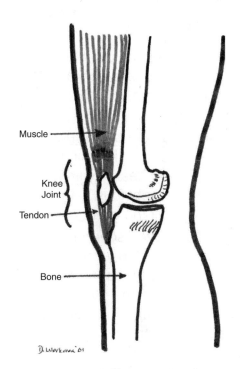

Figure 3.1   Muscles attach to tendons, and then tendons attach to bones. Often, when a muscle is injured, the tendon is also affected, and vice versa.

LIGAMENT INJURIES

Ligaments surround joints attaching bone to bone while allowing movement. They are strong fibrous tissues that are pliable. Their purpose is to keep the joints snug in their movement rather than loose and shifting. The ligaments play an important role in protecting the joint in its movement, and when a ligament is injured, or weakened to any degree, the joint is more susceptible to injury.

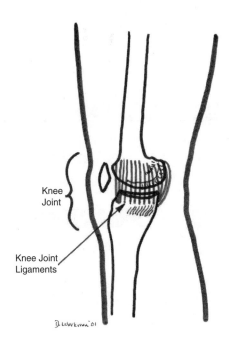

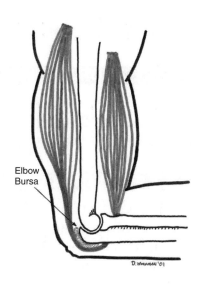

Figure 3.2   Ligaments stabilize two bones that meet to form a joint. They keep the joint snug unless they are injured in some way.

Figure 3.3   This figure shows an elbow bursa. Bursae are lubricant-filled bags positioned between two moving objects in the body to provide smooth movement without friction.

BURSAE INJURIES

Bursae are different from the soft tissues. They are various-sized sacs of lubricating fluid that are situated between moving parts within the body to reduce wear, heat, and friction that can cause injury. For example, where a muscle rubs against something, you will find a *bursa* to reduce the possible friction.

They are found in areas around the shoulder, knee, hip, and so forth, where much movement occurs. Misuse of the area can cause irritation of the bursae, resulting in inflammation (bursitis). If you have pain in a joint during movement, bursitis is one possibility.

MOST COMMON TYPES OF DRUM/PERCUSSION INJURIES

Muscle spasm: when a *muscle* goes into sudden, involuntary contraction
Bursitis: when a *bursa* is overworked, begins to break down, or is inflamed

Tendonitis: when a *tendon* is injured by being torn, frayed, or irritated

Nerve impingement: when something puts pressure on a *nerve,* causing a decrease in its ability to function

Strain: when *muscles* are injured by being torn or frayed

Sprain: when a *ligament* is injured by being torn or frayed

CONCERNING SPRAINS AND STRAINS

Musicians usually have only microscopic changes in this injury (relatively few fibers are affected) from playing. Most severe injuries and changes are a result of major trauma (lifting or moving equipment, falling, etc.).

DIGGING A LITTLE DEEPER

For more information on the most common types of drum/percussionist injuries and how to treat them, see Appendix C: muscle spasms (Section C.1), bursitis (Section C.2), tendonitis (Section C.3), nerve impingement (Section C.4), strain (Section C.5), and sprain (Section C.6).

CHAPTER 4

HAND AND WRIST PROBLEMS

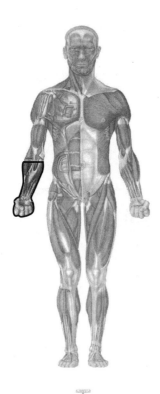

Muscles of Right Hand
(Palmar View)

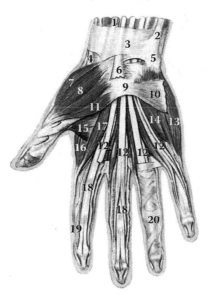

1. Flexor carpi radialis t.
2. Flexor carpi ulnaris t.
3. Flexor retinaculum
4. Abductor pollicis longus t.
5. Pisiform
6. Palmaris longus t.
7. Opponens pollicis m.
8. Abductor pollicis brevis m.
9. Flexor retinaculum
10. Palmaris brevis m.
11. Flexor pollicis brevis m.
12. Flexor digitorum superficialis tt.
13. Abductor digiti minimi m.
14. Flexor digiti minimi brevis m.
15. Adductor pollicis m.
16. Dorsal interosseous m.
17. Lumbrical m.
18. Flexor digitorum profundus tt.
19. Synovial sheath
20. Digital fibrous sheath

Ligaments of Right Hand
(Dorsal View)

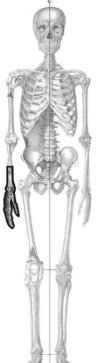

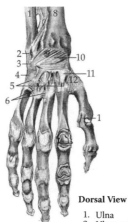

(Palmar View)

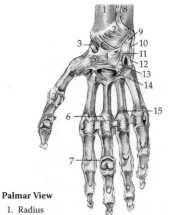

Dorsal View

1. Ulna
2. Ulnar collateral l.
3. Triquetral
4. Hamate
5. Dorsal carpometacarpal ll.
6. Dorsal metacarpal ll.
7. Articular capsule
8. Radius
9. Dorsal radiocarpal l.
10. Scaphoid
11. Trapezium
12. Carpometacarpal capsule
13. Collateral l.

Palmar View

1. Radius
2. Palmar radiocarpal l.
3. Flexor caro radialis t.
4. Flexor retinaculum
5. Trapezium
6. Palmar ll.
7. Articular capsule
8. Ulna
9. Flexor cari ulnaris t.
10. Pisiform
11. Pisohamate l.
12. pisometacarpal l.
13. Hamate
14. Palmar metacarpal ll.
15. Deep transverse metacarpal ll.

SIGNS AND SYMPTOMS

Dull ache in the muscles on top of the forearm. The pain is sharp while playing (especially traditional grip) or doing wrist-turning moves.

NAME OF INJURY

Muscle spasm (hand and wrist)

DESCRIPTION

Muscles increase in tightness until they cramp (usually pronator quadratus muscles, pronator teres muscles, or thumb muscles).

CAUSE

Prolonged constant movement of the muscles in a similar manner depletes them and causes them to freeze up (spasm).

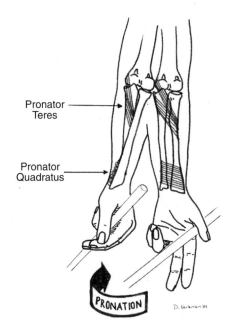

Figure 4.1 This figure illustrates how the pronator teres and pronator quadratus muscles pull the radius bone over the ulna bone to rotate (pronate) the hand as demonstrated in the traditional grip motion.

TREATMENT

Immediate Relief

Rest; ice and heat, alternating at fifteen minutes each (see Section A.1); and massage of the muscles at the top of the forearm. Aspirin has been known to help.

PREVENTION

Technique

The musician may be using too much rotation of the wrist (especially in the traditional grip and mallet playing) or a tight thumb grip. He or she must learn to use the fingers, wrist, and forearm more equally. Loosen the traditional grip fulcrum, allowing the stick to move more freely in the hand, letting it work for you.

Stretches

You must stretch the muscles of the forearm and thumb to keep them moving in their full range of motion for better circulation and strength (see Stretch 4.4).

Exercises

Do basic rudiments to strengthen the muscles, beginning slowly and gradually increasing speed with each repetition (see Exercise B.1). If you begin to feel tight in the involved area, stop and massage the muscles (see Section A.2). You may also use slightly heavier sticks to build strength in the hands.

Caution

Only use sticks one size heavier than your regular heavy sticks, or you may cause injury to the area (if a little is good, more is not necessarily better).

IF NO RELIEF

Massage to the deep muscles of the forearm and thumb by a certified massage therapist can help relieve the tightness. If no results appear, manipulation of the wrist and elbow and deep therapy to the muscles can be done by a doctor of chiropractic. If no relief is found, then he or she can refer you to the proper specialist.

PROGNOSIS

This injury has an excellent prognosis. It usually heals completely in about a week without much (if any) decrease in playing. If it doesn't subside, you may have a different injury and should consult your medical or chiropractic doctor for further evaluation.

OTHER POSSIBILITIES

Tendonitis (usually has no tenderness in the muscle belly).

DIGGING A LITTLE DEEPER

What are muscle spasms? See Section C.1.

SIGNS AND SYMPTOMS

Moderate to severe muscular incoordination or decreased ability to control well-known movements done numerous times on the instrument.

NAME OF INJURY

Focal dystonia (hand and wrist)

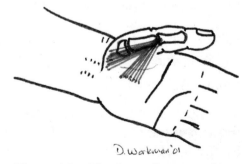

Figure 4.2 This figure illustrates a few thumb muscles that are involved in focal dystonia.

26

DESCRIPTION

Neurologic movement disorder. It demonstrates as painless loss of muscular coordination or voluntary motor control while doing well-trained movements on an instrument.

CAUSE

Believed to be caused by neurological malfunction brought on at least in part by anxiety and other emotional factors.

TREATMENT

Immediate Relief

Control of emotional aspects of playing such as performance anxiety and so forth through relaxation or thought-channeling exercises, or both. Mild stretching and slow, relaxed movements of the arms and hands may allow for better function, but ultimately this problem must be dealt with through long-term treatment by your doctor.

PREVENTION

Technique

The musician may be using too much thumb and wrist (especially in the matched grip while playing a snare drum or drum set) and must learn to use more fingers, elbow, and full body movement to balance out the work in his or her technique. Loosen the fulcrum, allowing the stick to move more freely in the hand and letting it work for you. Actions that illustrate this flow of movement include bouncing a basketball, throwing a baseball, jumping rope, and so forth.

Stretches

Stretch muscles of the thumb and forearm to keep the wrist and hand moving in their full range of motion and allow increased circulation and strength. This reduces opposing muscle pull while playing (see Stretch 4.3).

Exercises

Do basic rudiments to retrain the brain and hands on how to easily and smoothly move in a relaxed manner. It may take months or years to retrain yourself on how to play if the focal dystonia is highly progressed.

IF NO RELIEF

Massage to the deep muscles of the hand by a certified massage therapist or physical therapist can help relieve any tightness in the muscles involved. If there are no results, evaluation, manipulation of the hand, and deep therapy to the muscles can be done by a chiropractor. If there is no change in two to four weeks, he or she can refer you to the proper specialist.

PROGNOSIS

This injury can be career ending if it has been there for a long time. It usually requires extensive retraining of the brain–hand coordination.

OTHER POSSIBILITIES

Muscle spasms (usually painful on movement), rheumatoid arthritis of the thumb (painful and usually affecting all joints of the hand), osteoarthritis (painful, and the most likely type of arthritis from years of wear and tear).

DIGGING A LITTLE DEEPER

What is nerve impingement? See Section C.4.

SIGNS AND SYMPTOMS

Tingling, pins and needles, or numbness of the first three fingers; also weakness on striking drum (traditional grip) with elbow bent or straight.

NAME OF INJURY

Median nerve entrapment

DESCRIPTION

Pressure on median nerve by the muscles of the forearm, fracture (if recent trauma to the area), or inflammation causing decreased nerve function (i.e., numbness or tingling).

CAUSE

Muscle spasms, overuse of the elbow or wrist–finger complex (commonly in the snare arm of traditional players), causing prolonged pronation effort.

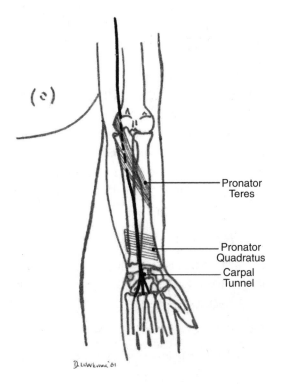

Figure 4.3 Pressure on a nerve can cause odd sensation along that nerve. This figure illustrates common pressure points for the nerve going to the middle fingers (median nerve): (1) pronator teres muscle, (2) pronator quadratus muscle, and (3) carpal tunnel.

TREATMENT

Immediate Relief

Rest twenty-four hours, using ice to decrease swelling of the area (see Section A.1) for two hours morning, noon, and night. Every session is to be preceded by light stretching of the forearm for five minutes (see the description of warming up in Chapter 3). Over-the-counter anti-inflammatories may also help.

PREVENTION

Technique

Decrease the rigidity of the traditional grip. Relax the hand just before the stick strikes the drum, allowing free stick movement.

Stretches

Do supination stretches of the forearm with the elbow extended (see Stretch 4.4).

Exercises

Try doing rudiments with your heavy playing sticks, beginning slowly and gradually speeding up (see Exercise B.1).

IF NO RELIEF

See a doctor of chiropractic or certified massage therapist for soft tissue work on the forearm muscles.

PROGNOSIS

Prognosis is good if treated within three months, but the amount of improvement decreases with time.

OTHER POSSIBILITIES

Carpal tunnel syndrome (affects middle fingers, mostly with movement while wrist is in extension) or supracondylar ligament (usually occurs with pronation and flexion of the forearm).

DIGGING A LITTLE DEEPER

What is a muscle spasm? What is nerve impingement? See Sections C.1 and C.4.

SIGNS AND SYMPTOMS

Pain and swelling on movement or resistance to movement of the thumb (particularly during extended periods of drum or mallet playing).

NAME OF INJURY

Pollicis (thumb) tendonitis

DESCRIPTION

Increased tension or trauma to the tendon, causing tearing of the tendon fibers to varying degrees.

CAUSE

Increased tension to the tendon from a strong overload or (more likely) a constant tension put on the tendon (i.e., muscle spasm unreleased) for long periods of time.

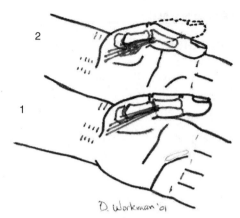

Figure 4.4 (1) Normal muscle tension. (2) A muscle knot is from the muscle contracting on itself. This shortens the muscle, possibly altering the natural posture of the joint (number 2: dotted line = normal, solid line = abnormal).

TREATMENT

Immediate Relief

Ice, elevation, immobilization with wrist or thumb splint. Massage to the muscles of the forearm (thumb side) and thumb.

PREVENTION

Technique

You must play more in neutral position—allow one to two centimeters in the space between the thumb and hand. Decrease wrist movement; use more fingers and forearm motion. Also keep the wrist in a more straight posture.

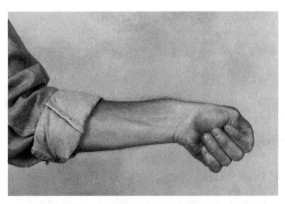

Figure 4.5 This stretch is one of the most effective for relieving tightness in the thumb extension muscles.

Stretches

Tuck the thumb into the fist and bend the wrist in the direction of the little finger (see Stretch 4.3).

Exercises

If it doesn't cause pain, do the thumb and pinkie pull exercise (see Exercise B.3).

IF NO RELIEF

See your physician for more aggressive treatment if there is no improvement after two weeks.

PROGNOSIS

The prognosis is excellent if treated early. It can become chronic or lead to stenosing tenosynovitis if not cared for properly and in a timely manner.

OTHER POSSIBILITIES

Stenosing tenosynovitis (long-standing tendonitis).

DIGGING A LITTLE DEEPER

What are muscle spasms? What is tendonitis? See Sections C.1 and C.3.

SIGNS AND SYMPTOMS

Pain, grinding, or clicking (crepitation) on the thumb side of the wrist and forearm or palm of hand, and pain in the area on movement.

NAME OF INJURY

Stenosing tenosynovitis

DESCRIPTION

Irritation or increased swelling of the tendon or sheaths at the wrist (carpal tunnels) or hand. This decreases space in the tunnel and irritates the nerves. There are two types: *De Quervain's* (thumb side of the wrist) and *trigger finger* (palm of hand by the finger or fingers).

CAUSE

Improper technique, increased playing time, or a sudden change to a more powerful stroke can cause irritation and swelling that can hurt the tissues.

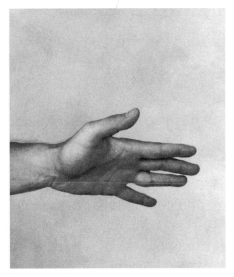 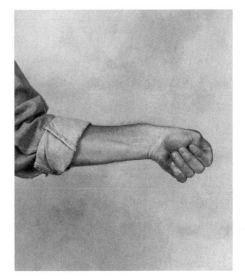

Figure 4.6   When the thumb is in extension (left) or the wrist is in ulnar deviation (right) you will experience pain if you have stenosing tenosynovitis.

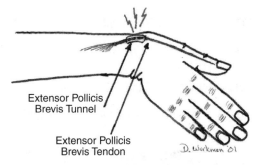

Extensor Pollicis
Brevis Tunnel

Extensor Pollicis
Brevis Tendon

D. Workman '01

Figure 4.7   Through misuse of various kinds, the tendon and synovium (tunnel) become irritated and swollen.

TREATMENT

Immediate Relief

Ice, elevation, immobilization with a wrist, thumb, or finger splint (found at most drugstores). Ice massage the muscles of the forearm (four to eight inches above the wrist on the thumb side).

PREVENTION

Technique

Try to play in a more neutral position as often as possible and decrease wrist movement. Use more fingers and forearm motion.

Stretches

Hand stretches (see Stretches 4.3 and 4.4).

Exercises

Hand exercise (see Exercises B.2, B.3, and B.5).

IF NO RELIEF

If there is no change within a week, see your physician.

PROGNOSIS

If caught early, the prognosis is good. If the injury is not responding to treatment, it may be chronic or severe, in which case, the prognosis is worse.

OTHER POSSIBILITIES

Arthritis, scaphoid problems, or radial nerve entrapment.

DIGGING A LITTLE DEEPER

What is tendonitis? See Section C.3.

SIGNS AND SYMPTOMS

Numb, tingly, or achy feeling in the hand or wrist (usually thumb and first finger), or both, that gets worse over weeks or months and during or shortly after repeated stressful motions of the hand or wrist.

NAME OF INJURY

Carpal tunnel syndrome

DESCRIPTION

Irritation of the median nerve as it goes through the carpal tunnel (see Figure 4.8). Overactive or inefficient movement through the tunnels causes heat, swelling, and pressure.

Figure 4.8 Tendons that operate the fingers go across the wrist on the palm side through carpal tunnels (X) on the right. (Ortho-McNeil Pharmaceutical, Inc., 2003)

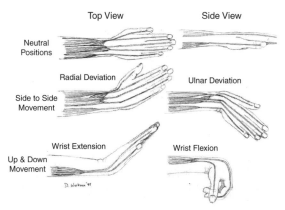

Figure 4.9 This figure illustrates various motions of the wrist. All positions except neutral (top row) cause the tendons to rub harder against the carpal tunnels. Greater angles or muscle tension cause greater irritation.

CAUSE

Commonly from long-term misuse (microtrauma) of the wrist for a period of weeks or months. Other causes are a sudden increase in speed, practice time, or stick size; tighter heads; change in instrument setup; and so forth.

TREATMENT

Immediate Relief

Ice the wrist for fifteen minutes on and fifteen minutes off in an elevated position (see Section A.1). Aspirin or ibuprofen has shown to be helpful. When practicing, rest ten minutes of each hour. Soft tissue work may be done on the wrist flexor muscles (see illustration at front of chapter) to relax them, decreasing pressure on the tendons and the tunnel.

PREVENTION

Technique

Try incorporating more finger and arm movement into your wrist strokes to reduce the amount of wrist bending (flexion/extension). Also consider using more wrist rotation. Do half of your speed and length of playing for three days. Finally, let the sticks do more of the work—don't try so hard to control them. Flip the stick and let it swing, bouncing independently of your hand (like a basketball). Find a good teacher.

Stretches

Do Stretch 4.1 four times per day.

Exercises

You may also try shoulder shrugs (see Stretch 4.2).

IF NO RELIEF

If there is no relief within two weeks of this treatment, see your doctor.

PROGNOSIS

If you catch the injury early (within four weeks), the prognosis is excellent, but if it becomes chronic (twelve weeks or more), the chances for full recovery decrease.

OTHER POSSIBILITIES

Carpal tunnel tendonitis (pain when wrist is straight during resisted flexion) or ulnar nerve entrapment (tingle or numbness mostly in the pinkie finger).

DIGGING A LITTLE DEEPER

What is nerve impingement? See Section C.4.

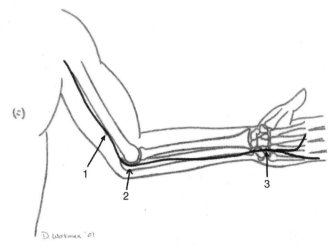

Figure 4.10 Pressure on a nerve can cause odd sensation along that nerve. This figure illustrates common pressure points for the hand (ulnar nerve): (1) posterior condylar groove, (2) medial epicondyle, (3) tunnel of Guyon.

SIGNS AND SYMPTOMS

Pain, tingling, or numbness in the fourth and fifth fingers. Possible pain in the shoulder blade (near the spine), upper back, or elbow.

NAME OF INJURY

Ulnar nerve entrapment

DESCRIPTION

The ulnar nerve (funny bone nerve) becomes irritated by trauma, pressure due to tight muscles, or wear and tear.

CAUSE

Constant motion that rubs the ulnar nerve (see Figure 4.3). Spasm of the muscles causes compression around the ulnar nerve. Tunnels that the nerve passes through become obstructed (i.e., posterior condylar groove [1], just above the elbow on the inside; cubital tunnel [2], the front side of the elbow; and the tunnel of Guyon [3], fat pad of the hand on the pinkie side). An obstruction may be due to a forceful hit to the area, tight muscles, or pressure on the area from the outside (i.e., clothing, jewelry, etc.), among other things.

TREATMENT

Immediate Relief

Forearm stretches (see Stretch 4.4) and anti-inflammatories. Ice the painful area (Section A.1) and avoid painful movements.

PREVENTION

Technique

You may be bending at the elbow too much while playing. Incorporate more wrist and finger use. If you have increased the force of your playing, it may have caused swelling or muscle spasm, or both, leading to pressure on the nerve.

Stretches

Forearm stretches (see Stretch 4.4).

Exercises

Warm-up exercises (see Exercise B.1).

IF NO RELIEF

See a certified massage therapist for soft tissue work to the forearm muscles if there is no change in a week. If there is no change in three weeks, see your doctor for evaluation and treatment.

PROGNOSIS

If the injury is one of muscle tightness, it should respond well and heal completely. Those injuries having to do with bone entrapment may need to be dealt with surgically.

OTHER POSSIBILITIES

Tunnel of Guyon entrapment.

DIGGING A LITTLE DEEPER

What is nerve impingement? See Section C.4.

SIGNS AND SYMPTOMS

Numbness and possible weakness in the ring and pinkie fingers are worse during and after playing hand instruments; there is also pain and tenderness under the muscle on the pinkie side of the palm.

NAME OF INJURY

Tunnel of Guyon entrapment

DESCRIPTION

The tunnel of Guyon is formed by a ligament (the pisohamate), spanning two of the wrist bones (the hamate and the pisiform; see Figure 4.11). Through this tunnel runs the ulnar nerve and artery. Increased pressure on

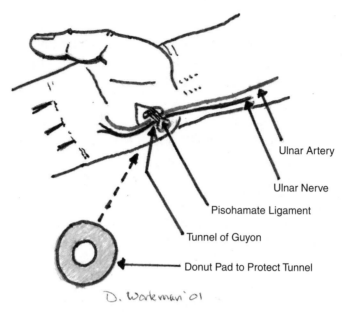

Ulnar Artery

Ulnar Nerve

Pisohamate Ligament

Tunnel of Guyon

Donut Pad to Protect Tunnel

D. Workman '01

Figure 4.11   The ulnar nerve (funny bone nerve) passes through the tunnel of Guyon. Damage or swelling of the tunnel may put pressure on the nerve and send odd sensations into the ring and pinkie finger.

the tunnel from swelling and so forth can cause nerve irritation, sending symptoms into the small fingers (fourth and fifth).

CAUSE

This injury is usually caused by a hard, direct blow to the heel of the hand (over the tunnel of Guyon). It can also be caused by repetitive trauma to the same area. Hand drumming is the most common drum activity causing this condition.

TREATMENT

Immediate Relief

The best immediate relief is rest, elevation, and ice (fifteen minutes on, fifteen minutes off) applied to the sore area (see Section A.1). Aspirin or other anti-inflammatories may also help. A donut-shaped pad may be applied to the hand (as in Figure 4.11) while playing to reduce the impact and further swelling of the area.

PREVENTION

Technique

Try playing without the damaged area striking hard parts of the drum.

Stretches

Do hand extensions to allow stretching of the tight muscles surrounding the injury and to decrease pressure on the tunnel (see Stretch 4.4.3).

Exercises

Grip a punctured tennis ball or racquetball (do three sets of ten repetitions with one-minute rests between sets). Focus on the pinkie finger (see Exercise B.2).

IF NO RELIEF

See your physician for treatment, and you should be referred to a hand specialist should that treatment not succeed.

PROGNOSIS

The prognosis is good if caught and treated within the first three months.

OTHER POSSIBILITIES

Carpal tunnel syndrome (no tenderness over the tunnel of Guyon area).

DIGGING A LITTLE DEEPER

What is nerve impingement? See Section C.4.

SIGNS AND SYMPTOMS

Painless lump one to three centimeters in diameter on the wrist (usually the back of the wrist). May be larger when the wrist is bent away from it and smaller when bent toward it. Also found in hands, feet, or ankles.

NAME OF INJURY

Ganglion cyst

DESCRIPTION

Weakness in the membrane around the joint, or herniation of the lining through a ligamentous area or defect (locations: wrist, palms, finger joints, and others), leads to a bulge or bubble of mucinous (yellow gelatin type) fluid. It is a cystic enlargement of a tendinous sheath on the back of the wrist (see Figure 4.12).

CAUSE

Unknown, but possibly a break or trauma causing fluid to enter.

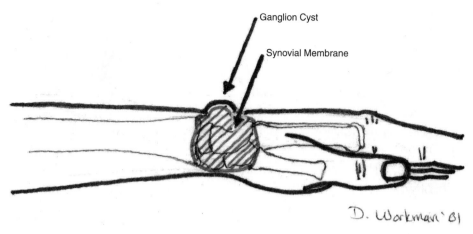

Figure 4.12   The synovial membrane wraps around the carpal bones to keep lubricating fluid in the wrist. Weakness in the membrane causes a bubble (ganglion cyst).

TREATMENT

Either leave it alone (since it usually doesn't affect movement and is typically painless), or have the fluid removed surgically or with a needle. *This must be done only by a doctor.*

PREVENTION

There are no prevention measures known to work at this time. Ganglion cysts are usually not painful and can be reduced, but they usually return.

IF NO RELIEF

See your physician if it is painful or if you want it removed.

PROGNOSIS

Many times, the cyst will reappear even after treatment.

OTHER POSSIBILITIES

Epidermal, sebaceous, or mucous cyst.

SIGNS AND SYMPTOMS

Pain in one or more joints of the arm in the morning or following activity. Can be one or both hands (usually after age thirty).

NAME OF INJURY

Osteoarthritis (hand)

DESCRIPTION

Aging of a joint before its time.

CAUSE

Repetitive joint-wearing movements, or macrotrauma, causing the joint or joints to be dysfunctional (gradual onset). Often called "getting old before your time." This injury is usually found in players who play hard.

TREATMENT

Immediate Relief

Heat does well in the morning to get the joint moving. If the pain follows exercise or activity, ice or aspirin, or both, are good choices for decreasing it.

PREVENTION

Technique

The best advice is to reduce stress to the already degenerative joint(s) by avoiding movements that are generally ergonomically inefficient.

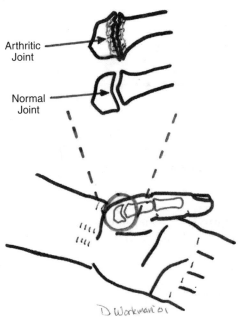

Figure 4.13   This figure illustrates an example of a normal joint and a joint with degenerative arthritis. Degenerative arthritis is the wearing down of the joint from improper use. Note the smooth curves at the bone's edge in the normal joint, while the arthritic joint shows jagged edges (bone spurs) and decreased space between the bones. Spurs are the bone's attempt to heal.

Stretches

Yoga is an excellent overall stretching technique for this ailment. Soft tissue massage to the muscles around the joint is also helpful. Chiropractic treatment improves the condition in most cases.

Exercises

General aerobic conditioning is best. Those exercises that cause less stress to the joint are most effective (swimming, biking, and walking).

IF NO RELIEF

If you have no improvement, have swelling in the joints, or have a family history of arthritis, you should consult a rheumatologist.

PROGNOSIS

Rheumatoid arthritis has a fair prognosis; it is in the blood, handed down from generation to generation. Degenerative arthritis has a bad prognosis.

You can slow its progress by changing the inefficient movements to those causing less stress, but you cannot make the joint new again—damage done will remain. However, you can slow its progression.

OTHER POSSIBILITIES

See the table showing the different types of arthritis (Table C.1). Low-grade joint pain is rather indicative of some kinds of arthritis.

DIGGING A LITTLE DEEPER

Rheumatoid Arthritis versus Degenerative Arthritis. See Section C.9.

SIGNS AND SYMPTOMS

Clear or bloody-looking fluid-filled bump under a thin layer of the skin.

NAME OF INJURY

Blisters (clear or blood)

DESCRIPTION

A small vesicle (fluid-filled sac) or a bulla (larger vesicle). May have clear, watery (serous) contents or bloody contents.

CAUSE

May be caused by a pinch or bruise, but most often due to persistent friction to an area of skin.

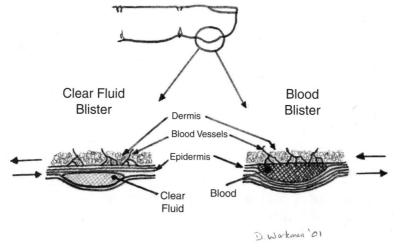

Figure 4.14   A blister is caused by rubbing of skin layers, producing irritation and fluid buildup between them. Deeper blisters may rupture small vessels and fill with blood, causing a blood blister.

TREATMENT

It is best to leave a blister alone until it pops (especially if it's smaller than one centimeter in diameter). However, you may pop it with a sterile needle just enough to allow the fluid to escape, keeping the skin intact. This protects the skin underneath from exposure or infection.

Immediate Relief

Lancing: First clean the skin with alcohol, poke one or two holes in the upper skin, drain the fluid, and leave the skin on. After it pops, or is lanced, it is best to apply antibiotic ointment and cover it with a bandage until it becomes less tender in a day or two (big or deep blisters take longer). If you are going to continue activity that rubs the blister (especially on the feet), put petroleum jelly over the bandage and cover it with a second bandage so they will slide on each other rather than rubbing.

PREVENTION

Technique

Blisters are usually a result of improper or inefficient movement. When the body operates inefficiently, friction can occur, causing rubbing of the skin layers on each other. This results in blisters or calluses, or both. A change in your technique will help. Contact a teacher (one without blistered hands) familiar with ergonomics. Most likely, you are gripping the sticks too tightly.

IF NO RELIEF

If the fluid coming from the blister isn't clear like water, or if it smells bad, seek advice from your physician. Also see your doctor if it gets infected (swollen, red, hot, increasingly painful over a short period of time).

PROGNOSIS

Excellent healing occurs if these procedures are followed and the source of the irritation is removed.

OTHER POSSIBILITIES

Boil (an infection that is deeper in the skin and more painful) or callus (solid knot of skin, not fluid filled).

DIGGING A LITTLE DEEPER

What is a blister? See Section C.7.

SIGNS AND SYMPTOMS

Thickening of skin in areas that rub against something (hands or feet). Usually cause pain, especially on pressure or rubbing of the area.

NAME OF INJURY

Callus

DESCRIPTION

A callus is a thickening of the skin anywhere on the body where repeated rubbing or friction occurs (usually on the hands or feet). Many times they appear gradually after blisters have come and gone. The skin markings (fingerprints) are unchanged, and the callus typically won't bleed if scraped or sanded. Although not usually painful at first, calluses will hurt, crack, or bleed if they continue to progress.

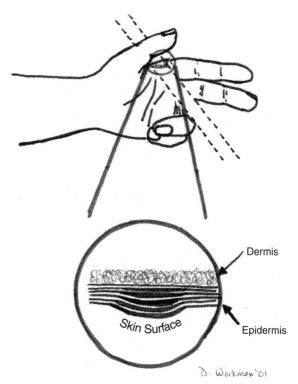

Figure 4.15 A callus is thickening of the outer skin (epidermis) in response to increased rubbing of the area. This protects it.

CAUSE

The skin rubs something repeatedly for an extended period of time (weeks or longer). A few causes are improper movement of the hand while playing, heavy sticks or mallets, hand drumming inefficiently, and so on.

TREATMENT

Immediate Relief

First, find and fix the cause of the callus (see Technique).

To remove the callus, cover it with a hot towel for about ten minutes, then remove and scrape off the dead skin with a pumice stone. Another method is to put Whitfield's Ointment and hydrocortisone cream on it at night, cover with a plastic bag until morning, and rub off the dead skin with a rough towel or firm brush. Do this as needed, but remember that the calluses are a result of using the body in an improper way, and if you don't fix the problem, you will never get rid of the callus. Check your technique.

PREVENTION

Technique

These sores usually result from playing instruments that require aggressive use of the hands (hand drumming, marching, trap set, etc.).

Exercises

Find weak areas and strengthen them. Usually you will find that the parts with calluses are doing the jobs of other areas. Balance out your technique so each area of the body pulls its own weight. Find a good teacher to work with you on your technique.

IF NO RELIEF

If you have done all of this and the calluses do not decrease within four weeks, see your medical doctor or dermatologist.

PROGNOSIS

Calluses usually heal without any real problems.

OTHER POSSIBILITIES

Corns (see Chapter 7) or blisters (usually come on quickly and are filled with clear fluid or blood).

RELATED AREAS

Many injuries can be related to areas of the body other than where you feel the pain. For example, pain in the shoulder may be the result of a problem with the neck or elbow area. If you cannot find the injury that fits your complaints in this chapter, please look in the chapters of the related areas indicated in Figure 4.16.

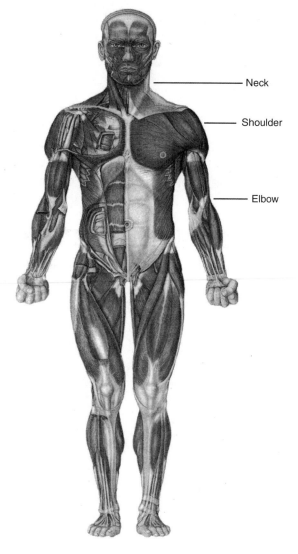

— Neck

— Shoulder

— Elbow

STRETCHES

THE PHILOSOPHY OF STRETCHING

Stretching is not something you do *to* the body; it is something you *allow* the body to do. All stretches must be done by relaxing and allowing the muscles to stretch. If you try to force the muscles to stretch, their immediate reaction is to protect themselves from tearing by pulling back. This can quickly turn into a tug-of-war of you against your muscles, and nothing good can happen. This is why many people stretch and stretch without any positive results, and sometimes they even injure themselves.

Figure 4.16   (Anatomical Chart Company, Lippincott Williams & Wilkins 2003)

GENERAL RULES FOR STRETCHING

Stretches are most effective when the body is warmed up first. This means you should do some mild exercise of the area to be stretched prior to beginning. For example, if you are stretching the legs, do some walking or running until the muscles get warm and loose (usually just before you begin to perspire). With the hands, try some basic rudiments—singles and doubles are best. If you are paying attention to your body, you will notice the area warming up as the blood is pumped into it. Or you can take a shower or sit in hot water prior to stretching—which is not as effective, but still good.

Do not

- pop your knuckles
- stretch when that part of the body is cold
- use bouncing or jerking motions while stretching
- force the stretch to the point where you cannot let the area relax

BASIC STRETCHES FOR THE WRIST AND HAND

STRETCH 4.1: "HANDS OVER HEAD" WRIST STRETCHES

This set of stretches is for general loosening of the arm muscles. If done correctly they will loosen and warm up the muscles that operate the wrists and fingers. By positioning your hands above your head, you get a better stretch in the arms and hands.

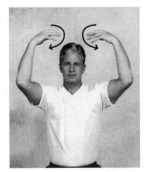

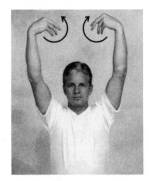

Figure 4.17 Rotate the arms and wrists (twenty rotations at one per second) in a relaxed way.

Figure 4.18 Bend the wrist forward and backward without forcing it (twenty times, one way per second). Repeat each wrist.

Figure 4.19 Rotate the wrist clockwise and counterclockwise in a relaxed way (twenty rotations at one per second).

STRETCH 4.2: SHOULDER SHRUGS

The muscles in what most people call the shoulders and neck are important in securing the arms to the body so that the hands can pull, push, move, and so on. If they are not operating properly, the arms and hands lose a great amount of strength, coordination, and endurance. These stretches are designed to restore circulation and movement to the stabilizers of the arms and shoulders.

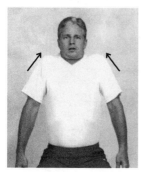

Figure 4.20 Pull both shoulders to the ears, hold tight for seven seconds, then relax for thirty seconds with shoulders dropped.

Figure 4.21 Drop and relax the shoulders completely, then roll them up and back slowly seven to ten times (one roll per two seconds).

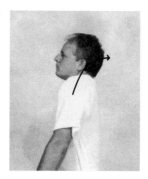

Figure 4.22 Rolling of the shoulders should be done slowly and smoothly, without forcing them.

STRETCH 4.3: THUMB STRETCHES

The thumb is constantly used in playing most percussive instruments. For this reason, it tends to suffer more than its fair share of injury. Most of these injuries have to do with tight, sore muscles that can decrease the ability to play and put undue pressure on the joints. The following stretches are specifically designed to loosen the muscles of the thumb most often affected. The thumb is typically overworked if the player doesn't balance the load properly between the wrist, arm, hand, and so forth.

4.3.1: Thumb Tuck

This stretch works on the muscles that bring the thumb away from the hand. When they are tight, pain is usually felt just above the wrist on the thumb side.

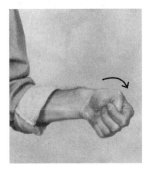

Figure 4.23 Tuck the thumb into the fist with a light grip.

Figure 4.24 Slowly and easily drop the fist toward the pinky with the arm straight and relax. Hold for twenty to thirty seconds (you should feel mild stretching).

Figure 4.25 Lightly shake the hand at your side to allow the muscles to relax. Repeat this routine three to five times with each hand.

4.3.2: Thumb Extension

This stretches the muscles that bring the thumb to the palm of the hand and can help relieve pain and tightness in the big muscle of the thumb.

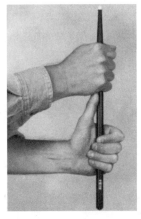

Figure 4.26 Grab the left thumb with the right hand while holding a stick.

Figure 4.27 Pull the thumb into extension, as illustrated in the figure. Relax and hold for twenty seconds. Repeat for abduction.

Figure 4.28 Lightly shake the hand to allow the muscles to relax. Repeat this routine three to five times with each hand.

STRETCH 4.4: FOREARM STRETCHES

The forearm muscles operate the wrist and fingers. Obviously, it is imperative that they are at their best for the percussionist to play well. These stretches are designed to loosen the forearm muscles. They are the most effective stretches I have found.

4.4.1: Pretzel Stretch

It is common for the musician to get too aggressive with this stretch with an "if a little is good, more is better" attitude. Remember to keep the fingers snug around the sticks just enough to hold on, and keep the wrists and forearms very loose.

  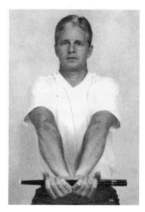

Figure 4.29   Extend both arms in front of you with palms facing up holding a stick.

Figure 4.30   Bring the hands to the chest, rotating down through the arm loop and straight out in an inverted position.

Figure 4.31   Hold the stretch for twenty seconds, relax for a second, then raise the arms and hold again (repeat entire stretch until loose).

4.4.2: Hand Flexors

Continue to lower the hands with each repetition until the hands feel limber and comfortable. As your hands go lower, the palm gets farther from the wall, which allows better stretching of the finger muscles. If you feel pain in the wrist, back off or stop.

Figure 4.32 Place palms on the wall about chest height, gradually leaning on them while relaxing; hold twenty seconds (you should feel the stretch).

Figure 4.33 Drop hands to the sides and lightly shake them to relax the muscles.

Figure 4.34 Place hands on the wall, six inches lower than last position, and repeat the stretch.

4.4.3: Hand Extensors

Raise the hands with each repetition of this stretch until the hands feel limber and comfortable. Do not push hard on the hands or you may injure the wrist. Just relax the wrists and allow enough pressure to stretch the muscles. If you feel pain in the wrist, back off or stop.

Figure 4.35 Place back of hands on the wall about chest height, gradually leaning on them while relaxing; hold twenty seconds (you should feel the stretch).

Figure 4.36 Drop hands to the sides and lightly shake them to relax the muscles.

Figure 4.37 Place hands on the wall, six inches higher than last position, and repeat the stretch.

With each of these three forearm stretches, you can reach other muscles by moving the hands out to each side slightly and repeating the stretch in the same manner.

CHAPTER 5

ELBOW PROBLEMS

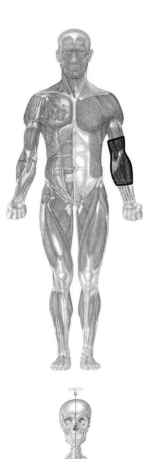

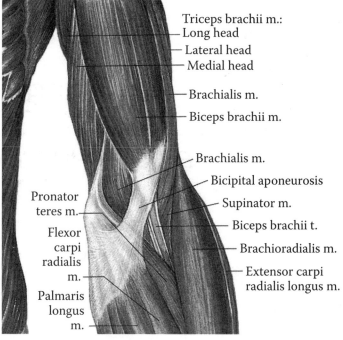

Triceps brachii m.:
Long head
Lateral head
Medial head

Brachialis m.

Biceps brachii m.

Brachialis m.

Bicipital aponeurosis

Supinator m.

Biceps brachii t.

Brachioradialis m.

Extensor carpi
radialis longus m.

Pronator
teres m.

Flexor
carpi
radialis
m.

Palmaris
longus
m.

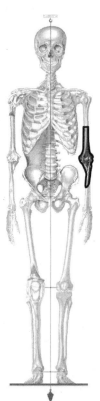

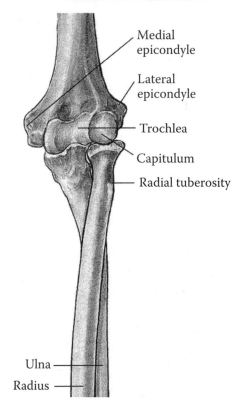

Medial
epicondyle

Lateral
epicondyle

Trochlea

Capitulum

Radial tuberosity

Ulna

Radius

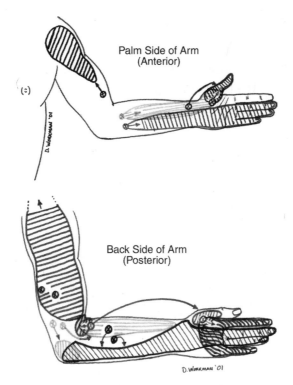

Figure 5.1 This figure shows common places for spasms and trigger points in the arm. The X represents the trigger point, and the shaded lines represent where the pain radiates.

SIGNS AND SYMPTOMS

Stabbing pain or ache in the forearm or upper arm. Limited arm movement with pain at extremes. Pain relieved with arm resting in neutral position. Tender spots in the muscle belly.

NAME OF INJURY

Muscle spasm (elbow)

DESCRIPTION

Overuse or improper use of the wrist and fingers, causing depletion and cramping of the muscle (e.g., long practices with heavy sticks or mallets or inefficient technique).

CAUSE

Doing too much too soon or too often, or both.

TREATMENT

Immediate Relief

Rest, ice the area of pain, and resist movements that produce the pain. Aspirin or other over-the-counter pain relievers have proved effective. Massage to the tight areas and trigger points helps to reduce the pain and spasm.

PREVENTION

Technique

Change your seat, shoes, instrument configuration, or sitting positions to decrease stress to the body. Drink plenty of water to flush out the muscles. Take time out to rest periodically each session (ten-minute rest for each hour), and allow one day a week when you don't play at all to let the body rejuvenate.

Stretches

Mild massage to the sore muscles followed by gentle stretching of the area (see Stretches 4.2 and 4.4). Allow pain to be your guide. In addition, when you play, change positions more often and try the recommended stretches as you begin feeling tight.

Exercises

Repeat the movements that caused the pain but at a lower intensity and for shorter periods of time (about half as long). Gradually increase the time and intensity over a period of weeks, stopping when the pain begins.

IF NO RELIEF

If no improvement occurs within one to two weeks, consult your doctor.

PROGNOSIS

This injury is easy to treat and fully resolves. However, if you wait to treat it, it can become chronic (requiring extensive treatment) and possibly lead to other, more serious, injuries. This injury can decrease your strength, endurance, and power.

OTHER POSSIBILITIES

Tendonitis (see descriptions of tennis elbow and golfer's elbow in this chapter) or phlebitis (inflammation of a vein—see your medical doctor).

DIGGING A LITTLE DEEPER

What are muscle spasms? What is a trigger point? See Sections C.1 and C.8.

SIGNS AND SYMPTOMS

Swelling or pain (burn, stab), or both, at the tip of the elbow while moving (active or passive). May be tender to touch. Stretching or using those muscles without movement doesn't increase pain.

NAME OF INJURY

Elbow bursitis

DESCRIPTION

Bursae are flat, coin-sized, lubricant-filled sacs positioned anywhere two tissues rub together. They provide smooth movement and prevent damage to the area. When an area gets overused, the bursae get hot and inflamed, causing bursitis.

CAUSE

Increased playing time or aggressiveness will produce tight muscles and friction to the areas of movement (bursae). Bursitis may also be caused by sudden trauma to a bursae area.

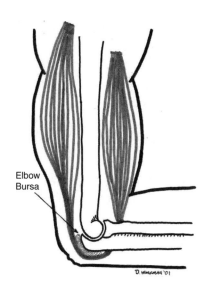

Figure 5.2 This figure shows the location of a bursa in the elbow. They are coin-sized, lubricant-filled sacs between rubbing tissues. They reduce friction and irritation.

TREATMENT

Immediate Relief

Rest, ice the area of pain, and resist movements that produce the pain. Aspirin has been shown to relieve some of the pain. When the joint cools down (two to five days), alternate ice (fifteen minutes) and heat (fifteen minutes—some say caster oil on the area during heating helps). Massage to the triceps reduces pressure on the bursa.

PREVENTION

Technique

Move elbows efficiently.

Stretches

Begin when pain is no longer acute, approximately five days (see Stretch 5.1).

Exercises

An excellent exercise after the pain is gone is to dribble a basketball for three minutes with each hand, alternating right and left for a total of fifteen to thirty minutes. Swimming the breaststroke for fifteen to thirty minutes daily is a good alternative. As pain allows, do triceps extensions—five to fifteen pounds, three sets of ten repetitions with a one-minute rest between repetitions. If you are unable to finish the last set, use a lower weight.

IF NO RELIEF

See your doctor if there is no improvement within one week. Extreme cases may need to be drained with a needle (*only to be done by a doctor*), although this is a last resort. This injury may possibly become infected.

PROGNOSIS

If treated early, chances for full recovery are excellent. However, if treatment is not completed, the injury may return.

OTHER POSSIBILITIES

Avulsion fracture (usually from a sudden injury—see a doctor immediately) or triceps tendonitis (pain starts mild and usually increases gradually over weeks).

DIGGING A LITTLE DEEPER

What is bursitis? See Section C.2.

SIGNS AND SYMPTOMS

Pain on the thumb-side bone of the elbow, particularly when bending the wrist backward or rotating the forearm outward against resistance.

NAME OF INJURY

Lateral epicondylitis (aka tennis elbow)

DESCRIPTION

Inflammation of tendons that extend the wrist. Tight and spastic muscles pull the tendons, tearing them at or from the bone (see Figure 5.3). This leads to tendonitis—an irritation of the tendons.

CAUSE

Repetitive misuse of, or increased pressure on, muscles that extend the wrist. Usually from a sudden increase in playing time, intensity, or stick size.

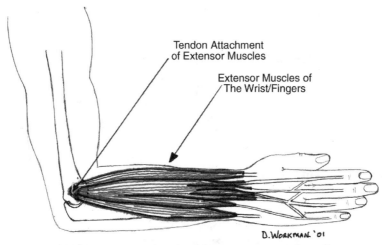

Tendon Attachment
of Extensor Muscles

Extensor Muscles of
The Wrist/Fingers

D.WORKMAN '01

Figure 5.3   When the muscles that extend the wrist and fingers are injured or in spasm, they put constant pull on the lateral epicondyle where they attach. This will cause an injury known as lateral epicondylitis, or tennis elbow.

TREATMENT

Immediate Relief

Rest the area for three to five days. Ice the skin directly over the area of pain for fifteen minutes, then remove the ice for fifteen minutes. Do this for two hours in the morning and in the evening (see Section A.1). Aspirin may help. A tennis elbow wrap may help, especially when playing. Massage the bulky muscles of the forearm for five minutes followed by ice for fifteen minutes to decrease the swelling after playing.

PREVENTION

Technique

Use lighter sticks or mallets. Improve hand technique—avoid playing with the wrists bent excessively forward or backward.

Stretches

Hand extensor stretches (see Stretch 4.4.3).

Exercises

Finger extensions (see Exercise B.4).

IF NO RELIEF

If no improvement occurs within one week, see your physician.

PROGNOSIS

Prognosis is excellent if relief begins within a week. It's good if relief begins within four to eight weeks and poor if relief begins after twelve weeks.

OTHER POSSIBILITIES

Bursitis or avulsion fracture (usually from a sudden injury—see a doctor immediately).

DIGGING A LITTLE DEEPER

What are muscle spasms? What is tendonitis? See Sections C.1 and C.3.

SIGNS AND SYMPTOMS

Pain on the inner-side (pinky) bone of the elbow, particularly when curling the wrist or rotating the forearm inward.

NAME OF INJURY

Medial epicondylitis (aka golfer's elbow)

DESCRIPTION

Inflammation of tendons and muscles that flex the wrist. Muscles get tight and spasm from overuse, and they pull the tendons from their insertion at the medial epicondyle of the humerus bone (see Figure 5.4), producing tendonitis.

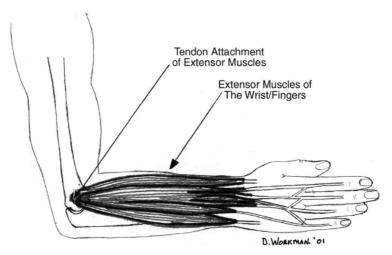

Tendon Attachment of Extensor Muscles

Extensor Muscles of The Wrist/Fingers

D. WORKMAN '01

Figure 5.4 This figure shows the areas of trigger points in the muscles that flex the wrist and fingers. When the muscles are injured or contracted, they cause constant pull or irritation, or both, where the tendon attaches at the medial epicondyle, causing medial epicondylitis, or golfer's elbow.

CAUSE

Repetitive misuse of or increased pressure on flexor muscles. Usually from increased playing time or stick size.

TREATMENT

Immediate Relief

Rest for three to five days. Ice for fifteen minutes then remove ice for fifteen minutes. Do this for two hours in the morning and in the evening (see Section A.1). Aspirin may help. A tennis elbow wrap eases pressure, especially when playing or lifting equipment. Massage the bulky muscles of the forearm for five minutes, followed by ice for fifteen minutes to decrease the swelling.

PREVENTION

Technique

Use lighter sticks or mallets. Improve technique: Avoid playing with the wrists bent excessively forward or backward.

Stretches

Wrist stretches (see Stretch 4.1).

Exercises

Finger flexion (See Exercise B.5).

IF NO RELIEF

If no improvement occurs within one week, see your physician.

PROGNOSIS

Prognosis is excellent if relief begins within a week. It's good if relief begins within four to eight weeks and poor if relief begins after twelve weeks.

OTHER POSSIBILITIES

Bursitis or avulsion fracture (usually from a sudden injury—see a doctor immediately).

DIGGING A LITTLE DEEPER

What are muscle spasms? What is tendonitis? What is a trigger point? See Sections C.1, C.3, and C.8.

RELATED AREAS

Many injuries can be related to areas of the body other than where you feel the pain. For example, pain in the shoulder may be the result of a problem with the neck or elbow area. If you cannot find the injury that fits your complaints in this chapter, please look in the chapters of the related areas indicated in the Figure 5.5.

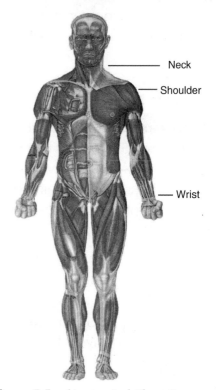

Neck

Shoulder

Wrist

Figure 5.5 (Anatomical Chart Company, Lippincott Williams & Wilkins 2003)

STRETCHES

THE PHILOSOPHY OF STRETCHING

Stretching is not something you do *to* the body; it is something you *allow* the body to do. All stretches must be done by relaxing and allowing the muscles to stretch. If you try to force the muscles to stretch, their immediate reaction is to protect themselves from tearing by pulling back. This can quickly turn into a tug-of-war of you against your muscles, and nothing good can happen. This is why many people stretch and stretch without any positive results, and sometimes they even injure themselves.

GENERAL RULES FOR STRETCHING

Stretches are most effective when the body is warmed up first. This means you should do some mild exercise of the area to be stretched prior to beginning. For example, if you are stretching the legs, do some walking or running until the muscles get warm and loose (usually just before you begin to perspire). With the hands, try some basic rudiments—singles and doubles are best. If you are paying attention to your body, you will notice the area warming up as the blood is pumped into it. Or you can take a shower or sit in hot water prior to stretching—which is not as effective, but still good.

Do not

- pop your knuckles
- stretch when that part of the body is cold
- use bouncing or jerking motions while stretching
- force the stretch to the point where you cannot let the area relax

BASIC STRETCHES FOR THE ARMS

STRETCH 5.1: TRICEP STRETCHES FOR THE ARMS

This set of stretches is for general loosening of the tricep muscles of the arms. They will loosen and warm up the muscles that straighten the elbow. If done correctly, the stretches will relieve pressure on the elbow bursae. By positioning the hands above your head, you get a better stretch.

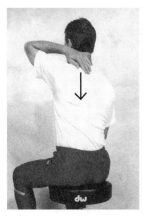  

Figure 5.6   While sitting (or lying face up), reach back over the head and slide the hand down the neck to the shoulders.

Figure 5.7   Relax the arm, and let it stretch for twenty to thirty seconds.

Figure 5.8   Allow the arm to straighten and hang down to loosen the muscles, then repeat until stretch is no longer felt.

CHAPTER 6

SHOULDER PROBLEMS

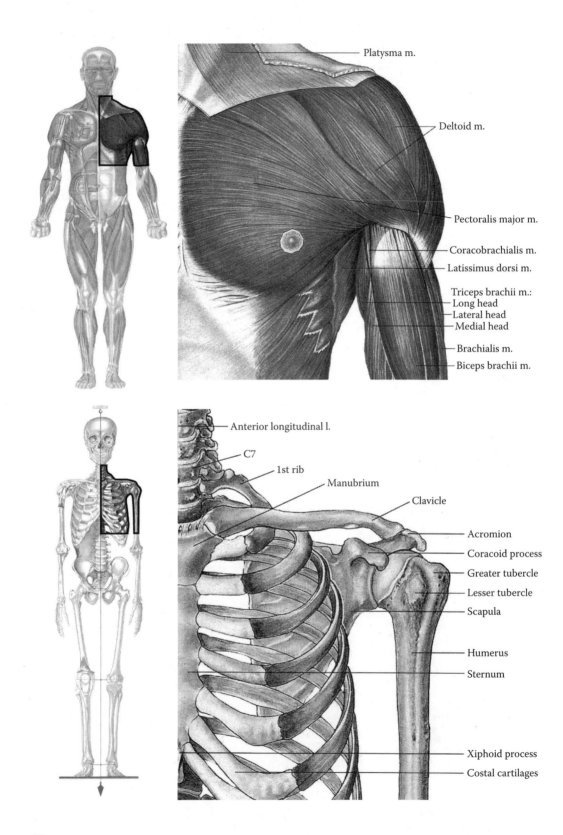

Platysma m.

Deltoid m.

Pectoralis major m.

Coracobrachialis m.

Latissimus dorsi m.

Triceps brachii m.:
Long head
Lateral head
Medial head

Brachialis m.

Biceps brachii m.

Anterior longitudinal l.

C7

1st rib

Manubrium

Clavicle

Acromion

Coracoid process

Greater tubercle

Lesser tubercle

Scapula

Humerus

Sternum

Xiphoid process

Costal cartilages

66

SIGNS AND SYMPTOMS

Pain and weakness when lifting arm, but good range of motion and strength. Tender top or outer shoulder area. Pain in the morning that goes away while exercising.

NAME OF INJURY

Muscle spasm (shoulder rotators)

DESCRIPTION

Overuse or improper use of the arms (e.g., prolonged practice in reaching or awkward positions with heavy sticks or mallets or inefficient technique). Muscle overuse causes depletion and contraction of muscle, which leads to cramps.

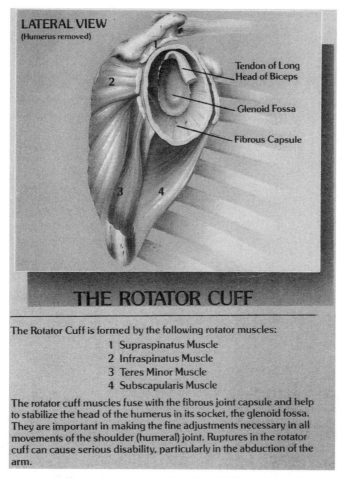

Figure 6.1 The rotator cuff muscles (commonly called SITS muscles) allow for fine movements of the shoulder. They are commonly injured muscles. (Ortho-McNeil Pharmaceutical, Inc., 2003)

CAUSE

Overuse of, trauma to, or increased stress on muscles of the shoulder (usually deltoid or supraspinatus muscles) over a short period of time (one day to two weeks). Increased load or amount of time using arm, or using unfamiliar or demanding equipment (e.g., improper mallet, marching bass drum, or ride cymbal).

TREATMENT

Immediate Relief

Ice and heat with massage. Rest twelve hours and stretch lightly and gradually (see the description of fibromyalgia in this chapter).

PREVENTION

Technique

Incorporate a longer warm-up session before playing or practicing to allow the muscles to acclimate. If necessary, bring drums and cymbals closer to your comfortable reach (especially the ride cymbal). Proper lifting techniques may help prevent this problem (see Section A.3).

Stretches

See the description of fibromyalgia in this chapter.

Exercises

See the description of fibromyalgia in this chapter.

IF NO RELIEF

If no improvement occurs within three days, see your doctor.

PROGNOSIS

The prognosis is excellent. See your doctor to be evaluated and to rule out any serious condition.

OTHER POSSIBILITIES

Bursitis (usually pain near the joint on movement of the shoulder) or tendonitis (usually severe pain on holding arm out from side).

DIGGING A LITTLE DEEPER

What are muscle spasms? See Section C.1.

SIGNS AND SYMPTOMS

Pain, stiffness, or tenderness of muscles and joints (achy) with tender points, especially in the neck, shoulders, thorax, or thighs.

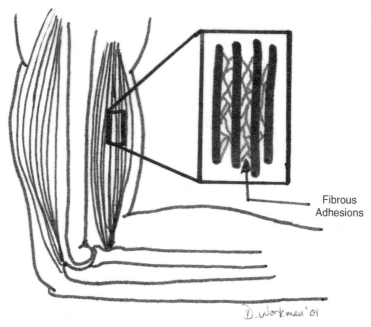

Figure 6.2 This figure shows fibrous adhesive tissue (red crisscrossing lines) binding the muscle fibers (black lines) together, making movement of the muscle fibers painful or impossible.

NAME OF INJURY

Fibromyalgia

DESCRIPTION

A rheumatic condition causing pain in the fibrous connective tissues of muscles, tendons, or ligaments.

CAUSE

Most commonly caused by mental or physical stress (either one major trauma or many small episodes for extended periods of time). May also be caused by poor sleeping or eating habits or damp, cold weather.

TREATMENT

Immediate Relief

If the problem is stress induced, reduce the stress or learn ways to deal with it more effectively. Heat to the painful area as well as moderate to deep soft tissue work are effective. Over-the-counter pain relievers seem to reduce the pain.

PREVENTION

Technique

Change instrument setup to decrease needless reaching. Lowering the ride cymbal to shoulder level or lower is especially effective. Try to keep movements close to the neutral range in any playing situation.

Stretches

See Stretches 6.2 and 6.3.

Exercises

Try lateral shoulder raises with light weights (five to ten pounds), three sets of ten forward, backward, and in windmill position (see Exercise B.6), or swimming (freestyle or backstroke) for fifteen to thirty minutes (see Exercise B.8).

IF NO RELIEF

See your physician if you have no relief.

PROGNOSIS

Treatment may be a long process. If all aspects are successfully addressed and causes eliminated, then the prognosis is good. If the condition persists without treatment, it will become chronic and increasingly more difficult to resolve.

OTHER POSSIBILITIES

Arthritis (joint pain) or bursitis (pain usually close to joint).

DIGGING A LITTLE DEEPER

What are muscle spasms? See Section C.1.

SIGNS AND SYMPTOMS

Burning, stabbing pain, increasing with movement of the shoulder. No increased pain when resting or using muscles without movement.

NAME OF INJURY

Shoulder bursitis

DESCRIPTION

Bursae are flat, coin-sized, lubricant-filled sacs positioned where two areas of the body rub together. They provide smooth movement and prevent damage to the area.

CAUSE

When an area gets overused, the bursae get increased friction, break down, and become hot and inflamed. This causes irritation of the bursae (known as bursitis).

TREATMENT

Immediate Relief

Rest, ice the area of pain, and resist movements that produce the pain. Aspirin has been shown to relieve some of the pain. When the joint cools down (two to five days), alternate ice (fifteen minutes) and heat (fifteen minutes). Some say that caster oil on the area during heating is helpful. Massage to the shoulder muscles helps reduce pressure on the bursae.

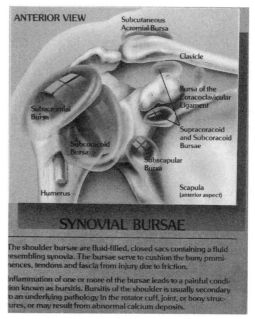

ANTERIOR VIEW

Subcutaneous Acromial Bursa

Clavicle

Bursa of the Coracoclavicular Ligament

Subacromial Bursa

Supracoracoid and Subcoracoid Bursae

Subcoracoid Bursa

Subscapular Bursa

Scapula (anterior aspect)

Humerus

SYNOVIAL BURSAE

The shoulder bursae are fluid-filled, closed sacs containing a fluid resembling synovia. The bursae serve to cushion the bony prominences, tendons and fascia from injury due to friction.

Inflammation of one or more of the bursae leads to a painful condition known as bursitis. Bursitis of the shoulder is usually secondary to an underlying pathology in the rotator cuff, joint, or bony structures, or may result from abnormal calcium deposits.

Figure 6.3 Bursae are flat, coin-sized, lubricant-filled sacs positioned where two areas rub together. They provide smooth movement to prevent irritation and damage to the area. (Ortho-McNeil Pharmaceutical, Inc. 2003)

PREVENTION

Technique

This is usually caused by excessive shoulder movement or by poor or extreme positioning, such as high ride cymbal, prolonged symphonic crash cymbals, mallet instruments, and so on. Improper lifting techniques are also a cause (see Section A.3).

Stretches

Begin when pain is no longer acute, approximately five days (see Stretch 6.1).

Exercises

Once the pain is gone, put arms straight out to sides. Rotate them in small circles slowly for fifteen times, then repeat, doing medium circles followed by large circles. Swimming the backstroke or freestyle for fifteen to thirty minutes daily is a great exercise. If you can do these exercises without pain, do lateral raises with light weights (less than ten pounds), three sets of ten repetitions with a one-minute rest between repetitions (as pain allows). If you are unable to finish the last set, use a lower weight.

IF NO RELIEF

See your doctor if there is no change within two weeks. Extreme cases may need to be drained by the doctor as a last resort. This injury may possibly become infected.

PROGNOSIS

If treated early, the prognosis for full recovery is excellent. However, if treatment is not completed, the injury may return.

OTHER POSSIBILITIES

Avulsion fracture (usually from a sudden injury or trauma—see a doctor immediately) or tendonitis of shoulder muscle areas (especially supraspinatus).

DIGGING A LITTLE DEEPER

What is bursitis? See Section C.2.

SIGNS AND SYMPTOMS

Sharp or dull ache in the shoulder, especially when raising arm to sides. Usually from constant microtrauma rather than one large (macro-) trauma.

Acute pain (in twenty-five- to forty-five-year-olds) around acromion (bone on top of shoulder). It is usually gone in a few days without return if treated as indicated next.

Chronic pain (in forty-five- to sixty-year-olds). Shows on x-ray. With arms out from sides, patient feels jerk and agonizing pain just below the shoulder (pain from 0 to 180 degrees; see the description of osteoarthritis of the shoulder at the end of this chapter). It also produces pain at the acromion and crepitation (grinding feeling) and pain when sleeping on that shoulder. The condition usually subsides within six months if treated as follows.

NAME OF INJURY

Tendonitis (shoulder)

DESCRIPTION

Micro- or macrotrauma to one or more of the shoulder rotator muscles results in inflammation of the tendon(s)—usually the supraspinatus tendon (see Figure 6.4).

CAUSE

Lifting heavy equipment when the muscles aren't ready or exposing the shoulder to prolonged use (months to years) while in a painful situation.

TREATMENT

Immediate Relief

Sudden onset: Put ice on it, don't move it, and see your doctor as soon as possible. Old, chronic problem (worse or same over time): Have it evaluated (usually x-ray) by a doctor before beginning any treatment. With a doctor's approval, the following program may be helpful.

PREVENTION

Technique

Avoid far-reaching and high movements. *Do not* lift heavy objects (more than twenty pounds) with the damaged arm until it is healed. When it has healed, it still won't be as good as before the injury. You will always need to be careful with it, allowing pain to be your guide. Proper lifting techniques will help prevent this (see Section A.3).

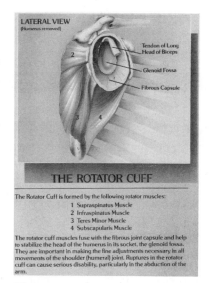

THE ROTATOR CUFF

The Rotator Cuff is formed by the following rotator muscles:
1 Supraspinatus Muscle
2 Infraspinatus Muscle
3 Teres Minor Muscle
4 Subscapularis Muscle

The rotator cuff muscles fuse with the fibrous joint capsule and help to stabilize the head of the humerus in its socket, the glenoid fossa. They are important in making the fine adjustments necessary in all movements of the shoulder (humeral) joint. Ruptures in the rotator cuff can cause serious disability, particularly in the abduction of the arm.

Figure 6.4 Supraspinatus tendonitis is very common in the shoulder. It is the tearing of the tendon fibers (shown in figure), which causes swelling and pain. (Ortho-McNeil Pharmaceutical, Inc. 2003)

Stretches

See Stretch 6.5. *Any stretches or exercises should be done under doctor supervision.* When strong enough, you may begin exercises.

Exercises

Once the pain is gone, do Exercises B.7 and B.8. As pain allows, progress to lateral raises (Exercise B.6) with light weights (less than ten pounds), three sets of ten repetitions with a one-minute rest between repetitions. If you are unable to finish the last set, use a lower weight.

IF NO RELIEF

If you feel that you have this injury, see a doctor as soon as possible. You cannot properly treat this injury without strict supervision.

PROGNOSIS

Acute tendonitis has an excellent prognosis if the tendon is not torn, and with proper treatment. Chronic tendonitis has a fair to good prognosis depending on the extent of the damage, and with proper treatment.

OTHER POSSIBILITIES

Tendon rupture (cannot move arm out to the side) or dislocation (unable to move it, and shoulder looks deformed or dropped down).

DIGGING A LITTLE DEEPER

What are muscle spasms? What is tendonitis? See Sections C.1 and C.3.

SIGNS AND SYMPTOMS

Pain in and around shoulder joint from sudden trauma or improper use over a prolonged period of time. Motion limited by pain, causing progressively limited motion and muscle weakness (may interrupt sleep).

NAME OF INJURY

Adhesive capsulitis (frozen shoulder)

DESCRIPTION

Progressively worse pain and gradual (weeks to months) decrease in shoulder motion from muscle and ligament contraction at the joint.

CAUSE

Usually caused by a single macrotrauma or a repetitive microtrauma. May be of unknown cause in some cases (usually in women older than age forty and men older than age fifty).

TREATMENT

Immediate Relief

Do not put off going to see your doctor on this one. It requires aggressive work for the shoulder to respond well. The following are things that will aid you as you are going through therapy.

PREVENTION

Technique

Avoid using extreme shoulder motions or postures for a few weeks until the pain subsides. Proceed to return to normal playing as pain permits.

Stretches

Regular stretching should be part of your daily routine, especially after an injury (see Stretches 6.2–6.4). Moderate pain is expected with

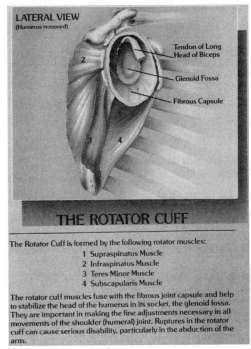

LATERAL VIEW
(Humerus removed)

Tendon of Long Head of Biceps
Glenoid Fossa
Fibrous Capsule

THE ROTATOR CUFF

The Rotator Cuff is formed by the following rotator muscles:
1 Supraspinatus Muscle
2 Infraspinatus Muscle
3 Teres Minor Muscle
4 Subscapularis Muscle

The rotator cuff muscles fuse with the fibrous joint capsule and help to stabilize the head of the humerus in its socket, the glenoid fossa. They are important in making the fine adjustments necessary in all movements of the shoulder (humeral) joint. Ruptures in the rotator cuff can cause serious disability, particularly in the abduction of the arm.

Figure 6.5   This figure shows injured muscles and ligaments of the shoulder joint contract, causing limited and painful shoulder movement. (Ortho-McNeil Pharmaceutical, Inc., 2003)

these stretches, but the pain should subside shortly after you let off of the stretch.

Exercises

Try lateral shoulder lifts (see Exercise B.7). Swimming is also good in place of, or in conjunction with, this treatment. The best movements are freestyle or backstroke for fifteen to thirty minutes (see Exercise B.8).

IF NO RELIEF

You should already be seeing your doctor for this injury; he or she will make the proper referral if you are not progressing.

PROGNOSIS

This injury requires extensive therapy to regain range of motion and strength. The therapy is very painful but effective. With proper treatment and patient compliance, full recovery is possible, but it is not typical.

OTHER POSSIBILITIES

Muscle spasm (tender areas in the muscle belly), bursitis (usually pain on movement of the shoulder), tendon rupture (usually the arm is too painful or is impossible to raise out to the side), or dislocation (usually the shoulder looks deformed or dropped down when the shirt is off, and the patient is unable to move the shoulder in any direction).

DIGGING A LITTLE DEEPER

What are muscle spasms? See Section C.1.

SIGNS AND SYMPTOMS

Pain in the shoulder joint, especially in the morning or following activity. Can be one or both arms or multiple areas of the body.

NAME OF INJURY

Osteoarthritis (shoulder)

DESCRIPTION

Aging of a joint before its time.

CAUSE

Repetitive small movements that wear on the joint (microtrauma) or large injury (macrotrauma), making the joint dysfunctional. It comes on gradually

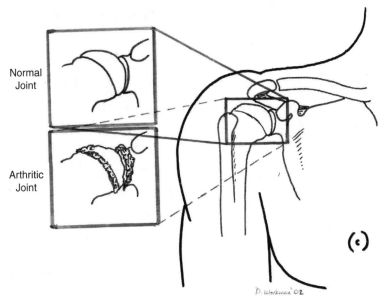

Figure 6.6 To the left is an example of a normal shoulder joint and one with degenerative arthritis, the wearing down of the joint from improper use. Note the smooth curves at the bone's edge in the normal joint, while the arthritic joint shows jagged edges (bone spurs) and decreased space between the bones. These spurs are the bone's attempt to heal.

and is often called "getting old before your time." It affects players who use their shoulders a lot.

TREATMENT

Immediate Relief

Heat does well in the morning to get the joint moving. If the pain follows exercise or activity, ice and aspirin are good choices.

PREVENTION

Technique

The best advice is to reduce stress to the already degenerative joint(s) by avoiding movements that are ergonomically inefficient.

Stretches

Yoga is an excellent overall stretching technique for this ailment in my opinion. Soft tissue massage to the joint has also been found to be helpful. Chiropractic treatment improves the condition in many cases.

Exercises

General aerobic conditioning is warranted. Those exercises that reduce stress to the joint are most effective (swimming, biking, and walking).

IF NO RELIEF

If you have no improvement over a period of months, swelling in the joints, or a family history of any type of arthritis, you should consult a rheumatologist.

PROGNOSIS

Rheumatoid arthritis has a fair prognosis; it is in the blood, handed down from generation to generation. Degenerative arthritis can have its progress slowed by changing the inefficient movements to those of less stress.

OTHER POSSIBILITIES

Different types of arthritis. Low-grade joint pain is rather indicative of some kind of arthritis.

DIGGING A LITTLE DEEPER

Rheumatoid Arthritis versus Degenerative Arthritis. See Section C.9.

RELATED AREAS

Many injuries can be related to areas of the body other than where you feel the pain. For example, pain in the shoulder may be the result of a problem with the neck or elbow area. If you cannot find the injury that fits your complaints in this chapter, please look in the chapters of the related areas indicated in Figure 6.7.

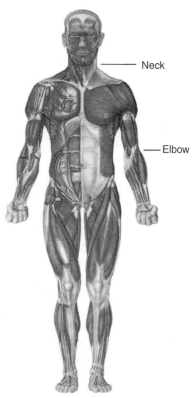

STRETCHES

THE PHILOSOPHY OF STRETCHING

Stretching is not something you do *to* the body; it is something you *allow* the body to do. All stretches must be done by relaxing and allowing the muscles to stretch. If you try to force the muscles to stretch, their immediate reaction is to protect themselves from tearing by pulling back. This can quickly turn into a tug-of-war of you against your muscles, and nothing good can happen. This is why many people stretch and stretch without any positive results, and sometimes they even injure themselves.

Figure 6.7 (Anatomical Chart Company, Lippincott Williams & Wilkins 2003)

GENERAL RULES FOR STRETCHING

Stretches are most effective when the body is warmed up first. This means you should do some mild exercise of the area to be stretched prior to beginning. For example, if you are stretching the legs, do some walking or running until the muscles get warm and loose (usually just before you begin to perspire). With the hands, try some basic rudiments—singles and doubles are best. If you are paying attention to your body, you will notice the area warming up as the blood is pumped into it. Or you can take a shower or sit in hot water prior to stretching—which is not as effective, but still good.

Do not

- pop your knuckles
- stretch when that part of the body is cold
- use bouncing or jerking motions while stretching
- force the stretch to the point where you cannot let the area relax

BASIC STRETCHES FOR THE SHOULDERS

STRETCH 6.1: GENERAL LOOSENING OF THE UPPER BACK, CHEST, ARMS, AND WRISTS

These stretches are for general loosening of the shoulders, across the chest, and behind the back (repeat each stretch five times with one-minute rest between repetition). These muscles stabilize the arms, so they are often tight from use. *Note:* If you are recovering from an injury, begin doing these stretches when the pain is no longer acute (five days or longer). At first, do them lightly and increase the stretch as the body will allow without pain.

 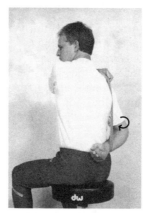 

Figure 6.8   In a sitting or standing position, slowly and easily allow the injured-arm hand to slide *down* the back, and hold the position with a towel or rope (twenty to thirty seconds).

Figure 6.9   Bring the arm around the chest and over the opposite shoulder. Holding a towel or rope, allow the injured arm to drop and relax for twenty to thirty seconds.

Figure 6.10   In sitting or standing position, slowly and easily allow the injured-arm hand to slide *up* the back, and hold the position with a towel or rope (twenty to thirty seconds).

STRETCH 6.2: ARMS AND CHEST STRETCH

Stand in a doorway and, with arms out to sides, lean forward and stretch the shoulders and chest, keeping arms relaxed.

Figure 6.11 Place hands in a doorway at chest height. Lean forward without pushing. Allow twenty to thirty seconds of relaxed stretch.

Figure 6.12 Rest thirty seconds while rotating shoulders to loosen the muscles. Do the same stretch, but position the arms higher or lower the door.

Figure 6.13 Between the stretches, roll the shoulders up and back in a circular motion to loosen the muscles.

STRETCH 6.3: SHOULDER ABDUCTION STRETCH

Loss of motion in the shoulder is common with shoulder injuries. This shoulder stretch is designed to restore the lateral raising motion. Shoulder problems heal slowly, so you should only increase the height 1-2 inches per session having a day of rest between sessions. Ice the shoulder for 15 minutes following the stretch session.

Figure 6.14 Stand with sore shoulder to the wall and begin walking the fingers up the wall.

Figure 6.15 When you hit the painful level, stop and slightly lean the armpit to the wall while relaxing (twenty to thirty seconds).

Figure 6.16 Bring the body back away from the wall and continue walking up a few steps. Repeat previous steps.

STRETCH 6.4: SHOULDER ROTATION STRETCHES

This stretch is to restore motion to the shoulder or to loosen it up prior to playing. This will not be painful unless the shoulder is injured. If it is injured, moderate pain is expected with these stretches, but the pain should subside shortly after you let off of the stretch (if not, discontinue the program and consult your doctor).

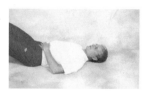

Figure 6.17   Lie on back or stomach with arm to the square, allowing it to drop without pushing (twenty seconds).

Figure 6.18   Lie on back or stomach with arm squared, pointing to feet, allowing it to drop without pushing (twenty seconds).

Figure 6.19   While still on back, allow the arm to rest and relax, then repeat the exercise three to five times.

STRETCH 6.5: INITIAL STRETCHES FOR THE INJURED SHOULDER

This particular program is best as a first stretch following an injury to the shoulder. If you cannot do this routine with relative comfort, do not proceed to any other stretches for the shoulder. *Any stretches or exercises should be under doctor supervision.* A regular stretching program should always be part of your daily routine, especially once you've been injured. When the pain has subsided, gradual and relaxed stretches of the area should begin to regain full range of motion.

Figure 6.20   Lean on a chair with the good arm and allow the injured arm to hang loosely. Rotate one direction, then the other (one to two minutes each direction).

Figure 6.21   As pain permits, allow the circles to get bigger (they should grow every few days).

Figure 6.22   When large circles are no problem and painless, go through the same routine with a weight around the wrist.

CHAPTER 7

FOOT AND ANKLE PROBLEMS

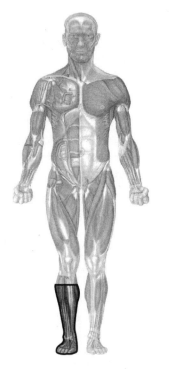

Muscles of Right Foot
(Plantar View)

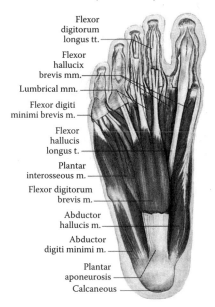

Flexor digitorum longus tt.

Flexor hallucix brevis mm.

Lumbrical mm.

Flexor digiti minimi brevis m.

Flexor hallucis longus t.

Plantar interosseous m.

Flexor digitorum brevis m.

Abductor hallucis m.

Abductor digiti minimi m.

Plantar aponeurosis

Calcaneous

Ligaments of Right Foot
(Dorsal View)

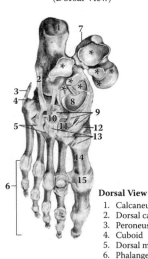

Ligaments of Right Foot
(Plantar View)

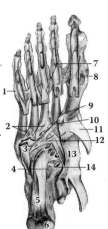

Plantar View
1. Collateral l.
2. Plantar metatarsal ll.
3. Flexor digiti minimi brevis t.
4. Plantar calcaneocuboid l.
5. Long plantar l.
6. Calcaneus
7. Deep transverse metatarsal ll.
8. Sesamoid bone
9. Peroneus longus t.
10. Plantar tarsometatarsal l.
11. Tibialis anterior t.
12. Plantar cuneocuboidl.
13. Tibialis posterior t.
14. Plantar calcaneonavicular l.

Dorsal View
1. Calcaneus
2. Dorsal calacneocuboid l.
3. Peroneus brevis t.
4. Cuboid
5. Dorsal metatarsal ll.
6. Phalanges
7. Talus
8. Navicular
9. Dorsal cuneonavicular ll.
10. Lateral cuneiform
11. Intermediate cuneiform
12. Medial cuneiform
13. Dorsal tarsometatarsal ll.
14. Metatarsus
15. Articular capsule
* Articular surfaces.

SIGNS AND SYMPTOMS

Knifelike pain and possible grabbing sensation in the lower leg muscles. Worse when pointing the toes down.

NAME OF INJURY

Muscle spasm (lower leg)

DESCRIPTION

Muscle overuse causes depletion of potassium, calcium, and sodium, leading to contraction and cramping of the muscle.

CAUSE

Doing too much too soon or too often, or both, or overuse or misuse of the foot and toes; for example, a large increase in marching, poor shoes, improper walking form, or inefficient bass drum technique.

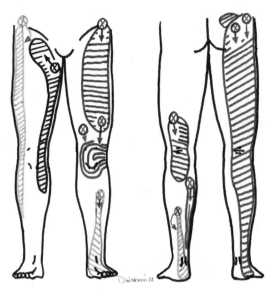

Figure 7.1 This figure shows common lower leg trigger point areas (X) with their areas of referred pain (shaded areas of same color or line pattern).

TREATMENT

Immediate Relief

Rest, ice the area of pain, and resist movements that produce the pain. Aspirin or other over-the-counter pain relievers have been shown to relieve some of the pain. Massage to the tight areas and trigger points will reduce the pain and spasm (see Sections A.1 and A.2).

PREVENTION

Technique

Change seat, shoes, or sitting positions to decrease stress to the body. Drink plenty of water and electrolyte drinks to flush out and restore the muscles. Take time out to rest periodically each session, and allow one day a week when you don't play at all to let the body rejuvenate.

Stretches

Gently stretch the affected muscles after mild massage. Allow pain to be your guide as you stretch (see Stretch 7.3). In addition, when you play, change positions as you begin feeling tight.

Exercises

Repeat the exercises that caused the pain but at a lower intensity for shorter periods of time (about half as long). Gradually increase the time and intensity over a period of weeks, stopping when the pain begins. A general health exercise program will help relieve and reduce the occurrence of this problem.

IF NO RELIEF

If no improvement occurs within one to two weeks, consult your doctor.

PROGNOSIS

These kinds of pains should never become a big problem because they are so easy to treat and fully resolve so well. However, if you do not address the problem, they can become chronic (requiring extensive treatment) and possibly lead to other, more serious, injuries. Not to mention, they decrease your endurance, coordination, and strength.

OTHER POSSIBILITIES

Compartment syndrome.

DIGGING A LITTLE DEEPER

What are muscle spasms? What are trigger points? See Sections C.1 and C.8, respectively.

SIGNS AND SYMPTOMS

Knifelike or grabbing pain in the sole of the foot, at the arch area. Pain when stretching the toes upward. Pain with or without using the foot (common when sleeping or during rest).

NAME OF INJURY

Muscle spasm (muscles of the toes)

DESCRIPTION

Tightening of the muscle (usually following a long workout) until it goes into involuntary contraction.

CAUSE

Overuse or improper technique of the foot. Muscle overuse causes electrolyte depletion and involuntary contraction, leading to cramps; for example, prolonged, intense bass drum playing or long walking, running, marching, or standing.

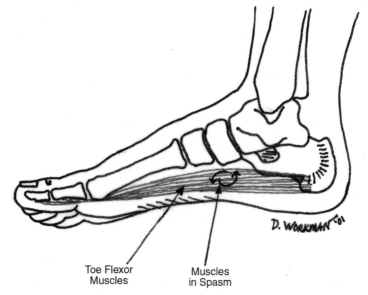

Toe Flexor
Muscles

Muscles
in Spasm

Figure 7.2   Trauma to, misuse of, or fatigue of the toe flexor muscles causes them to contract (spasm) into a knot.

TREATMENT

Immediate Relief

Stand or walk on it slowly. Do the wall stretch for the toes (see Stretch 7.2). Massage area, stroking from heel to toe on the bottom of the foot (see Section A.2).

PREVENTION

Technique

You might be using too much toe in your bass drum technique. Use more ankle motion and allow the foot to strike while at various angles of flexion.

Stretches

See Stretch 7.2.

Exercises

Crumple papers with your toes (see Exercise B.9.2), then move them with your toes from one pile to another for strength and dexterity. Walking (up to sixty minutes) also helps as you heal, depending on your physical condition (see Exercise B.10).

IF NO RELIEF

See your doctor if no relief occurs within two weeks.

PROGNOSIS

This usually heals well with no residual effects unless you fail to release the spasm (which may be deep in the muscle or be long-standing). This injury is like interest: It compounds daily, and if you do not deal with it as soon as possible, it will continue until you do.

OTHER POSSIBILITIES

Strain or sprain of the foot (usually following trauma of some sort), tarsal tunnel syndrome, heel spur (usually doesn't have pain during rest).

DIGGING A LITTLE DEEPER

What are muscle spasms? See Section C.1.

SIGNS AND SYMPTOMS

Pain and swelling on the back of the heel at or below the rim of the shoe. Aggravated while wearing shoes, especially during heavy use of the feet (i.e., marching). Tender when you touch back of heel (deep pain).

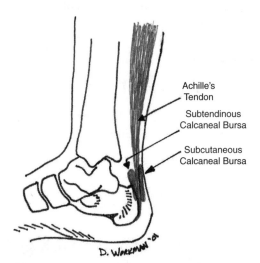

Achille's Tendon

Subtendinous Calcaneal Bursa

Subcutaneous Calcaneal Bursa

D. WORKMAN-01

NAME OF INJURY

Retrocalcaneal bursitis

DESCRIPTION

Bursae are flat, coin-sized, lubricant-filled sacs positioned anywhere two areas rub together to provide smooth movement and prevent damage. When an area gets overused, the bursae get hot and inflamed, causing bursitis.

Figure 7.3   This figure shows the location of bursae on the back of the heel. They are positioned between moving parts to prevent friction, wear, and injury.

CAUSE

Increased playing time or aggressiveness will produce tight muscles and friction to the areas of movement (bursae). Although less common, bursitis may also be caused by sudden trauma to a bursae area.

TREATMENT

Immediate Relief

Rest and ice the area of pain with leg elevated (see Section A.1). Resist movements that produce the pain. Aspirin has been shown to relieve some of the pain. When the joint cools down (two to five days), alternate ice (fifteen minutes) with heat (fifteen minutes). Some say that caster oil on the area while heating is helpful. Massage to the lower leg muscles helps reduce pressure on the bursae (see Section A.2).

PREVENTION

Technique

Avoid misusing the ankle and choose shoes carefully (see Section C.10).

Stretches

Begin when pain is no longer acute (approximately five days). Do stretches of the calf muscles (see Exercise B.11) for twenty seconds, five times with one-minute rest between repetition.

Exercises

Swimming is the best exercise to begin with after the pain is gone. Hold to the side of the pool and kick the feet moderately for fifteen to thirty minutes in the morning and in the evening. Walking is always an excellent exercise for the lower legs (fifteen to thirty minutes is usually adequate).

IF NO RELIEF

See a doctor if no improvement occurs within two weeks. Extreme cases may need to be drained with a needle (only by a doctor), although this is a last resort. This injury may possibly become infected.

PROGNOSIS

If treated early, the prognosis for full recovery is excellent. However, if treatment is not complete, the injury may return.

OTHER POSSIBILITIES

Heel spur, Achilles tendonitis, or ligament tear (partial).

DIGGING A LITTLE DEEPER

What is bursitis? See Section C.2.

SIGNS AND SYMPTOMS

Needle-type pain on the back of the heel (at or slightly above the rim of the shoe) mostly during active use of the foot (toe walk, bass pedal work, etc.).

NAME OF INJURY

Achilles tendonitis

DESCRIPTION

Pulling of the Achilles tendon fibers to the point that they tear to some degree and swell, causing an inflammation of the Achilles tendon.

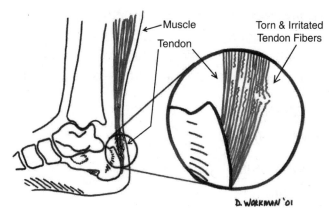

Figure 7.4   The muscles of the lower leg combine into one common tendon and attach to the heel. One large injury or repetitive misuse causes pain, swelling, or tearing of the tendon fibers. This is called Achilles tendonitis (circled area shows the location of pain).

CAUSE

The main cause is a sudden stretching of tendon fibers without having the muscles in that area warmed up. It can also be caused by a sudden increase in activity or intensity in using that body part. In addition, rubbing of the shoe on the back of the heel area (Achilles) may cause irritation.

TREATMENT

Immediate Relief

Perform the home ice program on the area of pain (see Section A.1). Decrease activity or intensity. Stay off of your feet as much as possible in the first week or two to allow the healing process to start. Then, for up to four more weeks, avoid stairs, hard-soled shoes, aggressive athletics, or heavy marching. If you must play or march, apply ice between sets or when possible. If you feel pain, *stop,* or you will be causing more damage.

PREVENTION

Technique

If you march, you can prevent further agony by making sure your shoes have soft midsoles and good support and are comfortable (see Section C.10). If you play the drum set and have this injury, analyze your pedal— Does it move smoothly? How much pressure do you have to apply to it? You can get more volume with less effort by incorporating more leg, ankle, and toe coordination.

Stretches

After the pain subsides (five to ten days or so), begin some mild stretching (see Stretch 7.3), but stay away from the pain.

Exercises

Do heel raises (see Exercise B.14) and soft tissue work after the pain is gone to loosen up the plantar fascia (see Section A.2).

IF NO RELIEF

If your pain is not making an exit after two weeks of this treatment, see your doctor.

PROGNOSIS

This can be a very serious injury and must be taken very seriously to avoid possible rupture or chronic long-standing problems with the foot. This one has potential to end your career.

OTHER POSSIBILITIES

Bursitis or rupture (partial).

DIGGING A LITTLE DEEPER

What is tendonitis? See Section C.3.

SIGNS AND SYMPTOMS

Nonspecific achy discomfort up and down the lower leg; constant but worse at the end of or during activity (in more progressed cases).

NAME OF INJURY

Shin splints

DESCRIPTION

Some say this is the beginning of a stress fracture. Others say it's the tendon or deep tissue (fascia) pulling away from the shinbone (tibia).

CAUSE

Tight muscles from increased friction or intensity of activity produce tightness, which causes a pull on the tendons over time. The tight muscles lose their elasticity, and when under activity, they do not allow enough stretch. This pulls the tendon from the bone it attaches to.

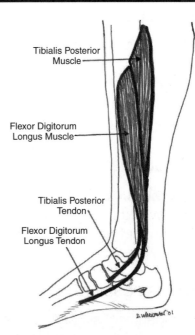

Tibialis Posterior Muscle

Flexor Digitorum Longus Muscle

Tibialis Posterior Tendon

Flexor Digitorum Longus Tendon

Figure 7.5 Some believe that shin splints are caused when muscles or tissue of the lower leg pull away from the bone (tibia), as illustrated in this figure.

TREATMENT

Immediate Relief

Use home ice program (Section A.1) up to three times a day for the first forty-eight hours. When pain allows, resume activity at about half of your usual intensity, then do soft tissue massage on the lower leg muscles after each activity or workout to reduce the muscle tightness (see Section A.2). Over-the-counter anti-inflammatories may relieve some pain.

PREVENTION

Technique

If you march, remember to do it on a soft surface if at all possible, and use proper shoes (see Section C.10). The vast majority of people with this pain have pronation (flat foot) or supination (high arch) problems. Although uncommon, constant use of the timpani pedals can irritate the shin muscles.

Stretches

General stretches for the leg and foot (see Stretch 7.3) are good for this condition. In addition, specialized stretches should help (see Stretch 7.4).

Exercises

Do exercises to strengthen the lower leg muscles (see Exercise B.13).

IF NO RELIEF

Give it two weeks, and if there is no change, see your doctor for a definitive diagnosis.

PROGNOSIS

Get to it quickly and constantly, and your chances of full recovery are good. However, this is a tough injury if it goes on for months or years. In that case, you should have some deep soft tissue work done by a professional with sports injury experience.

OTHER POSSIBILITIES

Compartment syndrome or stress fracture of the tibia (sharp pain when tapping on the front of the shin—see your doctor).

DIGGING A LITTLE DEEPER

What are muscle spasms? What is tendonitis? See Sections C.1 and C.3.

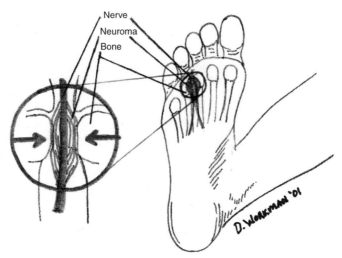

Figure 7.6   This figure shows the most common location for a Morton's neuroma (between the third and fourth toes). The shaded area shows where the symptoms will most likely manifest. Scar tissue from rubbing the area increases pressure on the nerve, causing pain or other symptoms.

SIGNS AND SYMPTOMS

Dull discomfort under the ball of the foot or toes, with possible electric (or loss of) sensation. Tender to touch behind and between third and fourth toes.

NAME OF INJURY

Morton's neuroma

DESCRIPTION

A neoplasm of nerve cell origin, abnormal growth of nerve tissue (see Figure 7.6).

CAUSE

Rubbing of the bones of the middle toes causes irritation around the nerve. This produces scar tissue (neuroma) around the nerve that squeezes it and causes more irritation. It may cause clicking between toes when walking.

TREATMENT

Immediate Relief

Get off the foot. Ice the area after activity to relieve pain. An orthosis can prevent pronation, support the transverse arch, and relieve pressure on the nerve. Ask your podiatrist about a metatarsal bar to decrease pressure on the nerve.

PREVENTION

Technique

This injury is largely due to prolonged walking or foot use combined with failure of the foot to function properly or improper shoes (see Section C.10). Be sure you have shoes with stability features and a wide and well-padded toe area. Marching players must wear shoes meeting these requirements. On a drum set, try reducing the tension on your bass pedal and applying less pressure to the hi-hat pedal.

Stretches

Keep lower leg biomechanics and muscle tone in balance (see Stretch 7.3).

Exercises

See Exercise B.9.

IF NO RELIEF

See your podiatrist if no improvement occurs after one week of this treatment.

PROGNOSIS

This injury has a good prognosis but may eventually require surgery.

OTHER POSSIBILITIES

Bone bruise (on metatarsal head).

DIGGING A LITTLE DEEPER

What is nerve impingement? See Section C.4.

SIGNS AND SYMPTOMS

Pain, burning feeling, or tenderness in the arch, or ball of the foot, and possibly the heel. Worse if you tap just under and behind the medial malleolus (bone on inner side of ankle).

NAME OF INJURY

Tarsal tunnel syndrome

DESCRIPTION

Foot tingling or pain from pressure on the posterior tibial nerve between the medial malleolus and the flexor retinaculum laciniate ligament (tissue that wraps around the ankle) (see Figure 7.7).

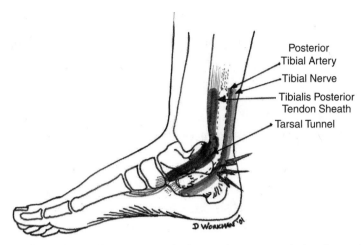

Figure 7.7   This figure shows the posterior tibial nerve being strangled at the medial malleolus (the bone on the inside of the ankle), causing tingle, numbness, burning feeling, and so forth from that point down into the foot.

CAUSE

This is usually caused by using the foot unnaturally. For example, pronation of the foot (aka flat foot) causes tension of the flexor retinaculum, pushing the nerve against the bone (see Figure 7.7). Less common causes include a broken bone in the area or trauma to the nerve.

TREATMENT

Immediate Relief

Use the ice program in Section A.1. If the pain comes during or following marching. Advil or aspirin may help relieve the pain.

PREVENTION

Technique

Set players may be causing the problem by spreading their pedals too far apart, causing the feet to flatten out at the arch. If you do a lot of marching, try to keep the feet straight (no duck feet) and take heed to the shoe advice (see Section C.10). Make sure your shoes provide adequate arch support (try a good stability running or walking shoe). Avoid loose shoes or loafers. Wear shoes that are low on the ankle so as not to rub the nerve.

Stretches

Inversion motion ankle stretches help the peroneus muscles, balancing the muscles of the ankle (see Stretch 7.1).

Exercises

Do pronation exercises (Exercise B.9). This strengthens the muscles of the foot and arch.

IF NO RELIEF

If no relief occurs within two weeks, see your podiatrist. You may need orthotics (shoe inserts) or surgery, or both.

PROGNOSIS

Prognosis is good. The symptoms will most likely decrease with this treatment. However, if pronation is the cause, this problem will recur if you do not improve the structural integrity of the foot with exercise, orthotics, or both.

OTHER POSSIBILITIES

Diabetes mellitus (see a doctor ASAP for an evaluation).

DIGGING A LITTLE DEEPER

What is nerve impingement? See Section C.4.

SIGNS AND SYMPTOMS

Tenderness, tightness, pain, possible bulge in any area of the lower leg or foot (pain out of proportion). Worse during foot activity or forward–backward foot stretch. Less pain after activity (if not, see a doctor immediately).

NAME OF INJURY

Compartment syndrome (exercise induced)

DESCRIPTION

More common in timpani players, set players using heel-down technique (front leg pain), and marching players (back of the leg).

Note: If this is sudden onset from trauma, go to the emergency room. This is a potential leg-loss problem (surgical release of pressure may be needed). The following treatment suggestions should be followed with your doctor's approval.

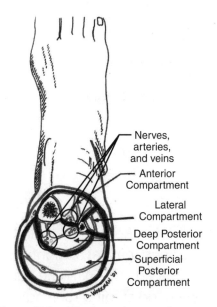

Nerves, arteries, and veins

Anterior Compartment

Lateral Compartment

Deep Posterior Compartment

Superficial Posterior Compartment

Figure 7.8   The lower leg muscles are divided into compartments (shown in this figure), each surrounded by tough material called fascia. When swelling occurs in a compartment, pressure decreases blood flow or nerve function, or both, causing compartment syndrome.

CAUSE

Trauma to the area, increased intensity or repetition, or inefficient technique, producing muscle swelling. This increases muscle compartment pressure, squeezing the veins and stopping the blood from leaving (causing pressure and pain).

TREATMENT

Immediate Relief

Follow the procedures for rest, ice, and elevation. Massage lightly, starting below the pain and moving in the direction of the heart. Lightly stretch the muscles involved (see Stretch 7.4).

PREVENTION

Technique

If you are a timpani player, perhaps you are standing too close to the instrument while operating the pedal. Step back a step. If you are a set player, alternate heel-up–heel-down technique or relax the foot when it is not in motion.

Stretches

General stretches (see Stretch 7.4).

Exercises

Whatever movement hurts the area is the one you must do after the pain is gone and the muscles have relaxed some. Start with doing lower leg exercises (see Exercises B.12–B.14), then begin walking or jogging, and finally lifting weights.

IF NO RELIEF

If this is gradual onset over a period of weeks or months, treat as indicated. If no change occurs in a few days, see your doctor for examination of the area.

PROGNOSIS

Prognosis is fair. Keep it at bay and it should resolve. There is a chance that you were born susceptible to this problem. If this is the case, keep it stretched and strengthened daily.

OTHER POSSIBILITIES

Acute compartment syndrome (sudden traumatic onset—numb foot, extreme pain, toe weakness, or "woody" hardness of muscles) or shin splints.

DIGGING A LITTLE DEEPER

What is nerve impingement? See Section C.4.

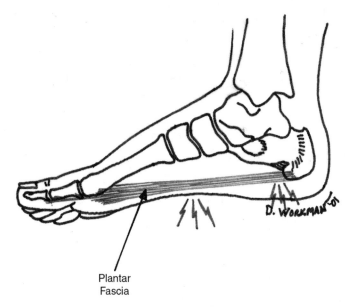

Plantar
Fascia

Figure 7.9 The plantar fascia attaches at the toes and heel to support the arch. Repetitive pressure or one large injury to the area may cause irritation or injury to the fascia (plantar fasciitis).

SIGNS AND SYMPTOMS

Persistent sharp, stabbing pain in the bottom of the heel or arch side of the foot, or both. Typically increases at the beginning of activity and decreases during activity. Most noticeable during first few steps in the morning.

NAME OF INJURY

Plantar fasciitis

DESCRIPTION

The plantar fascia is a fibrous tendon-like structure stretching from the bottom of the heel to each toe. It gives some support to the arch while you're on your feet.

CAUSE

Usually caused by a sudden increase in activity or intensity within a short period of time (e.g., beginning of marching season), resulting in microtears in the plantar fascia. It may be caused by a sudden injury, producing tears and swelling in the fascia; it is also associated with excessive pronation.

TREATMENT
Immediate Relief

Ice the bottom of the foot (see Section A.1). Stay off of it or avoid walking on it for a few days if possible. When the pain goes away, slowly work the foot back into activity.

PREVENTION
Technique

If you have a high arch, use soft-soled shoes. If you have a flat arch, wear a more stable shoe. Running or walking shoes with arch support are best (see Section C.10). If you march, you may want to use shoes as described and also use foot orthotics.

Stretches

Balance the pressure of the muscles attaching to the heel. Stretch the calf muscles (gastrocnemius and soleus) and the foot muscles (the toe flexors). See Stretches 7.2 and 7.3.

Exercises

Strengthen the foot muscles (see Exercises B.9 and B.11).

IF NO RELIEF

Give treatment a couple of weeks, and if you get no relief (or if problem keeps recurring over time), see your podiatrist for possible orthosis fitting or further investigation of an underlying problem.

PROGNOSIS

It responds well to this treatment. Very few cases require more aggressive procedures than those mentioned here.

OTHER POSSIBILITIES

Bone bruise, spasm of foot muscles, tarsal tunnel syndrome, or heel spur (pain at rear of the foot only).

SIGNS AND SYMPTOMS

Sharp pain on the bottom of the heel, especially when under exertion. Pain gets worse over a period of months or years and increases with activities involving walking, running, and jumping.

NAME OF INJURY

Heel spur

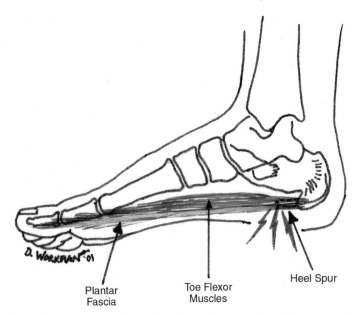

Plantar
Fascia

Toe Flexor
Muscles

Heel Spur

Figure 7.10   The heel spur occurs where the plantar fascia and toe flexor muscles attach (see figure). Pressure from the foot hitting the ground and the calf muscles pulling the heel in the opposite direction contribute to the problem.

DESCRIPTION

Pulling of the plantar fascia attachment at the heel, causing inflammation, swelling, and pain in that area. It is common on both feet. Not all heel spurs are painful.

CAUSE

Force on the plantar fascia (from pronation, increased activity or intensity, or biomechanical changes) pulls it away from its heel attachment, causing the bone to grow (creating a bone point commonly called a heel spur).

TREATMENT

Immediate Relief

Use the RICE technique as described in Section A.1 (twenty minutes, three to four times per day). Use a round, felt donut (two inches in diameter with a one-half-inch hole in it), putting the hole where the pain spot is to prevent pressure on that area. Massage to the sole of the foot and lower leg muscles helps reduce pull on the spur (see Section A.2).

PREVENTION

Technique

Tight lower leg muscles can increase pressure on the plantar fascia and can ultimately increase the chances of a heel spur. For this reason, supportive shoes can help in both prevention and cure of a heel spur. Wear a running or walking shoe with good arch support (see Section C.10).

Stretches

You may loosen the muscles of the feet by rolling a soda bottle under the feet. Also see stretches for muscle spasm of the foot (see Stretch 7.3).

Exercises

See exercises for muscle spasm and plantar fasciitis.

IF NO RELIEF

Give it two weeks, and if there is no improvement, see your doctor.

PROGNOSIS

You can treat the pain, but the heel spur will remain. The best treatment is reducing the initial pain and then correcting any cause of the spur to prevent further irritation.

OTHER POSSIBILITIES

Note that not all heel spurs are painful, and not all heel pain is caused by a heel spur, which can be caused by calcaneal bursitis (usually quicker onset), plantar fasciitis (acute or insidious onset), fracture (acute onset), tumor (insidious onset), or arthritides.

SIGNS AND SYMPTOMS

Clear or bloody-looking fluid-filled bump under a thin layer of the skin.

NAME OF INJURY

Blisters (clear or blood)

DESCRIPTION

A small (zero to one centimeter) vesicle (fluid-filled sac) or a bulla (larger vesicle, one centimeter). May have clear (serous), watery contents or bloody contents. If pus filled, suspect infection.

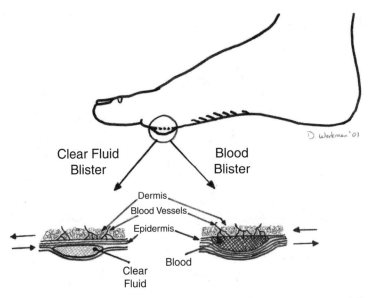

Figure 7.11 A blister is caused by rubbing of the skin, producing irritation and fluid buildup between the layers. Deeper blisters may rupture small vessels and fill with blood (blood blister).

CAUSE

May be caused by a pinch or bruise, but is often due to persistent friction to an area of skin, causing separation of skin layers where fluid collects. It is very common with poor-fitting (mostly tight) shoes.

TREATMENT

It is best to leave a blister alone until it pops (if smaller than one centimeter). However, you may pop it with a sterile needle just enough to allow the fluid to escape.

Immediate Relief

Lancing: First clean the skin with alcohol, poke one to two holes in the upper skin, drain the fluid, and leave the skin on to protect from infection. After it pops, or is lanced, it is best to apply antibiotic ointment and cover it with a bandage until it becomes less tender in a day or two (big or deep ones may take longer). If you are going to continue activity that will rub on the blister area (especially on the feet), it's best to put petroleum jelly over the bandage and cover it with a second bandage so they will slide on each other (or use moleskin).

PREVENTION

Technique

Blisters are a result of improper or inefficient biomechanics (body movement). If the body moves inefficiently, friction can occur, causing blisters and (later) calluses. Change to more comfortable shoes, bandage the blister, and wear double socks (until shoes are worn in).

IF NO RELIEF

If the fluid coming from the blister isn't clear like water, or if it smells bad, seek advice from your podiatrist or medical doctor. Also see your doctor if it gets infected (swollen, red, or hot; you feel increased pain over a short period of time, fever, nausea, chills, etc.).

PROGNOSIS

Blisters heal well and quickly if these procedures are followed and the source of the irritation is removed.

OTHER POSSIBILITIES

Boil (deeper in the skin, more painful, and is an infection).

DIGGING A LITTLE DEEPER

What is a blister? See Section C.7.

SIGNS AND SYMPTOMS

Thickening of skin, usually painful when pressing or rubbing the area.

NAME OF INJURY

Callus or corn

DESCRIPTION

Callus: Thickening of the skin where repeated rubbing or friction occurs (usually the hands or feet). The skin markings remain, and it typically won't bleed if scraped or sanded. They are less painful than corns. **Corn:** Similar to a callus, size of a pea, usually on the feet. Has a hard, clear, sharply outlined

Callus   Dermis   Corn   "Core"

Epidermis   D. WORKMAN '01

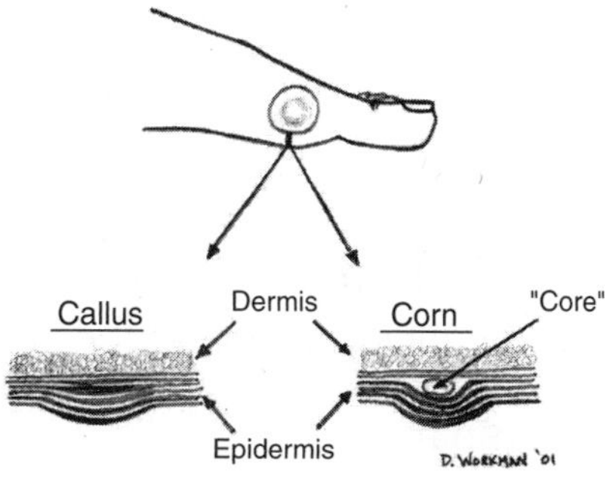

Figure 7.12   This figure compares a callus (left) and a corn (right). Both are a response to skin rubbing. The callus is thickening of the outer skin, and the corn is that plus a clear round core in the center.

core (usually on toes). "Hard" corns are usually on the protruding surfaces of the foot, and "soft" corns usually occur between the toes. Either may ache spontaneously or have sharp pain with pressure.

CAUSE

The skin rubs an area constantly (weeks or more). Commonly due to shoes that are too small, too narrow, or poorly ventilated (bad foot technique also).

TREATMENT

Immediate Relief

Find the cause (biomechanics or shoes, etc.) and correct it. Do not cut into calluses or corns. Home treatments include putting five or six aspirins in a bowl with one teaspoon of water and one teaspoon of lemon. Place some of the paste on each corn, place a plastic bag over the foot, and cover foot with hot towel for ten minutes. Then scrape off the dead skin with a pumice stone. Another method is to put Whitfield's Ointment and hydrocortisone cream on the callus at night, cover with a plastic bag, put a sock over the bag until morning, then rub off as much of the callus as you can with a rough towel or firm brush. If corns are between the toes, place a piece of felt between them to air out the sore. Do as needed. Apply medication to the corn, not the surrounding skin.

PREVENTION

Technique

Common in musicians who use the feet, such as when marching, using trap set, and so forth. Wear comfortable shoes with proper fit. You may also be using the foot inefficiently. Set players may have their pedals in an awkward position. Your walking form may contribute (see a podiatrist or chiropractor). Various pads help take the pressure off of the sore.

Stretches

Do general stretches of the lower legs and feet to assist in the gait correction (see all stretches at the end of this chapter).

Exercises

Find weak areas and strengthen them. Usually a walking program to practice gait work is very effective.

IF NO RELIEF

See a doctor of podiatric medicine.

PROGNOSIS

This heals without return if the cause is resolved and it is treated as indicated.

OTHER POSSIBILITIES

Bursae irritation under the corn.

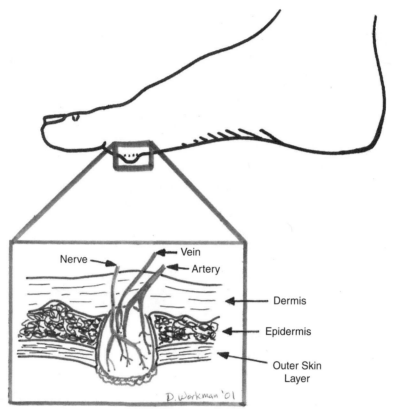

Figure 7.13 This figure illustrates the anatomy of a typical plantar wart. Note the blood and nerve supply. This means that it will bleed and hurt if cut into (as opposed to a callus, which does not have blood and nerve supply).

SIGNS AND SYMPTOMS

Fleshy black growth on the foot, round with flattened appearance (usually one millimeter to one centimeter in diameter). This is a common wart on the sole of the foot.

NAME OF INJURY

Plantar warts

DESCRIPTION

Benign skin tumor occurring singly or in groups on the sole of the foot. Flattened by pressure and surrounded by cornified epithelium.

CAUSE

Warts (papilloma virus) thrive in warm, moist environments. They usually invade the body through a break in the skin and multiply constantly. If left alone, they will spread or enlarge, or both.

TREATMENT

Immediate Relief

May take months to get rid of (usually two to five months). Before going to bed, soak the wart in warm water for ten minutes and then apply plantar wart ointment (from any drugstore; ask the pharmacist). You may apply petroleum jelly to the surrounding skin to prevent a chemical burn from occurring on the healthy surrounding tissue. Cover the treated wart with a bandage. Use a pumice stone to scrape away dead skin in the morning.

Note: Keep the feet in a dry environment, and do not touch the wart. Some believe that warts spread more when you are under stress or when eating poorly.

IF NO RELIEF

If you have no improvement within two months, see a podiatrist.

PROGNOSIS

Recovery is common, but all warts are notorious for returning. Warts are self-limiting but may take years to resolve if left untreated. They have a high rate of recurrence.

OTHER POSSIBILITIES

Corns or calluses (plantar warts tend to display pinpoint bleeding when the surface is shaved off; corns and calluses don't) or skin tumors.

SIGNS AND SYMPTOMS

Burning, itching blisters and cracking skin on the feet, especially between the toes. Can be different places on each foot or just on one foot.

NAME OF INJURY

Athlete's foot

DESCRIPTION

Fungal infection of the foot (especially on the sole and between the toes) that grows best in warm, moist conditions (a nonventilated or poorly ventilated shoe).

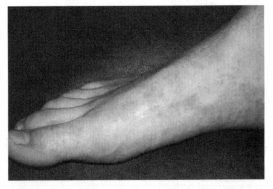

Figure 7.14   This photo is what common athlete's foot (Tinea pedis) looks like. The red dots burn and itch and are accompanied by dry, flaky skin.

CAUSE

Warm, moist environment created by sweaty socks and shoes that don't breathe.

TREATMENT AND PREVENTION

Immediate Relief

This ailment takes weeks (about four) to cure. Symptoms may cease within two weeks, but treatment must continue for foot to fully recover. Act quickly. Three to four times a day, soak your infected area in warm salt water (Dunburos solution) for about ten minutes. After each soak, apply athlete's foot medication (found at the drugstore). You may also use aluminum chloride (or baking soda in a paste consistency) in water solution; apply between the toes with cotton. Keep your toenails clean and trimmed.

Shoes are very important in curing athlete's foot. Remove the factory insert that is infected and put in a new one from the drugstore. Sandals or some other highly breathable design or material will allow the foot to stay dry, thus stopping and preventing the disease. Avoid plastic or waterproof shoes.

Try to wear different shoes each day to let them completely air out. Use an antifungal powder inside the shoe. After you shower, thoroughly dry feet with a clean towel and allow them to air-dry as long as possible. In fact, as much as possible, go without shoes and socks to allow feet to air out.

IF NO RELIEF

Contact your podiatrist or dermatologist if no relief occurs after six weeks of treatment.

PROGNOSIS

Chance of healing is excellent if treatment is followed properly, and athlete's foot will not return if good foot hygiene becomes a habit.

OTHER POSSIBILITIES

Dermatitis (symmetrical and can be on top of toes), psoriasis, or bacterial infection (usually from athlete's foot).

SIGNS AND SYMPTOMS

Red, swollen, and very tender toe where the edge of the toenail curves down into the sides of the toe (most commonly the big toe).

NAME OF INJURY

Ingrown toenail

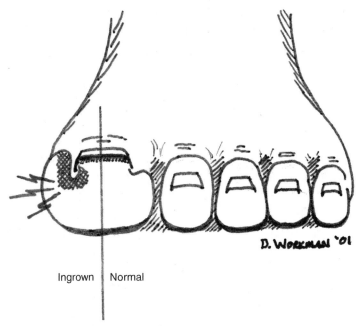

Ingrown | Normal

Figure 7.15   When the sharp toenail rubs excessively against the surrounding skin, swelling, pain, and infection can occur (as shown in this figure). To combat this, keep the area clean and the nail away from the skin until it is healed.

DESCRIPTION

The toenail rubs the skin (usually by curving into it) until it breaks through, causing tenderness and irritation. This may lead to infection.

CAUSE

Tight shoes or socks can increase friction as the toe rubs its neighbors or the shoe. This produces irritation, swelling, and possible cutting into the skin (which will cause it to grow into or through the skin). It can also be caused by trauma to the cells that make the toenail.

TREATMENT

Immediate Relief

Use ice and over-the-counter products to decrease swelling (consult your doctor first). Don't trim the nail shorter than the tip of the toe. Soak and dry foot, and put a small piece of cotton between the toe and the nail. Change the dressing daily until the skin heals.

PREVENTION

Technique

Get shoes with a spacious toe box and a soft upper and midsole (especially when marching). Check the fit. See if the shoe gives two centimeters of space between the toe and the end of the shoe. You may have a technique that pushes the toe into the front of the shoe, causing the problem. If sitting, you may need to lower the heel a bit to keep the foot a little flatter or lower the throne to prevent leaning into the foot.

IF NO RELIEF

If no improvement occurs within a week, have a podiatrist work on the nail. *Do not try this yourself*. If you notice increased swelling or red or purple color, see a podiatrist *as soon as possible* to rule out infection and to prevent infection from spreading into the bone.

PROGNOSIS

The prognosis is excellent. It takes about two weeks to completely recover, but it heals well. Recurrence is common if you have concave nails, if you don't have surgical correction, or if you refuse to change the behavior that causes it (i.e., shoes, pressure on the toes).

OTHER POSSIBILITIES

The presentation of this injury is very specific. If you have any questions, contact your doctor.

SIGNS AND SYMPTOMS

Pain on the top of the foot in the middle area. Usually worse during activity, less pain during rest. May also be worse at night.

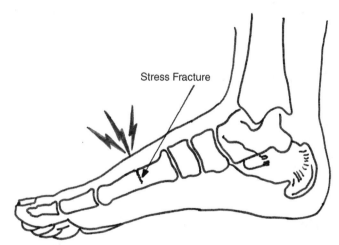

NAME OF INJURY

Stress fracture

DESCRIPTION

Constant trauma to the foot (mostly in ways it was not designed to handle) produces small breaks in the outer bone (cortex), causing a stress reaction and pain.

Figure 7.16   A stress fracture is a fairly common problem. On x-ray, it is difficult to see at first, but it shows up better a few weeks later after the healing progresses. This figure is an illustration of a metatarsal stress fracture (most commonly the third metatarsal).

Continued irritation will produce more breaking, resulting in a stress fracture and increased pain until something is done to stop it.

CAUSE

Excessive repetitive trauma such as marching (i.e., flat feet or fallen arches) or other biomechanical problem causes abnormal stresses to the foot and may hurt the bone. This is common in marching.

TREATMENT

Immediate Relief

Bruising over the area is a sign of significant damage—*see a physician immediately.* See home ice program in Section A.1. Aspirin helps. Decreased activity is imperative, and do not put weight on the foot (use crutches). I also suggest that your podiatrist examine the foot for possible biomechanical problems.

PREVENTION

Technique

If you suffer from flat feet, work on keeping your feet straight and toes lined up ahead of you. If you are on your feet a lot (marching), then it is necessary that you always wear good supportive shoes, with orthotic inserts if necessary (see Section C.10).

Stretches

Stretches and exercises are to be done only after the foot pain has disappeared. Balance out the muscles of the lower leg by doing Stretch 7.3.

Exercises

Do foot-strengthening exercises (see Exercises B.11 or B.12).

IF NO RELIEF

If the pain is not relieved in one week, see your physician as soon as possible.

PROGNOSIS

This heals well if you treat it early and effectively. The key is to stay off of it long enough to allow proper healing, then gradually bring it back to normal activity and performance level.

OTHER POSSIBILITIES

Bruise (usually is visible and involves some recent trauma) or Morton's neuroma (very similar).

RELATED AREAS

Many injuries can be related to areas of the body other than where you feel the pain. For example, pain in the shoulder may be the result of a problem with the neck or elbow area. If you cannot find the injury that fits your complaints in this chapter, please look in the chapters of the related areas indicated in Figure 7.17.

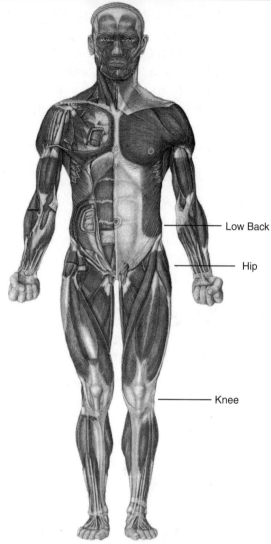

Low Back

Hip

Knee

Figure 7.17 (Anatomical Chart Company, Lippincott Williams & Wilkins 2003)

STRETCHES

THE PHILOSOPHY OF STRETCHING

Stretching is not something you do *to* the body; it is something you *allow* the body to do. All stretches must be done by relaxing and allowing the muscles to stretch. If you try to force the muscles to stretch, their immediate reaction is to protect themselves from tearing by pulling back. This can quickly turn into a tug-of-war of you against your muscles, and nothing good can happen. This is why many people stretch and stretch without any positive results, and sometimes they even injure themselves.

GENERAL RULES FOR STRETCHING

Stretches are most effective when the body is warmed up first. This means you should do some mild exercise of the area to be stretched prior to beginning. For example, if you are stretching the legs, do some walking or running until the muscles get warm and loose (usually just before you begin to perspire). With the hands, try some basic rudiments—singles and doubles are best. If you are paying attention to your body, you will notice the area warming up as the blood is pumped into it. Or you can take a shower or sit in hot water prior to stretching—which is not as effective, but still good.

Do not

- pop your knuckles
- stretch when that part of the body is cold
- use bouncing or jerking motions while stretching
- force the stretch to the point where you cannot let the area relax

BASIC STRETCHES FOR THE ANKLES AND FEET

STRETCH 7.1: LATERAL LEG MUSCLE STRETCHES (TO HELP ANKLE STABILITY)

Many times ankle instability or injury is in part due to weak and tight lateral leg muscles (peroneal muscles). These ankle stretches will loosen the peroneal muscles and improve the balance and strength of the ankle. If you feel ankle pain, don't push as hard.

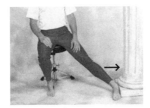

Figure 7.18   Sit with leg extended at a forty-five-degree angle with the wall and with the foot against the wall, as shown in this figure.

Figure 7.19   Gradually roll the foot to the outside, as shown in this figure, until you feel the stretch in the lower leg. Hold for twenty to thirty seconds.

Figure 7.20   Allow the foot to relax and shake it after each repetition to loosen the muscles. Repeat the stretch for five to ten times.

STRETCH 7.2: STRETCHES FOR THE BOTTOM OF THE FOOT

Kneel on the floor, then sit on your heels with the toes in a stretched position. You should feel the stretch in the arch of the foot. With each repetition you should be able to stretch farther with less pain.

  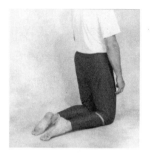

Figure 7.21   Kneel on the floor with toes in stretched position. Sit on heels, as shown in this figure.

Figure 7.22   Rock back on the heels, moving the heels closer to the floor until you feel a stretch in the bottom of the foot. Hold the stretch for twenty to thirty seconds.

Figure 7.23   Allow the foot to lay flat on the floor in a relaxed position for thirty seconds, then repeat the stretch until loose (three to five times).

STRETCH 7.3: FOOT AND CALF STRETCHES

This stretch is designed to balance the tension of the muscles attaching to the heel—the calf muscles (gastrocnemius and soleus) and the foot muscles (flexor digitorum brevis). These are strong muscles, and they will stretch only if you *relax* them and *push* them into the stretch.

Figure 7.24   Start by leaning against a wall for balance with ball of foot on a curb or book and the other leg supporting.

Figure 7.25   Allow the body weight to push the heel to the floor until stretch is felt. Hold stretched position for twenty to thirty seconds. *Do not bounce!*

Figure 7.26   Allow the leg to hang in a relaxed position while shaking it to loosen the muscles. Repeat five to ten times on each leg.

STRETCH 7.4: DEEP CALF MUSCLE STRETCHES (SOLEUS AND TIBIALIS POSTERIOR MUSCLES)

This stretch is designed to stretch the deep muscles of the lower leg. These are very strong muscles, and they will stretch only if you *relax* them and *push* them into the stretch. For a broader stretch, keep toes pointed in on the first one. For each stretch, relax the leg and let the muscle release. Hold position for twenty to thirty seconds—*do not bounce!*

7.4.1. The Soleus Stretch

The soleus muscle is difficult to stretch and needs stretching often. It is one of the muscles that are always in use while you are on your feet.

Figure 7.27 Begin in the position shown in this figure, with the foot and leg relaxed. Drop the heel as far as it will go—don't use force.

Figure 7.28 Bend the knee slightly, as shown in this figure. Hold the position for twenty to thirty seconds while relaxing.

Figure 7.29 Come back up, shake the foot to relax it, then repeat the stretch five to ten times, relaxing more each time.

7.4.2. The Tibialis Posterior Stretch

This muscle is very important in supporting the arch of the foot. If it gets fatigued and is in spasm, it is less effective in this role, and the foot is more easily injured. The stretches in Figures 7.30 through 7.32 will require a person to help you.

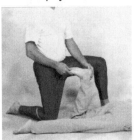 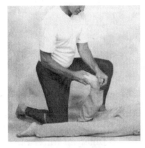 

Figure 7.30 Begin in the position shown in this figure, with the affected foot up. Relax the foot completely.

Figure 7.31 The foot is stretched by someone pushing toes down with right hand while holding the heel steady for about two minutes.

Figure 7.32 After thirty seconds relaxing, the stretch is repeated. Do this about five to ten times.

CHAPTER 8

KNEE PROBLEMS

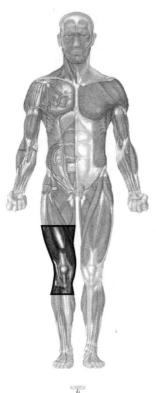

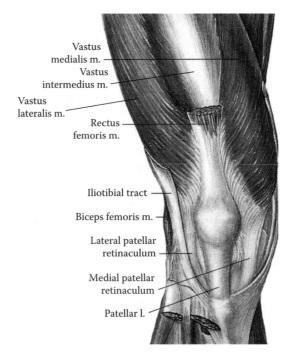

Vastus
medialis m.

Vastus
intermedius m.

Vastus
lateralis m.

Rectus
femoris m.

Iliotibial tract

Biceps femoris m.

Lateral patellar
retinaculum

Medial patellar
retinaculum

Patellar l.

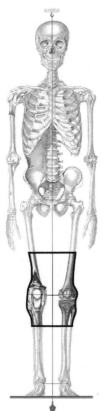

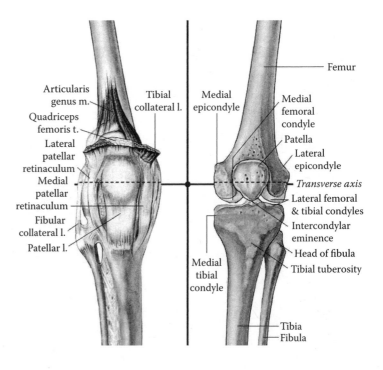

Articularis
genus m.

Quadriceps
femoris t.

Lateral
patellar
retinaculum

Medial
patellar
retinaculum

Fibular
collateral l.

Patellar l.

Tibial
collateral l.

Medial
epicondyle

Medial
tibial
condyle

Femur

Medial
femoral
condyle

Patella

Lateral
epicondyle

Transverse axis

Lateral femoral
& tibial condyles

Intercondylar
eminence

Head of fibula

Tibial tuberosity

Tibia
Fibula

SIGNS AND SYMPTOMS

Knifelike pain and possible grabbing in the upper leg muscles. Worse when walking up stairs or hills. Usually tender to the touch. Will not show bruise or increased temperature.

NAME OF INJURY

Muscle spasm (upper leg)

DESCRIPTION

Muscle overuse causes depletion of the muscle's energy and contraction of muscle fibers, leading to cramps.

CAUSE

Doing too much too soon or too often, or both. Overuse or improper use of the knee; for example, large increase in marching, poor shoes, improper walking form, or inefficient bass drum technique on the drum set.

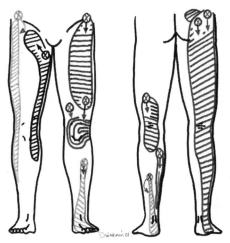

Figure 8.1 This figure shows the muscles around the knee. The tender spots (X) are "trigger points," and the lined areas are where the pain can radiate to by touching the trigger points.

TREATMENT

Immediate Relief

Rest and ice the area of pain. Resist movements that produce the pain. Aspirin or other over-the-counter pain relievers may offer some relief. Massage to the tight areas and trigger points will reduce the pain and spasm (see Section A.2).

PREVENTION

Technique

Change your seat height (usually the drummer is sitting too high, causing the legs to constantly bear the weight of the body), shoes, or sitting positions to decrease stress to the body. Drink plenty of water to flush out the muscles. Take time out to rest periodically each session, and allow one day a week when you don't play at all to let the body rejuvenate.

Stretches

Do some mild massage to the sore muscles (see Section A.2) followed by gentle stretching of the area—allow pain to be your guide. The stretches can be found at the end of Chapter 7 (Stretches 7.3 and 7.4) and at the end of this chapter (Stretches 8.1 and 8.2). When you play, change positions as you begin feeling tight.

Exercises

Repeat the movement that caused the pain but at a lower intensity for shorter periods of time (about half as much). Gradually increase the time and intensity over a period of weeks, stopping when the pain begins. In this way you will strengthen the injured muscles and prevent repeated injury in the future.

IF NO RELIEF

If no improvement occurs within one or two weeks, consult your doctor.

PROGNOSIS

These kinds of pains should never become a big problem because they are so easy to treat and they fully resolve so well. However, if you do not address these problems, they can become chronic (requiring extensive treatment) and possibly lead to other, more serious injuries. In addition, they decrease your endurance.

OTHER POSSIBILITIES

Contusion or bruise (usually caused by a direct hit to the area and accompanied by a red or purple mark on the skin).

DIGGING A LITTLE DEEPER

What are muscle spasms? What are trigger points? See Sections C.1 and C.8, respectively.

SIGNS AND SYMPTOMS

Pain beneath the kneecap during movement of the knee, especially while climbing up and down stairs. Possible swelling, redness, and heat in the knee area (most common in women).

NAME OF INJURY

Chondromalacia patella (patellar tracking problem)

DESCRIPTION

The kneecap rubs the edges of the femoral condyle (see Figure 8.2), causing friction and heat, leading to swelling and pain. This process builds on itself until the problem can no longer be ignored.

CAUSE

Change in or inefficient development of the path of the kneecap, causing imbalance or misalignment.

TREATMENT

Immediate Relief

Rest and avoid stairs and knee-bending activities. Ice (fifteen minutes) on the kneecap while elevating the knee if possible. Massage the muscles of the upper front leg just above the knee, working mostly on any tender areas (see Section A.2). Aspirin may reduce the pain.

PREVENTION

Technique

If problems occur while playing set, try changing your foot technique, sitting higher, or moving farther away from the bass drum to allow the knee better alignment while playing. If the pain is marching induced, consider decreasing the movement some and taking breaks each hour for a ten-minute ice session to the knee.

Stretches

Quadratus femoris stretches (see Stretch 8.1). Stretch the contracted side twice as long as the other. Start lightly and slowly increase the intensity as pain allows.

Exercises

Straight leg raises (see Exercise B.16).

IF NO RELIEF

Give two to three weeks for improvement. If no improvement occurs within

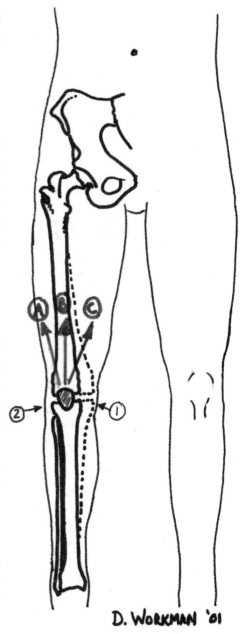

D. WORKMAN '01

Figure 8.2 Two things contribute to improper knee tracking. First, notice that the muscles (a, b, and c) pull to influence the movement of the kneecap. If one is too tight, the kneecap will veer in that direction and rub on the bone. Second, notice that the female knee (dotted line, no. 1) has more of an angle than the male knee (solid line, no. 2), which causes the kneecap to rub the bone more intensely in women.

four weeks, see the doctor of your choice (MD, DC, DPM) for an exercise program, orthotics, or further diagnostic tests on the knee.

PROGNOSIS

You must improve the way the knee moves, changing the behavior that has caused the problem (technique, exercises, orthotics, etc.), or this will not improve. If you can correct the problem early, and allow proper healing, it will not restrict you.

OTHER POSSIBILITIES

Bursitis, knee joint derangement, ligament instability, or joint effusion.

SIGNS AND SYMPTOMS

Severe pinpoint knee pain just below the kneecap (patella). Worse when doing activity requiring the knee to bend (squatting, climbing stairs, running sprints or hills, etc.). Tender to the touch on the area, with possible swelling.

NAME OF INJURY

Osgood-Schlatter's disease

DESCRIPTION

Continued or increased pulling where the thigh muscles attach causes irritation or tears of the tendon or pulls the bone away.

CAUSE

Anything that causes increased pressure to the area through knee bending and pressure. May be related to a growth spurt in children who have not completed puberty (seven to nineteen years old). Child: patellar tendonitis; adult: usually caused by a very forceful activity.

TREATMENT

Immediate Relief

Ice the painful area (see Section A.1). Decrease the activity that causes pain until it doesn't hurt. Soft tissue massage or trigger point work on the painful areas of

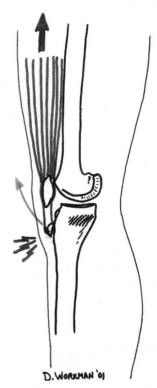

Figure 8.3 During puberty, the bone where the thigh muscles attach is still weak, and increased pressure from those muscles can tear the tendons or pull the bone away (avulsion fracture).

the quadratus femoris is effective in giving more slack to the area (see Section A.2). Aspirin or other over-the-counter medications will help reduce the pain and swelling; however, they will not solve the problem caused by the continuous muscle pull.

PREVENTION
Technique
Most commonly found in teenagers who march long hours and have various other activities that stress the knee area. It is important to take breaks every hour or so depending on the intensity of the workout and to use the home ice program (see Section A.1).

Stretches
Hamstring and quadratus femoris stretches (see Stretches 8.1 and 8.2). Check the muscle balance between the hips and the lower back muscles (they have a tug-of-war with each other over the position of the pelvis).

Exercises
Exercises that don't require knee bends past twenty-five degrees are the most effective because they put less pressure on the joint.

IF NO RELIEF
See your primary care physician if no improvement occurs within two weeks of this treatment.

PROGNOSIS
This injury should be closely guarded so it doesn't progress to full detachment (avulsion). With proper care, the prognosis is excellent: Full recovery without residual pain can be expected. However, a lump will most likely remain below the knee where the bone heals.

OTHER POSSIBILITIES
Bursitis of the patellar tendon (pain is just above this injury) or chondromalacia patella (pain directly under the kneecap).

SIGNS AND SYMPTOMS
Tender to palpation of the bursae areas (see Figure 8.4) most noticeable after extended activity of the area.

NAME OF INJURY
Knee bursitis

DESCRIPTION

Bursae are positioned between tissues that rub against each other and have potential for friction irritation. When overworked (from over-repetition or increased pressure), they get swollen and sore.

CAUSE

Prolonged or increased intensity (i.e., heavier loads, tight muscles compressing the area, etc.) of movement around the bursae or movement of areas that are not used to it.

TREATMENT

Immediate Relief

Apply the RICE technique (see Section A.1) to the area that hurts. Cool it down for two or three days if possible and move without intensity (slower or without the instrument).

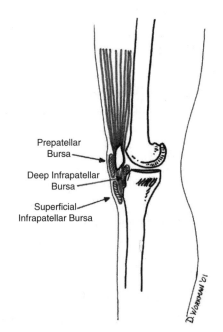

Figure 8.4 Bursae (blue) are lubricant-filled sacs positioned between tissues that rub together to reduce friction. If misused, they can become inflamed or damaged, causing pain in the area.

PREVENTION

Technique

Pain in the hip or any joint further down may be helped by a more stable shoe or orthotics (see Section C.10). This will help improve the way the foot moves and give it a more stable foundation, especially when marching.

Stretches

Quadricep and hamstring stretches increase muscle length and flexibility, decreasing pressure on the bursae (see Stretches 8.1 and 8.2).

Exercises

After the pain is gone, begin doing the movement that used to hurt, but do it at half of your normal exertion. Gradually increase the exertion over a period of time. If you feel pain, you are overdoing it, so you must decrease your intensity or stop for a time to allow some recovery. Continue this routine until you are back to full ability without pain.

IF NO RELIEF

You may already have a chronic problem, and you should see a medical doctor, chiropractor, or specialist in that particular area.

PROGNOSIS

Prognosis is good if the injury is caught and treated early on and to its completion. But the longer it is allowed to persist, the slower it will respond and the less chance you have for full recovery. It may recur frequently or never go away completely.

OTHER POSSIBILITIES

Tendonitis or sprain or strain of the area (usually from a trauma of some sort).

DIGGING A LITTLE DEEPER

What is bursitis? See Section C.2.

SIGNS AND SYMPTOMS

Pain in tendon areas, especially just above or below the joint. Painful on exertion (or any movement if the injury is bad) and pressure to the area.

NAME OF INJURY

Tendonitis (knee)

DESCRIPTION

Increased load on the tendon, possibly constant, which causes irritation or tears that produce swelling and pain.

CAUSE

Most likely from increased activity or increased load over a short period of time.

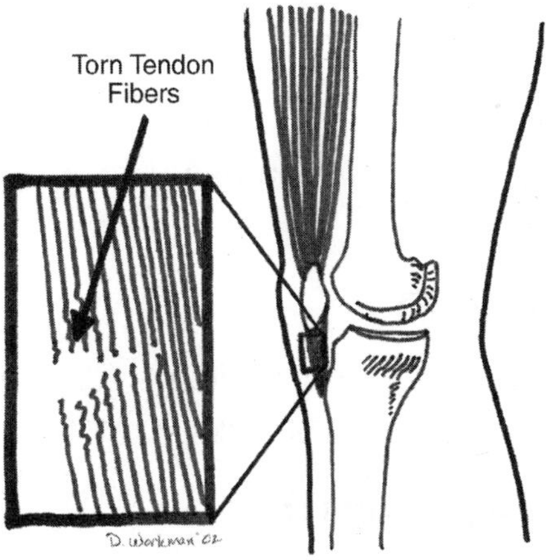

Torn Tendon Fibers

D. Workman '02

Figure 8.5 The tendons secure muscles to their attachment (usually bone), as shown in the figure. Many tendons attach at the knee to give movement, strength, and protection to the area.

TREATMENT

Immediate Relief

Apply the RICE therapy to the injury (see Section A.1). Decrease activity or intensity. Stay off of your feet as much as possible in the first week or so to allow the healing process to start. Then, for up to four more weeks, you can do light activity but avoid stairs, aggressive athletics, or heavy marching.

If you must play or march, apply ice to the painful area between sets or whenever possible. The same rules go for those of you who haul your own equipment.

PREVENTION

Technique

If you march, you can prevent further agony by making sure your shoes have soft midsoles and good support and are comfortable (see Section C.10). If you play the drum set and have this injury, analyze your technique. How much pressure do you have to apply to your pedals? Also review your playing technique. Can you get more volume by using less effort? Yes: Incorporate more leg, ankle, and toe coordination.

Stretches

After the pain subsides (five to ten days or so), begin some mild stretching, but stay away from the pain (see Stretch 8.1).

Exercises

Do quadriceps extensions and soft tissue massage (see Section A.2) to the painful areas of the quadriceps muscles after the pain is gone to loosen up the tight muscles and reduce the constant pressure to the tendon (see Exercise B.15).

IF NO RELIEF

If your pain is not making an exit after two weeks of this treatment, see your doctor.

PROGNOSIS

This can be a very serious injury and must be taken very seriously to avoid possible rupture or chronic long-standing problems with the knee.

OTHER POSSIBILITIES

Bursitis or rupture (minor).

DIGGING A LITTLE DEEPER

What is tendonitis? See Section C.3.

SIGNS AND SYMPTOMS

Pain, ache, cramp, or tenderness in the leg when walking, playing, or exercising.

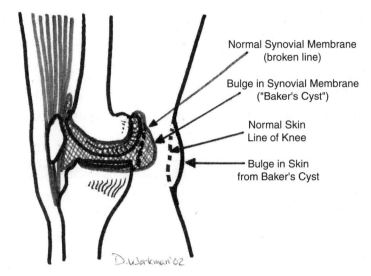

Figure 8.7 This figure illustrates the underlying synovial membrane bulge found in a Baker's cyst.

TREATMENT

Immediate Relief

Rest, apply ice with mild pressure, and elevate the knee.

PREVENTION

Technique

Avoid putting undue stress on the knee with heavy activity (e.g., marching, moving equipment, standing long periods of time, etc.).

Stretches

Any leg stretches alleviating pressure on the knee capsule are all right for this injury if no other problem exists in the knee. The stretches can be found at the end of Chapter 7 (Stretches 7.3 and 7.4) and at the end of this chapter (Stretches 8.1 and 8.2).

Exercises

Do all exercises of the legs to provide general stability to the knees (see Exercise B.15).

IF NO RELIEF

These injuries are not known to go away spontaneously. With or without relief, you need to see your physician to make sure that the knee capsule and the internal structure is intact.

PROGNOSIS

This injury is not harmful in itself, but it may cause pain and recur if not taken care of.

OTHER POSSIBILITIES

Lipoma (fatty tumor that moves with the skin; usually of little or no concern).

SIGNS AND SYMPTOMS

Pain in kneejoint(s), achy in nature. Pain on motion of the joint, worse in the morning and after activity, and decreasing during the day or during activity.

NAME OF INJURY

Osteoarthritis (knee)

DESCRIPTION

Pain in a joint of the body with swelling and pain (usually worse in the morning and improves during the day with movement). Not much pain during activity but increased pain following. It usually progresses to tenderness, grinding, and painful loss of range of motion.

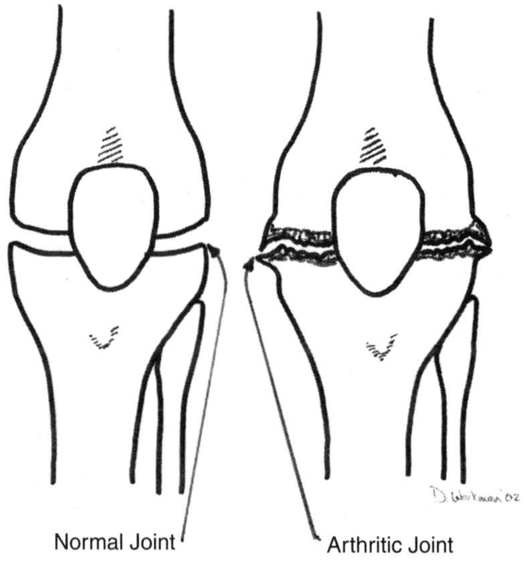

CAUSE

Repetitive, inefficient movements or macrotrauma, causing the joints to be dysfunctional (gradual onset). Often called "getting old before your time." This injury is usually found in players who are on their feet a lot.

Normal Joint   Arthritic Joint

Figure 8.8   This figure shows an example of a normal knee joint and one with degenerative arthritis (wearing down of the joint from improper use). Note that there are smooth curves at the bone's edge in the normal joint, while the arthritic joint shows jagged edges (bone spurs) and decreased space between the bones at the joint.

TREATMENT

Prevention is really the key in this injury, because if you feel it, it's been there a while. And although you can arrest it, there is no proven way to reverse the damage already done.

Immediate Relief

Ice (see Section A.1), rest, and use firm, supportive furniture. Aspirin or muscle relaxants are believed to be helpful in controlling the pain.

PREVENTION

Technique

Degenerative arthritis in the knee is usually due to long-term misuse of the knee, as when marching or hauling equipment. Proper lifting techniques will also help prevent this injury (see Section A.3).

Stretches

Do general stretching of the major muscle groups surrounding the affected joint (see Stretches 7.3, 7.4, and 8.1). The main focus is to relieve pressure from opposing muscle pull.

Exercises

General knee exercises will help strengthen the muscles (see Exercise B.15). Strong muscles greatly aid the joint in its motion and protect its ligaments and intricate parts from unnecessary wear that leads to osteoarthritis.

IF NO RELIEF

Treat for two weeks, then see your doctor (if no change) for his or her opinion and professional diagnosis to rule out various arthropathies (among other things).

PROGNOSIS

Damage done cannot be reversed. The sooner you treat it, the better.

OTHER POSSIBILITIES

Other types of arthritis (see your doctor).

DIGGING A LITTLE DEEPER

Rheumatoid Arthritis versus Degenerative Arthritis. See Section C.9.

RELATED AREAS

Many injuries can be related to areas of the body other than where you feel the pain. For example, pain in the shoulder may be the result of a problem with the neck or elbow area. If you cannot find the injury that fits your complaints in this chapter, please look in the chapters of the related areas indicated in Figure 8.9.

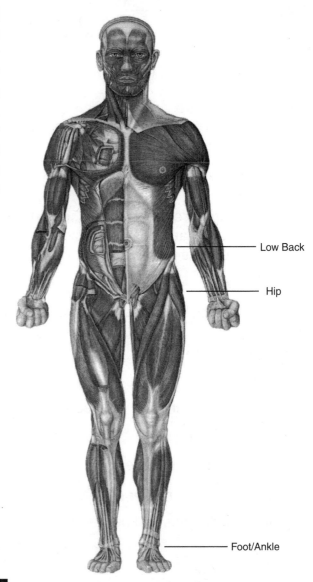

Low Back

Hip

Foot/Ankle

Figure 8.9 (Anatomical Chart Company, Lippincott Williams & Wilkins 2003)

STRETCHES

THE PHILOSOPHY OF STRETCHING

Stretching is not something you do *to* the body; it is something you *allow* the body to do. All stretches must be done by relaxing and allowing the muscles to stretch. If you try to force the muscles to stretch, their immediate reaction is to protect themselves from tearing by pulling back. This can quickly turn into a tug-of-war of you against your muscles, and nothing good can happen. This is why many people stretch and stretch without any positive results, and sometimes they even injure themselves.

GENERAL RULES FOR STRETCHING

Stretches are most effective when the body is warmed up first. This means you should do some mild exercise of the area to be stretched prior to beginning. For example, if you are stretching the legs, do some walking or running until the muscles get warm and loose (usually just before you begin to perspire). With the hands, try some basic rudiments—singles and doubles are best. If you are paying attention to your body, you will notice the area warming up as the blood is pumped into it. Or you can take a shower or sit in hot water prior to stretching—which is not as effective, but still good.

Do not

- pop your knuckles
- stretch when that part of the body is cold
- use bouncing or jerking motions while stretching
- force the stretch to the point where you cannot let the area relax

BASIC STRETCHES FOR THE KNEES

Stretch 8.1: Stretches for the Hip Flexors and Knee Extenders

Tight muscles of the upper leg can put increased pressure on the knee and lead to knee pain. These stretches will help loosen the upper leg muscles and reduce pressure and pain. It is very important that you push the pelvis forward to get the most from this stretch.

Figure 8.10 Stand on your good leg with your painful one bent at the knee, holding the ankle as shown in the figure. Balance by holding onto something.

Figure 8.11 Arch your lower back and push the pelvis forward and down until you can feel the stretch. *Do not bounce!* Hold the stretch for twenty to thirty seconds.

Figure 8.12 Relax the hips for thirty seconds by shaking the leg. Repeat the stretch five to ten times.

Stretch 8.2: General Stretches for the Back of the Legs (Hamstrings)

This stretch will loosen muscles from the bottom of the skull to the tips of the toes. You must allow the body to roll up and collapse in a completely relaxed state—*do not bounce or pull!* During the twenty-second stretch, breathe shallowly, then loosen the muscles by taking a deep breath when you come up. Your hands should be able to get closer to the toes with each repetition.

Figure 8.13 Sit with tailbone snug against a wall with legs straight in front of you in a relaxed position.

Figure 8.14 Drop chin to chest and gradually roll into a ball as shown in the figure. When you feel the stretch, stop, relax, and hang for twenty seconds.

Figure 8.15 Come up to a sitting position, take a deep breath, and rest for thirty seconds while shaking the legs and upper body.

CHAPTER 9

HIP AND PELVIS PROBLEMS

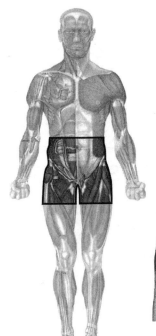

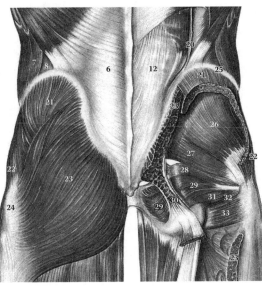

6. Thoracolumbar fascia
7. External abdominal oblique m.
8. Internal abdominal oblique m.
12. Erector spinae mm.:
20. Thoracolumbar fascia (removed)
21. Gluteus medius m.
22. Tensor fasciae latae m.
23. Gluteus maximus m.
24. Greater trochanter
25. Iliac crest
26. Gluteus minimus m.
27. Piriformis m.
28. Superior gemellus m.
29. Obturator internus m.
30. Sacrotuberal l.
31. Inferior gemellus m.
32. Obturator externus m.
33. Quadratus femoris m.

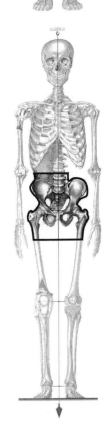

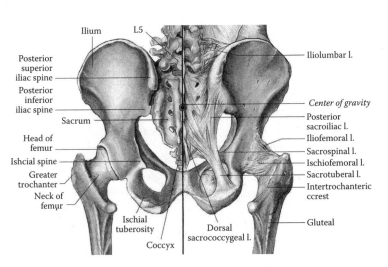

Ilium
L5
Iliolumbar l.
Posterior superior iliac spine
Posterior inferior iliac spine
Center of gravity
Posterior sacroiliac l.
Sacrum
Iliofemoral l.
Head of femur
Sacrospinal l.
Ishcial spine
Ischiofemoral l.
Sacrotuberal l.
Greater trochanter
Intertrochanteric ccrest
Neck of femur
Gluteal
Ischial tuberosity
Dorsal sacrococcygeal l.
Coccyx

SIGNS AND SYMPTOMS

Pain in the buttock (usually one side) with possible pain, tingle, burning feeling, or weakness down that same leg. The pain is usually worse during or just after sitting, when touching the toes, or when applying pressure on the buttock.

NAME OF INJURY

Piriformis syndrome

DESCRIPTION

Sciatic nerve is impinged by a deep hip rotator muscle spasm (usually the piriformis muscle), causing the previously described symptoms.

CAUSE

Sitting for long periods of time (car, bus, or plane rides) or increased workout (e.g., sprints, stairs, or sports requiring much bending of the hip).

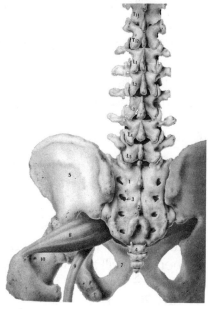

Figure 9.1 The sciatic nerve passes by the piriformis muscle, and if that muscle is in spasm, it puts pressure on the nerve and produces leg pain (aka sciatica). (Ortho-McNeil Pharmaceutical, Inc. 2003)

TREATMENT

Immediate Relief

Try moderate heat in the morning (twenty minutes maximum), movement to loosen up the muscle (walking, etc.), or soft tissue work to the deep buttock muscles (see Section A.2).

PREVENTION

Technique

This is usually a sitting problem, so you may want to evaluate your throne or seat. If they are too hard or irritating to sit in, they will irritate the buttock muscles. Marching may also irritate the area. If you are a marimba player, check your playing posture. Too much bending at the waist fatigues these muscles because they have to work to keep the body in an off-balanced position. Proper lifting techniques will also help prevent this injury (see Section A.3).

Stretches

Hamstring stretches and piriformis stretches (see Stretch 9.2).

Exercises

Walk on a level surface at a moderate pace for fifteen minutes to an hour to loosen up and begin the strengthening process. Swimming is also good in the initial stages to loosen up the muscle by repetitive mild contraction and relaxation. Making these muscles stronger by heavy workout will not necessarily prevent the problem. You must focus more on keeping them loose by stretching and avoiding improper use.

IF NO RELIEF

See your primary care physician for an examination if condition doesn't improve in two to four weeks.

PROGNOSIS

If you have this problem and it isn't related to a more extensive problem of the nerve, it will resolve completely.

OTHER POSSIBILITIES

Lumbar intervertebral disc syndrome with radiculopathy (usually trauma induced or secondary to degenerative arthritis of the lower spine).

DIGGING A LITTLE DEEPER

What are muscle spasms? See Section C.1.

SIGNS AND SYMPTOMS

Knifelike pain and possible grabbing in the upper leg muscles. Worse when walking up stairs or hills or when lifting knee the to the chest. Very tender to the touch if severe. No bruise or increased temperature.

NAME OF INJURY

Muscle spasm/fatigue (hip flexor muscle)

DESCRIPTION

Muscle overuse depletes the muscle's energy, causing constant contraction of the muscle and cramps.

CAUSE

Doing too much too soon or too often, or both. Overuse or improper use of the knee or hip; for example, large increase in marching, poor shoes, improper walking form, or inefficient bass drum technique for drumset.

TREATMENT

Immediate Relief

Rest, ice the area of pain, and resist movements that produce the pain. Aspirin or other over-the-counter pain relievers have been shown to relieve some of the pain. Massage to the tight areas and trigger points will reduce the pain and spasm (see Section A.2).

PREVENTION

Technique

Change your seat height (usually the drummer is sitting too low, causing the legs to lift the knee while already in a contracted position), shoes, or sitting positions to decrease stress to the body. Drink plenty of water to flush out the muscles. Take time out to rest periodically, and pick one day a week when you don't play at all to let the body rejuvenate. Proper lifting techniques will also help prevent this injury (see Section A.3).

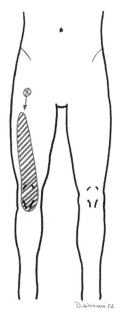

Figure 9.2 Trigger points in the muscle (X) are very painful pockets of lactic acid. When they are pressed, they produce a referred pain to other areas (shaded area).

Stretches

Apply mild massage to the sore muscles followed by gentle stretching of the area (see Stretch 9.1). Allowing pain to be your guide is extremely important. In addition, when you play, change positions as you begin feeling tight.

Exercises

Repeat the exercises that caused the pain, but at a lower intensity for shorter periods of time (about half as long). Gradually increase the time and intensity over a period of weeks, stopping when the pain begins. In this way you will strengthen the injured muscles and prevent repeated injury in the future.

IF NO RELIEF

If no improvement occurs within one or two weeks, consult your doctor.

PROGNOSIS

This should never become a big problem because it is so easy to treat and fully resolve. However, if you do not address the problem, it can become chronic (requiring extensive treatment) and possibly lead to other, more serious injuries — not to mention that it can decrease your endurance, power, and coordination.

OTHER POSSIBILITIES

Contusion or bruise (usually caused by a direct hit to the painful area and accompanied by a red or purple mark on the skin).

DIGGING A LITTLE DEEPER

What are muscle spasms? What are trigger points? See Sections C.1 and C.8, respectively.

SIGNS AND SYMPTOMS

Sudden, extreme, unrelenting pain in the buttock. Spontaneous, or provoked by movement on poorly cushioned seat. Pain into the night, no leg symptoms, tender buttock, and possible pain when on tiptoes.

NAME OF INJURY

Ischio-gluteal bursitis (aka weaver's bottom)

DESCRIPTION

Irritation from trauma or excess movement, causing friction that produces irritation and inflammation and possible chronic scarring to the bursae that sit between the moving parts around the ischial tuberosity (sitting bones).

CAUSE

Sitting for long periods of time on a poorly cushioned, vibrating, or wobbly seat. This can happen to drumset players with poor thrones and long playing sessions. It can also happen to musicians who spend a lot of time on an airplane or a bus.

TREATMENT
Immediate Relief

Rest, get off of your buttocks (lay on side or stomach), apply ice to the area, and try some over-the-counter ibuprofen. The swelling can take weeks to reduce. If you don't allow the injury to heal, you may get chronic bursitis that recurs over and over again.

PREVENTION
Technique

Proper lifting techniques will help prevent this injury (see Section A.3).

Stretches

Pressure and motion on the bursae cause irritation; stretching the tight muscles will reduce some pressure. The hamstrings and the lower back

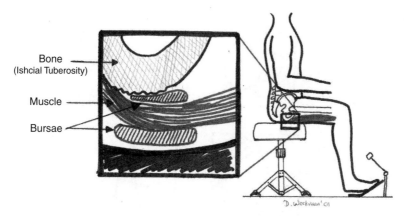

Figure 9.3 Constant sitting on a moving surface can cause the bursae next to the sitting bones (ischial tuberosities) to get inflamed. The pain is intense and can adversely affect the musician's career. Note the area of the bones and bursae when sitting (as shown in this figure).

muscles battle for position of the pelvis. They must be relaxed to allow the pelvis to sit correctly (see Stretch 9.2). This way, the sitting bones (ischial tuberosities) get the least agitation and the hamstrings can relax.

Exercises

You must wait until the pain is gone from the area (usually one to two weeks), then start mild stretching and exercise. Let pain be your guide. First you should do easy motion and isometric exercises. Then move on to exercises that allow movement of the muscles without putting pressure on the injury (e.g., swimming, walking, running, etc.). Proceed to strengthening the hamstrings and the lower back muscles to stabilize the pelvis, providing a firm foundation for the body (see Exercise B.18).

IF NO RELIEF

See your primary care physician if no relief occurs within two weeks of this program.

PROGNOSIS

If you catch it in the acute phase (within a few months), you have an excellent chance of ridding yourself of this problem for good. However, the longer you have put up with this problem, the less chance you have of full recovery without recurrence.

OTHER POSSIBILITIES

Sciatica (pain usually into the leg), lumbar intervertebral disc herniation (lower back pain mostly on back movement), or infection (usually have fever or painful swelling at the point of pain).

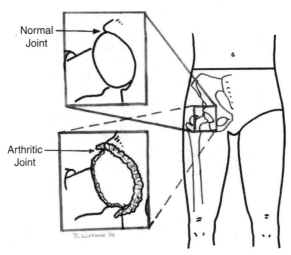

Normal Joint

Arthritic Joint

Figure 9.4   This figure shows an example of a normal hip joint and one with degenerative arthritis—the wearing down of the joint from improper use. Note that these are smooth curves at the bone's edge in the normal joint, while the arthritic joint shows jagged edges (bone spurs) and loss of space at the joint. These spurs are believed by some to be the bone's attempt to heal the damage.

DIGGING A LITTLE DEEPER

What is bursitis? See Section C.2.

SIGNS AND SYMPTOMS

Pain in the hip area, causing sensation of pain in the knees or back, or both. No change in pain during exercise, but there is stiffness in the joint at rest. Separation of the thighs causes pain. Grinding sounds occur during hip motion.

NAME OF INJURY

Osteoarthritis (hip)

DESCRIPTION

Wear and tear of the hip joint, causing early aging of the joint.

CAUSE

Trauma to the joint in the past or repetitive microtrauma over the years. A person may be susceptible to this injury through his or her genetics.

TREATMENT

Immediate Relief

Try mild heat in the morning to warm up the joint and reduce the pain. After exercise or increased activity for the joint, immediately put ice on the area for fifteen minutes while elevating it. Aspirin may help relieve the pain. Massage to the surrounding muscles may relieve pressure on the joint (see Section A.1). At night, try some muscle ointment to the area to reduce the pain.

PREVENTION

Technique

This condition most commonly results from marching over a period of years, perhaps with improper equipment. Drumset players may have the pedals too far apart, causing more wear on the joint. Proper lifting techniques help prevent this injury (see Section A.3).

Stretches

See stretches for the back, hamstrings, quads, hips, and gluteus muscles (see Stretches 8.1, 8.2, 9.1, 9.2, and 10.1). In addition, yoga has been found to be very helpful, although many find it somewhat painful.

Exercises

Strengthen the hip muscles through various exercises, preferably those that don't put weight on the joint (swimming, biking, etc.). Always exercise to the point of pain, but do not exercise during pain.

IF NO RELIEF

If you get no improvement of the symptoms within two weeks, see the physician of your choice for an examination. If it is improving, even slightly, continue this program.

PROGNOSIS

This injury is not one that is reversible. The goal is to reduce the pain, slow down the degeneration process, and reduce pressure to the joint, allowing longer and less painful use.

OTHER POSSIBILITIES

Muscle spasms of the hip rotators (shows normal hip on x-ray) or sciatica.

DIGGING A LITTLE DEEPER:

Rheumatoid Arthritis versus Degenerative Arthritis. See Section C.9.

SIGNS AND SYMPTOMS

Tingle, burn, or pain down one or both legs (possibly to the toes). May also have weakness in the leg(s).

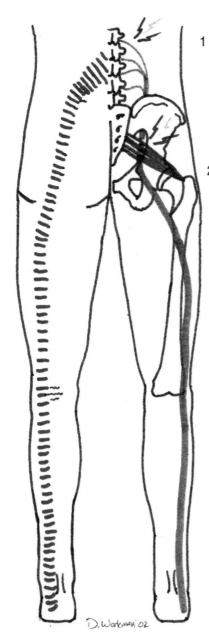

Figure 9.5 This illustration demonstrates two of the common causes of sciatica: (1) bulging or herniated lower back discs and (2) pressure on the nerve from a spastic muscle (usually the piriformis muscle). Sciatica can be down the leg as far as the toes in the pattern shown on the left (nerve in solid line, and pain pattern in dashes).

NAME OF INJURY
Sciatica

DESCRIPTION
Pressure on the sciatic nerve or one of its branches by something (e.g., herniated disc, fracture, scar tissue, muscle spasm, swelling, tumor, etc.).

CAUSE
Sciatica is a description of pain caused by a number of things. The following are the most common causes of sciatica: Trauma to the back (fall or accident) with possible popping noise or a tearing sensation in the spine area may indicate that the disc was herniated (see description of lumbar intervertebral disc herniation in Chapter 10). Prolonged sitting or walking a lot of stairs or hills (or similar movements requiring large bending at the hip) may cause spasm of the gluteus muscles or rotators of the hip (see description of piriformis syndrome in this chapter). These spasms cause tightness around the sciatic nerve that goes down the leg, causing it to get "dizzy" (tingle) or to "pass out" (numbness).

TREATMENT

Immediate Relief
Determine the cause of the sciatica, go to that injury, and follow the instructions outlined in that section. Proper lifting techniques will also help prevent this injury (see Section A.3).

OTHER POSSIBILITIES
Herniated intervertebral disc, piriformis syndrome, or tumor.

DIGGING A LITTLE DEEPER
What is nerve impingement? See Section C.4.

RELATED AREAS

Many injuries can be related to areas of the body other than where you feel the pain. For example, pain in the shoulder may be the result of a problem with the neck or elbow area. If you cannot find the injury that fits your complaints in this chapter, please look in the chapters of the related areas indicated in Figure 9.6.

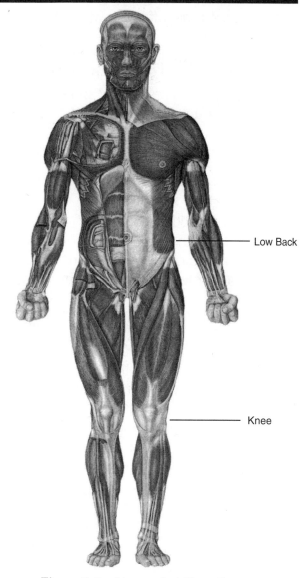

Low Back

Knee

Figure 9.6 (Anatomical Chart Company, Lippincott Williams & Wilkins 2003)

STRETCHES

THE PHILOSOPHY OF STRETCHING

Stretching is not something you do *to* the body; it is something you *allow* the body to do. All stretches must be done by relaxing and allowing the muscles to stretch. If you try to force the muscles to stretch, their immediate reaction is to protect themselves from tearing by pulling back. This can quickly turn into a tug-of-war of you against your muscles, and nothing good can happen. This is why many people stretch and stretch without any positive results, and sometimes they even injure themselves.

GENERAL RULES FOR STRETCHING

Stretches are most effective when the body is warmed up first. This means you should do some mild exercise of the area to be stretched prior to beginning. For example, if you are stretching the legs, do some walking or running until the muscles get warm and loose (usually just before you begin to perspire). With the hands, try some basic rudiments—singles and doubles are best. If you are paying attention to your body, you will notice the area warming up as the blood is pumped into it. Or you can take a shower or sit in hot water prior to stretching—which is not as effective, but still good.

Do not

- pop your knuckles
- stretch when that part of the body is cold
- use bouncing or jerking motions while stretching
- force the stretch to the point where you cannot let the area relax

BASIC STRETCHES FOR THE HIPS AND PELVIS

STRETCH 9.1: HIP FLEXOR STRETCHES

The muscles that bring the knees to the chest are the hip flexors. Many different percussion instruments make these muscles work hard, causing them to get tight and possibly go into spasm. These stretches are designed to restore their length and elasticity. Other helpful stretches are found in Chapter 8 (see Stretch 8.1).

Figure 9.7 Kneel on a soft surface, leaning back on your hands as shown in the figure. Gradually lower your body back until you feel the stretch.

Figure 9.8 When you feel the stretch in the front of your legs, relax and hold for twenty to thirty seconds. Push the pelvis forward if you want.

Figure 9.9 Stand up and shake both legs in a relaxed manner. Repeat the stretch five to ten times.

STRETCH 9.2: HAMSTRING AND HIP ROTATOR STRETCHES

9.2.1: Hamstring Stretches

The hamstrings are commonly injured muscles of the legs. For this reason, it is important to keep them loose and flexible by doing stretches such as these and those at the end of chapter 8.

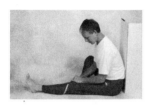

Figure 9.10 Sit with the tailbone snug against the wall, legs straight out in front of you, and toes pointing up.

Figure 9.11 Bend at the waist, and let gravity pull your head to your knees. When you feel the stretch, stay there for thirty seconds.

Figure 9.12 Return to a sitting position, and relax (thirty seconds) while moving the upper body and legs. Repeat stretch five to ten times.

9.2.2: Hip Rotator (Piriformis Muscle) Stretches

The hip rotators are rarely thought of until they are in pain and spasm. That pain is often felt deep in the buttock or *perceived* to be in the front of the hip (where the front pocket is). The stretch for these muscles is also not well known. It is most effective when accompanied by deep soft tissue work of the gluteal muscles (painful).

Figure 9.13 Get into a push-up position with the knee bent under the chest, as shown in this figure.

Figure 9.14 Gradually lower the upper body, allowing it to collapse over the knee. Control the lowering motion with the hands. Hold the stretch for twenty to thirty seconds, relaxed.

Figure 9.15 Come up slightly from the stretched position, and rest for thirty seconds. Repeat the stretch five to ten times. You should be able to go lower each time.

CHAPTER 10

LOWER BACK AND ABDOMEN PAIN PROBLEMS

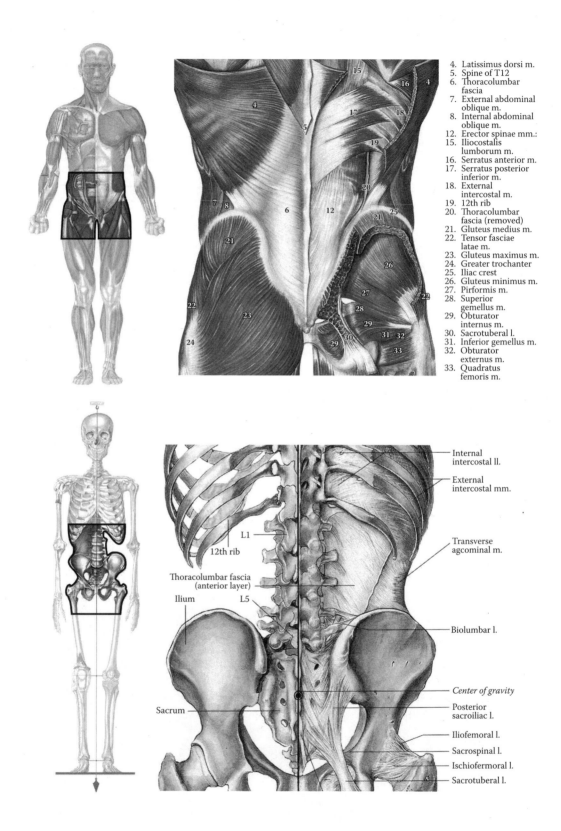

4. Latissimus dorsi m.
5. Spine of T12
6. Thoracolumbar fascia
7. External abdominal oblique m.
8. Internal abdominal oblique m.
12. Erector spinae mm.:
15. Iliocostalis lumborum m.
16. Serratus anterior m.
17. Serratus posterior inferior m.
18. External intercostal m.
19. 12th rib
20. Thoracolumbar fascia (removed)
21. Gluteus medius m.
22. Tensor fasciae latae m.
23. Gluteus maximus m.
24. Greater trochanter
25. Iliac crest
26. Gluteus minimus m.
27. Pirformis m.
28. Superior gemellus m.
29. Obturator internus m.
30. Sacrotuberal l.
31. Inferior gemellus m.
32. Obturator externus m.
33. Quadratus femoris m.

Internal intercostal ll.

External intercostal mm.

Transverse agcominal m.

L1

12th rib

Thoracolumbar fascia (anterior layer)

Ilium

L5

Biolumbar l.

Center of gravity

Sacrum

Posterior sacroiliac l.

Iliofemoral l.

Sacrospinal l.

Ischiofermoral l.

Sacrotuberal l.

SIGNS AND SYMPTOMS

Knifelike pain or grabbing in the lower back muscles. Worse when walking up stairs or hills. Very tender to the touch if severe. No bruise or increased temperature.

NAME OF INJURY

Muscle spasm (lower back)

DESCRIPTION

Muscle overuse causes muscle depletion, constant contraction, and cramps.

CAUSE

Doing too much too soon or too often, or both. Overuse or improper use of the lower back: for example, large increase in marching, poor shoes, improper walking form, or inefficient bass drum technique.

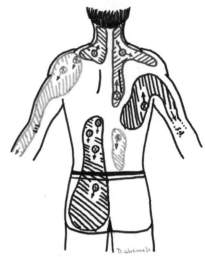

Figure 10.1 Low back pain is commonly caused by pockets of lactic acid (called trigger points) within the muscle (X in this figure). They are tender when pressed on and often send a pain sensation to other referred areas (shaded by diagonal lines).

TREATMENT

Immediate Relief

Rest, ice the area of pain (see Section A.1), and resist movements that hurt the area. Aspirin or other over-the-counter pain relievers have been shown to help decrease the pain. Massage to the tight areas and trigger points will reduce the pain and spasm (see Section A.2).

PREVENTION

Technique

Change your seat height (usually the drummer is sitting too high, causing the legs to constantly hold the weight of the body), shoes, or sitting positions to decrease stress to the body. Drink plenty of water to flush out the muscles. Take time out to rest each session, and pick one day a week when you don't play to let the body rejuvenate. Proper lifting techniques also help prevent this injury (see Section A.3).

Stretches

Try some mild massage to the sore muscles (see Section A.2) followed by gentle stretching with Stretches 8.1, 8.2, 9.1, 9.2, and 10.1. Allow pain to be your guide.

Exercises

Repeat the exercises that caused the pain but at a lower intensity and for shorter periods of time (about half as long). Gradually increase the time and intensity over a period of weeks, stopping when the pain begins. In this way you will strengthen the injured muscles and prevent repeated injury in the future.

IF NO RELIEF

If no improvement occurs within one to two weeks, consult your doctor.

PROGNOSIS

This problem should never become big, because it is easy to treat and heals well. However, if left alone, it can become chronic (requiring extensive treatment) and possibly lead to more serious injuries. This injury will decrease your endurance, coordination, and power.

OTHER POSSIBILITIES

Contusion or bruise (usually caused by a direct hit to the painful area and accompanied by a red or purple mark on the skin).

DIGGING A LITTLE DEEPER

What are muscle spasms? What is a trigger point? See Sections C.1 and C.8, respectively.

SIGNS AND SYMPTOMS

General mild back pain that doesn't go away and has no apparent cause. One side of the back, hips, shoulders, or legs is higher than the other (one leg is shorter than the other).

NAME OF INJURY

Scoliosis

DESCRIPTION

The spine curves like an "S" to varying degrees when seen from the back and is occasionally accompanied by a rotating of the spine (rotatory).

CAUSE

Scoliosis is believed to be genetic. It causes imbalance of the spine, producing various pains in the back due to muscle spasms and posture compensation. Treatment is to reduce pain. Most cases are of unknown cause, and 80 percent correct themselves to some degree before reaching a level

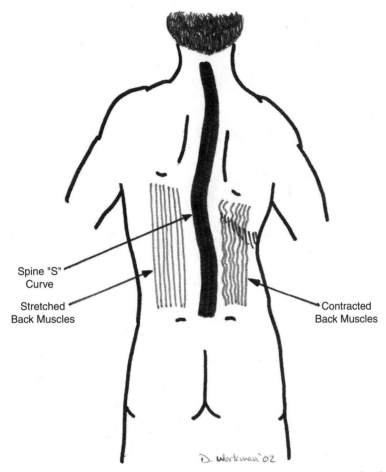

Spine "S" Curve

Stretched Back Muscles

Contracted Back Muscles

D. Workman '02

Figure 10.2 This figure shows a typical view of a scoliosis. Notice the uneven shoulders and hips (belt line). Drawn in are the imbalances of the muscles (solid lines), showing one side shorter than the other.

at which bracing or surgical correction is needed (usually just after puberty).

TREATMENT

Immediate Relief

Heat (thirty minutes) and massage (see Section A.2) the general muscles of the back.

PREVENTION

Technique

People with scoliosis will find it difficult to sit, stand, or march with heavy objects for long periods of time. If you have scoliosis, all things will affect you more than they affect those without scoliosis. So, you will need to be in good shape and at your correct weight and have the ability to deal with discomfort. Proper lifting techniques will also help prevent injury (see Section A.3).

Stretches

Be active in general, and do consistent back stretching, especially for the tight areas of the curve. Use Stretches 8.1, 8.2, 9.1, 9.2, and 10.1. Yoga or other types of stretching routines are very effective.

Exercises

As with stretches, exercising the entire back should be a regular routine done to stabilize the area and avoid common injury.

IF NO RELIEF

Your primary care physician can assist you in diagnosis and relief of the symptoms of scoliosis.

PROGNOSIS

Symptomatic relief is the main goal. There are those who claim that they can correct the scoliosis curve, but research is not sufficient to prove it at this time.

OTHER POSSIBILITIES

An x-ray shows proof of this condition.

SIGNS AND SYMPTOMS

Tingle, burning feeling, or pain down one or both legs (possibly to the toes). May also have weakness in the leg(s).

NAME OF INJURY

Sciatica

DESCRIPTION

Pushing on the sciatic nerve or one of its branches by something (e.g., herniated disc, fracture, scar tissue, muscle spasm, swelling, tumor, etc.).

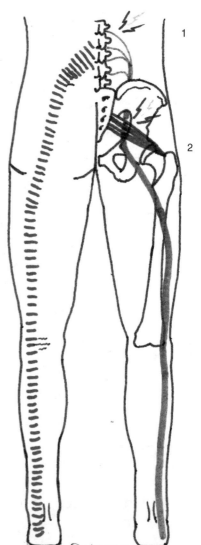

Figure 10.3 This figure demonstrates two of the common causes of sciatica: (1) bulging or herniated lower back discs and (2) pressure on the nerve from a spastic muscle (usually the piriformis muscle). Sciatica can be down the leg as far as the toes. Down the leg, the sciatic nerve is represented here by a solid line, and the pain pattern is represented by dashes.

CAUSE

Sciatica is a description of pain caused by a number of things. The following are the most common causes of sciatica: Trauma to the back (fall or accident) with possible popping noise or tearing sensation in the spine area may indicate that the disc was herniated (see description of lumbar intervertebral disc herniation in this chapter); prolonged sitting or walking a lot of stairs or hills (or similar movements requiring large bending at the hip) may cause spasm of the gluteus muscles or rotators of the hip (see description of piriformis syndrome in Chapter 9). These spasms cause tightness around the sciatic nerve that goes down the leg, causing it to get "dizzy" (tingle) or to "pass out" (numbness).

TREATMENT

Immediate Relief

Determine the cause of the sciatica, go to that injury, and follow the instructions outlined in that section. Proper lifting techniques will also help prevent this injury (see Section A.3).

OTHER POSSIBILITIES

Herniated intervertebral disc, piriformis syndrome, or tumor.

DIGGING A LITTLE DEEPER:

What is nerve impingement? See Section C.4.

SIGNS AND SYMPTOMS

Moderate to severe lower back pain; worse when sitting. May be unable to move because of pain. Possible pain, tingle, or numbness down one or both legs (as far as the toes). Affects walking and moving.

NAME OF INJURY

Lumbar intervertebral disc herniation

DESCRIPTION

The center (nucleus) of the intervertebral disc is affected in a way that forces the nuclear material out of the disc, usually into the tunnel that the nerve passes through to get down the leg. This causes pressure on the nerve and pain that you feel in the lower back and down the leg. The back and buttock muscles go into spasm, causing more pain and rigidity.

CAUSE

Suddenly falling on buttocks or lifting something that causes immediate and usually severe lower back pain. You may feel a tearing sensation or hear a pop just before you feel the severe pain.

TREATMENT

Immediate Relief

Get off your feet and do the home ice therapy (see Section A.1). Try some mild soft massage to the area of pain, stop if the massage is painful (see Section A.2).

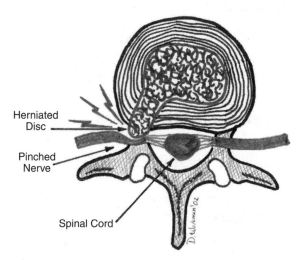

Figure 10.4 Shown in this figure is the top view of a herniated disc. Note how the disc material (arrow) pushes out, squashing the nerve against the bone and causing pain down the leg.

PREVENTION

Technique

No playing. This could increase the pain or worsen the injury. After the injury is healed to the point that you can play, concentrate on incorporating movements and postures that don't cause pain. Proper technique will allow you to play longer. Proper lifting techniques will also help prevent this injury (see Section A.3).

Stretches

As pain permits (usually around two weeks later), you can begin a general regime of lower back and leg stretches. Use Stretches 8.1, 8.2, 9.1, 9.2, and 10.1.

Exercises

The best exercises to start with are the lower back exercises found in this book (see Exercises B.17 and B.18). Do them to tolerance, and they will relieve the pain and strengthen the back. Later you can begin biking, swimming, or walking (low impact exercises) and, as pain permits, move to more aggressive exercises such as weightlifting, running, and so on.

IF NO RELIEF

If you are not feeling any relief within two to four days, you may have a herniated disc. See your primary care physician (chiropractors do well with this injury).

PROGNOSIS

This injury may lead to surgery if it is bad enough and if conservative treatment is not successful in reducing the symptoms. This injury must be taken seriously; you cannot just blow it off and continue to play (pain probably won't let you do so anyway).

OTHER POSSIBILITIES

Piriformis syndrome (deep tender buttock muscles), internal derangement (damage to the spine or cord), or infection (not a sudden injury, has temperature, etc.).

DIGGING A LITTLE DEEPER

What is nerve impingement? See Section C.4.

SIGNS AND SYMPTOMS

Pain in the lower back, achy, with occasional sharp pains on waist movement. Possible tingle, pain, burning feeling, or numbness down leg(s).

NAME OF INJURY

Lumbar intervertebral disc degeneration

DESCRIPTION

A large trauma or numerous irritations over a long period of time damage the disc and cause it to compress. This narrows the nerve tunnel between the bones and irritates the nerve that goes down the leg. The muscles of the back and buttock go into spasm to protect the area, causing a cycle of increased pressure on the nerve.

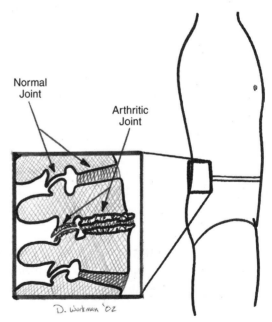

CAUSE

Macrotrauma (one big accident): usually a fall on the buttocks, a hit to the back, or pain directly from lifting an object. Microtrauma: repetitive, small irritations to the back over time (i.e., lifting, sitting, marching, etc.) or from improper ergonomics.

Figure 10.5 Note that the normal joint has smooth, rounded, clean corners and edges, while the arthritic one shows rough, thick edges, bone spurs, and decreased space between the bones, indicating degenerative disc (degenerative arthritis, wearing down of the joint from improper use). The spurs are the bone's attempt to heal the damage.

TREATMENT

Immediate Relief

Use the RICE program (see Section A.1).

PREVENTION

Technique

This is usually caused by old injuries (micro- or macrotrauma) to the back. Improper repetitive movements and positioning cause tight muscles, allowing basic movements to cause injury. Repetitive improper positions and movements wear down the spine and disc to cause bone degeneration. These positions include standing or sitting for long periods of time in poor posture (causing muscle fatigue and spasm), carrying heavy loads, and using equipment that works against you (shaky or hard thrones, poor shoes, difficult harnesses, etc.). Proper lifting techniques will help prevent this injury (see Section A.3).

Stretches

Do the lower back, hamstrings, and quadriceps stretches that are provided in Stretches 8.1, 8.2, 9.1, 9.2, and 10.1.

Exercises

Try the lower back exercises found in Exercise B.17.

IF NO RELIEF

These symptoms could be caused by something other than the disc (see Other Possibilities section that follows). If you are not getting relief within two weeks, see your chiropractor or medical doctor for an examination.

PROGNOSIS

By the time you feel pain from a degenerative disc, it has gone too far. You may reduce the pain, but you cannot reverse the damage done. You must always take care of it.

OTHER POSSIBILITIES

Piriformis syndrome, internal disorder (kidney, cancer, aneurysm, etc.), or disc herniation (usually from one large trauma).

DIGGING A LITTLE DEEPER

Rheumatoid Arthritis versus Degenerative Arthritis. See Section C.9.

SIGNS AND SYMPTOMS

Sudden onset of pain in the lower back area after some type of overexertion or trauma, causing a dull, constant ache in the lower back with occasional sharp attacks upon various movements.

NAME OF INJURY

Lumbar sprain or strain

DESCRIPTION

Tearing of the muscles or tendon fibers, or both, with a sudden or deliberate movement.

CAUSE

Lifting heavy objects or straining to reach something while in an awkward position.

TREATMENT

Immediate Relief

Perform the home ice program (see Section A.1) and light, soft massage to the muscles without causing any pain (see Section A.2). Don't move the back any more than necessary.

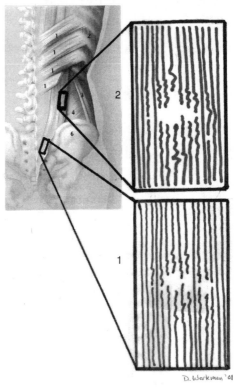

Figure 10.6 (1) A sprain is a tear in the tendons or ligaments, whereas (2) a strain is a tear in the muscle fibers. Muscles typically heal more quickly than tendons or ligaments because they have greater circulation (among other reasons). (Ortho-McNeil Pharmaceutical, Inc. 2003).

PREVENTION

Technique

Move gear properly. Proper lifting techniques will help prevent this injury (see Section A.3).

Stretches

Begin light stretching to the lower back and hamstrings as pain permits after at least forty-eight hours of rest and ice; use Stretches 8.1, 8.2, 9.1, 9.2, and 10.1.

Exercises

When you can stretch without pain, begin mild exercises (walking, swimming, etc.), gradually increasing resistance as pain permits (see lower back exercises in Exercises B.17 and B.18).

IF NO RELIEF

If you don't notice the pain decreasing in the first two or three days, see your doctor (chiropractic or medical).

PROGNOSIS

You can expect full healing in most cases with little or no residual pain if the injury is treated quickly and properly.

OTHER POSSIBILITIES

Intervertebral disc herniation, muscle spasm, tumor, and so forth.

DIGGING A LITTLE DEEPER

What is a strain or sprain? See Sections C.5 and C.6.

SIGNS AND SYMPTOMS

Lower back pain that feels like a knife in the spine, worse when bending backward (extension). Tight muscles in the lower back.

NAME OF INJURY

Facet syndrome

DESCRIPTION

Facet joints scissor onto each other, stressing or spraining the ligaments.

CAUSE

Marching with heavy apparatus causes lower back hyperextension. Bad posture while playing causes hyperlordosis (slouchy lower back).

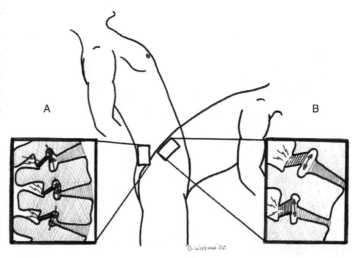

TREATMENT

Immediate Relief

Immobilization by using a lumbosacral brace during activity, especially those activities causing pain. Ice the lower back in the area

Figure 10.7 (A) When the lower back is arched back (extension), the facet joints jam together, causing pain. (B) When the lower back is bent forward (flexion), the facets are pulled apart, stressing the ligaments and causing irritation and pain.

of pain (see Section A.1) and perform mild stretches of the lower back after warm-up (hot bath or hot packs for twenty minutes).

PREVENTION

Technique

If marching with heavy apparatus (cymbals, quads, bass drum, etc.), you must avoid arching the lower back (especially when tired), which puts a scissoring pressure on the joints, causing damage to the ligaments (see Figure 10.7). Proper lifting techniques will also help prevent this injury (see Section A.3).

Stretches

Stretches to the lower back and hamstrings that are provided in Stretches 8.1, 8.2, 9.1, 9.2, and 10.1, will reduce pressure on the lower back joints.

Exercises

Strengthening the abdomen (stomach muscles) relieves pressure on the lower back joints (facets) (see Exercise B.19). It is also helpful to strengthen the upper back (rhomboids and latissimus dorsi) (see Exercise B.20). Hold your shoulders back when carrying the bass drum or quads—don't let the instrument or harness pull on them.

IF NO RELIEF

See your physician. Chiropractors commonly treat this problem.

PROGNOSIS

As with most injuries, catching it and treating it early provides better healing. Under proper care, the pain should be about gone in four weeks—longer in severe cases, and shorter in mild cases. Chronic cases (been there months or years) require more deep massage to loosen up tight muscles that squeeze the facets. A chiropractor or massage therapist who is familiar with working on athletes does this best. It is usually painful but effective.

OTHER POSSIBILITIES

Lumbar intervertebral disc syndrome (pain with all motions, not just extension, and commonly has leg symptoms), infection, or internal disorder (see your medical doctor if you have symptoms such as fever or abdomen pain).

DIGGING A LITTLE DEEPER

What is a sprain? See Section C.6.

SIGNS AND SYMPTOMS

Pain (acute or chronic) in the very bottom of the tailbone that is severely aggravated by sitting or standing. It may include lower back pain, constipation, or pain when having a bowel movement.

NAME OF INJURY

Coccydynia

DESCRIPTION

Something irritates the coccyx ligaments that attach it to the sacrum (tailbone). Swelling, pain on any movement of the coccyx (coughing, pooping, sitting, or standing).

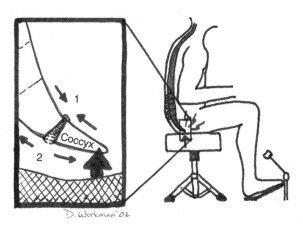

CAUSE

May be the result of prolonged sitting posture over time or (most likely) a sudden trauma to the area.

Figure 10.8 Shown in this figure is the slouching position of the body that puts pressure on the coccyx bone at the bottom of the spine, causing (1) the bones to jam on one side and the (2) ligaments to be stressed on the other—both cause pain.

TREATMENT
Immediate Relief

Acute injury: Use home ice therapy (see Section A.1). Rest in a position that doesn't put pressure on the coccyx bone (usually sitting on a donut-shaped pillow with a hole for the bone). It may help to strap both cheeks of the buttocks together tighter so they don't pull on the bone. A laxative may help by making going to the bathroom less of a strain. Aspirin has also been reported to help take the edge off of the pain.

PREVENTION
Technique

A donut-shaped ring for your throne would help. When you sit, don't slouch—sit straight to keep the lumbar curve (lordosis) maintained. Proper lifting techniques will also help prevent this injury (see Section A.3).

Stretches

When pain permits, stretch the lower back and gluteal muscles to help reduce pressure on the coccyx area. See Stretches 8.1, 8.2, 9.1, 9.2, and 10.1.

Exercises

As soon as pain permits, focus on strengthening the muscles of the lower back to help maintain proper posture (see Exercise B.18).

IF NO RELIEF

If no improvement occurs at all after a few days of rest, see your primary care physician. If the pain elevates, see your physician immediately.

PROGNOSIS

How it heals is variable depending on the individual, the cause, and the activity. If you stay off it, allow it to heal, and then solve the problem that caused it in the first place, you should have no recurrence.

OTHER POSSIBILITIES

Sacroiliac joint sprain (the pain is just below the beltline but not as low as the rectum) or fracture (can occur in either the sacrum or the coccyx, but is usually from a major trauma to the area).

DIGGING A LITTLE DEEPER

What is a sprain? See Section C.6.

SIGNS AND SYMPTOMS

Pain in the lower back, achy in nature. Pain on motion of the joint, worse in the morning and after activity, decreases during the day or during activity.

NAME OF INJURY

Osteoarthritis (spine–lower back)

DESCRIPTION

Pain in a joint of the body, with swelling and pain (usually worse in the morning and improves with movement during the day). Not much pain during activity but increased pain after. It usually progresses to tenderness, grinding, and painful loss of range of motion.

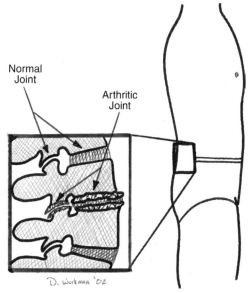

Figure 10.9 Note that the normal joint shown in this figure has smooth, rounded, clean corners and edges, while the arthritic one shows rough, thick edges, bone spurs, and decreased space between the bones. This indicates a degenerative disc (degenerative arthritis, wearing down of the joint from improper use). The spurs are the bone's attempt to heal.

CAUSE

Repetitive inefficient movements or macrotrauma, causing the joint or joints to be dysfunctional (gradual onset). Often called "getting old before your time." This injury is usually found in players who are on their feet a lot.

TREATMENT

Immediate Relief

Ice (see Section A.1), rest, and use firm and supportive furniture. Aspirin or muscle relaxants may help control the pain.

PREVENTION

Technique

Since lower back and neck pain usually stems from having poor sitting or standing posture, sitting on a poor throne, or playing while fatigued, it is crucial that you don't do these things. Proper lifting techniques will help prevent this injury (see Section A.3).

Stretches

General stretching of the major muscle groups around the spine and muscles surrounding the affected joint will help. The main idea is to relieve pressure on the joint from opposing muscle pull. Use Stretches 8.1, 8.2, 9.1, 9.2, and 10.1.

Exercises

Postural exercises (see Appendix B) will help strengthen the muscles. Strong muscles greatly aid the joint in its motion and protect its ligaments and intricate parts from unnecessary wear that leads to osteoarthritis.

IF NO RELIEF

Give treatment for two weeks, then see your doctor for his or her opinion and professional diagnosis to rule out (among other things) other arthropathies.

PROGNOSIS

Prevention is really the key, because if you feel it, it's been there too long. You can slow the process, but there is no proven way to reverse the damage already done. The damage done cannot be undone. The sooner you treat it, the better.

OTHER POSSIBILITIES

Other types of arthritis (see your doctor).

DIGGING A LITTLE DEEPER

Rheumatoid Arthritis versus Degenerative Arthritis. See Section C.9.

SIGNS AND SYMPTOMS

Pain near or in the genital area at the crease in the upper leg (in men). Pain worse when going to the bathroom, coughing, sneezing, and so forth.

NAME OF INJURY

Inguinal hernia (direct or indirect)

DESCRIPTION

A weakness develops in the opening leading into or out of the inguinal canal (see Figure 10.10), causing the inner layers to protrude through, especially on exertion.

CAUSE

Lifting too heavy an object, coughing, or stressfully exerting, internally causing pressure to the opening.

TREATMENT

Immediate Relief

Rest on your back (standing or sitting puts pressure on the opening). Ice the area mildly to reduce swelling (ten minutes) (see Section A.1). Avoid strenuous activity until the injury is completely healed.

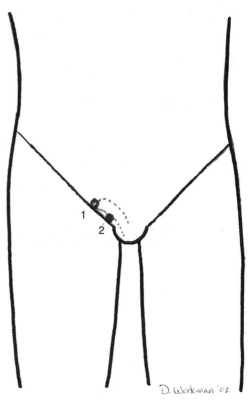

Figure 10.10 The two inguinal rings: (1) internal and (2) external for the opening and closing of the inguinal canal (located between the two in solid line). Shown in this figure as numbers 1 and 2 are the prime areas of the male hernia (inguinal area).

PREVENTION

Technique

If you have to hold or lift heavy objects while playing, you may consider a less stressful instrument or position. You can strengthen the abdominal and pelvic area, but that doesn't ensure against a reinjury of the area. Proper lifting techniques will also help prevent this injury (see Section A.3).

Exercises

After fully healed, you may try general abdominal strengthening only with your doctor's approval—do not overdo it. Once you have injured the area, you are more susceptible to reinjury.

IF NO RELIEF

If you get no relief in a day or two of this treatment, or if it continues to return, see your primary care physician. Should you feel a bubble or protrusion in the inguinal area (see Figure 10.10) or in the scrotal sac, see your medical doctor *immediately*.

PROGNOSIS

Once you have injured this area, you will need to be careful of it in the future. In many times this injury is in need of surgical correction that usually heals well.

OTHER POSSIBILITIES

The pain you feel is usually very specific to this particular injury.

SIGNS AND SYMPTOMS

Burning, itching swelling, or heavy feeling in the rectum and anus. Blood on tissue is also common when wiping after bowel movement.

NAME OF INJURY

Hemorrhoids

DESCRIPTION

Swelling of the hemorrhoidal veins in the rectum and anus causes pressure and swelling of the anus (closing it tighter), increasing irritation when defecating. There are two types of hemorrhoids: internal (deep inside the anal sphincter) and external (visible from outside or at the anal sphincter, look like ragged skin tabs or firm round nodules of skin, red and very tender).

CAUSE

Pressure of the hemorrhoidal veins from inside (e.g., being pregnant, stressed, or overweight; straining at the stool; or swelling) and irritation of the anal tissue around them (e.g., hard stools that scratch on the way out).

TREATMENT

Immediate Relief

Sit in a warm bath, then dry gently and put cold witch hazel on a cottonball. Hold to the anal opening until cottonball is warm. If hemorrhoids are swollen and protruding outside the anus, you must gently push them back in or blood clots can develop in the area.

PREVENTION

Technique

No heavy lifting; no drinking coffee, beer, or cola or eating strong spices. Eat plenty of fiber and drink large amounts of water. Do not scratch the area; that will irritate it and cause increased swelling. Use nonperfumed, white, moist toilet paper. A dab of petroleum jelly around the area will help make defecation smoother, causing less irritation and swelling and lessening the need to push. Lie on your left side. Sit on a donut cushion, especially when you are playing. Proper lifting techniques will also help prevent this injury (see Section A.3).

Exercises

It is important to do a general exercise routine to lose weight. However, avoid lifting heavy weights and anything else that causes you to hold your breath and push.

IF NO RELIEF

See a medical doctor or proctologist if you have tried these methods and over-the-counter hemorrhoid aids and have no relief within two weeks. You should also see one if you are bleeding during that time. If you are bleeding a lot, see your medical doctor immediately.

PROGNOSIS

Prognosis is good if you care for them before they get too large or chronic (more than three months).

OTHER POSSIBILITIES

Anal fissures (linear ulcer on skin around anus).

RELATED AREAS

Many injuries can be related to areas of the body other than where you feel the pain. For example, pain in the shoulder may be the result of a problem with the neck or elbow area. If you cannot find the injury that fits your complaints in this chapter, please look in the chapters of the related areas indicated in Figure 10.11.

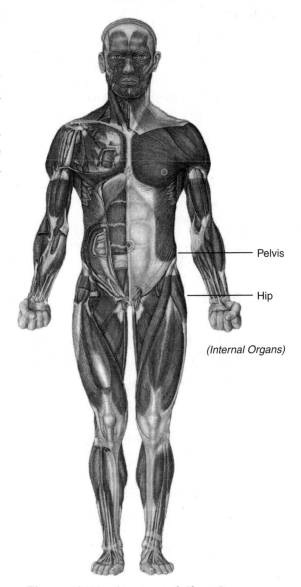

Pelvis

Hip

(Internal Organs)

Figure 10.11 (Anatomical Chart Company, Lippincott Williams & Wilkins 2003)

STRETCHES

THE PHILOSOPHY OF STRETCHING

Stretching is not something you do *to* the body; it is something you *allow* the body to do. All stretches must be done by relaxing and allowing the muscles to stretch. If you try to force the muscles to stretch, their immediate reaction is to protect themselves from tearing by pulling back. This can quickly turn into a tug-of-war of you against your muscles, and nothing good can happen. This is why many people stretch and stretch without any positive results, and sometimes they even injure themselves.

GENERAL RULES FOR STRETCHING

Stretches are most effective when the body is warmed up first. This means you should do some mild exercise of the area to be stretched prior to beginning. For example, if you are stretching the legs, do some walking or running until the muscles get warm and loose (usually just before you begin to perspire). With the hands, try some basic rudiments—singles and doubles are best. If you are paying attention to your body, you will notice the area warming up as the blood is pumped into it. Or you can take a shower or sit in hot water prior to stretching—which is not as effective, but still good.

Do not

- pop your knuckles
- stretch when that part of the body is cold
- use bouncing or jerking motions while stretching
- force the stretch to the point where you cannot let the area relax

BASIC STRETCHES FOR THE LOWER BACK

STRETCH 10.1: STRETCHES FOR THE INJURED LOWER BACK

These stretches must be done slowly, correctly, and consistently. If you have an injured back and go at these exercises aggressively, you will not do yourself any good. If your pain increases the day after stretching, you are doing the stretches too aggressively. For the injured lower back, these stretches should be a daily routine to avoid pain.

10.1.1: The Back Flattener

This stretch has two parts. The first thing is to allow your lower back muscles that keep the arch up to completely relax. At the same time, surrounding muscles must straighten the back enough so it can lie flat on the floor, taking pressure off of the lower spine. More important, this stretch trains the lower back muscles to release tension that compresses the spine.

Figure 10.12 To start, lie flat on the floor in a relaxed position, and take a few minutes to allow the muscles to let go.

Figure 10.13 Allow the lower back to drop to the floor while using the surrounding muscles to flatten it. Hold that position for twenty to thirty seconds.

Figure 10.14 Return to original position, relax for thirty seconds, and repeat the steps five to ten times.

10.1.2: Knee to Chest Stretch

During this stretch, try to relax and bring the knee closer to the chest. If it is forced or pulled, it will fight back to protect the lower back.

Figure 10.15 Begin in a relaxed position on your back with arms around one knee and the other leg slightly bent.

Figure 10.16 Slowly bring the knee to your chest while relaxing the lower back muscles. When you feel the deep lower back stretch, hold for twenty seconds.

Figure 10.17 With both feet on the floor, relax the lower back and legs for thirty seconds. Repeat the stretch five to ten times with each leg.

10.1.3: Raise and Pull Stretch

During this stretch, you must think of pulling just your upper body up and forward. Pretend your legs are paralyzed, and let the pelvis drag on the floor. This pulls the lower vertebra directly apart, taking pressure off of the spinal discs.

Figure 10.18 Start by lying flat on the ground, as shown in this figure, with the body fully relaxed.

Figure 10.19 Raise only the upper body up and forward, leaving the hips and legs relaxed on the floor. Lock your elbows into your sides, and relax in that position for thirty seconds.

Figure 10.20 This figure shows the same routine as shown in Figure 10.19, with the arms fully extended for a more aggressive stretch. Return to the original position. Repeat five to ten times.

10.1.4: "Crunch" Sit-ups

This is both an exercise for the abdomen and a stretch for the lower back. As you concentrate on bringing the lower ribs closer to the belly button, you will work the abdomen muscles while forcing the lower back to relax to aid the movement.

Figure 10.21 Start by lying in the position shown in this figure, locking hands between the head and neck.

Figure 10.22 Bring the lower ribs to the pelvis while relaxing the lower back muscles. Do not pull on the neck to accomplish this; you must use only the abdomen. The hands are there only for support.

Figure 10.23 Hold at the top for one second, and return to the original position and repeat without hesitation. Do three sets of fifteen to thirty or until you feel the abdominal muscles being worked.

CHAPTER 11

MIDBACK AND CHEST PROBLEMS

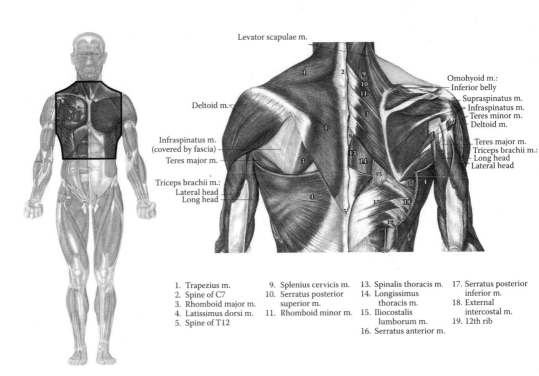

Levator scapulae m.

Deltoid m.

Infraspinatus m.
(covered by fascia)
Teres major m.

Triceps brachii m.:
Lateral head
Long head

Omohyoid m.:
Inferior belly
Supraspinatus m.
Infraspinatus m.
Teres minor m.
Deltoid m.

Teres major m.
Triceps brachii m.:
Long head
Lateral head

1. Trapezius m.
2. Spine of C7
3. Rhomboid major m.
4. Latissimus dorsi m.
5. Spine of T12

9. Splenius cervicis m.
10. Serratus posterior
    superior m.
11. Rhomboid minor m.

13. Spinalis thoracis m.
14. Longissimus
    thoracis m.
15. Iliocostalis
    lumborum m.
16. Serratus anterior m.

17. Serratus posterior
    inferior m.
18. External
    intercostal m.
19. 12th rib

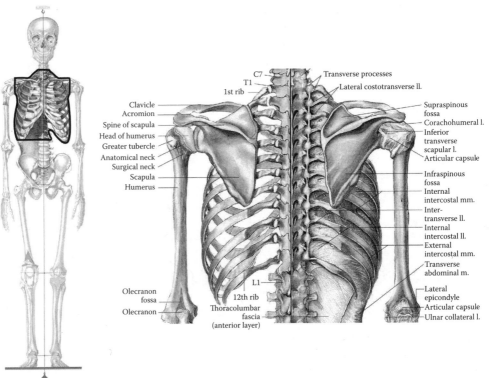

C7
T1
1st rib

Transverse processes
Lateral costotransverse ll.

Clavicle
Acromion
Spine of scapula
Head of humerus
Greater tubercle
Anatomical neck
Surgical neck
Scapula
Humerus

Supraspinous
fossa
Corachohumeral l.
Inferior
transverse
scapular l.
Articular capsule

Infraspinous
fossa
Internal
intercostal mm.
Inter-
transverse ll.
Internal
intercostal ll.
External
intercostal mm.
Transverse
abdominal m.

Olecranon
fossa

Olecranon

L1
12th rib
Thoracolumbar
fascia
(anterior layer)

Lateral
epicondyle
Articular capsule
Ulnar collateral l.

SIGNS AND SYMPTOMS

Knifelike pain and possible grabbing in the upper back or midback muscles. Worse when bending or using arms. Very tender to the touch if severe. Will not demonstrate bruise or increased temperature.

NAME OF INJURY

Muscle spasms (midback)

DESCRIPTION

Muscle overuse causes depletion of the muscle's energy and contraction of muscle, which leads to cramps.

CAUSE

Doing too much too soon or too often, or both. Overuse or improper use of the midback; for example, large increase (10 per-

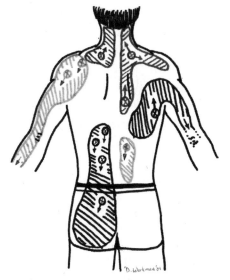

Figure 11.1 Upper back and midback pain are commonly caused by muscle spasms and trigger points (X). When pressed on, they give a referred pain to other areas (shaded lines). Your midback may cause pain in other areas.

cent or more) in sitting at the drum set, change in drum setup, marching, drum harnesses, improper walking form, or inefficient technique on mallet or timpani instruments. Your throne may be causing the problem, especially if it is wobbly or hard. A bad chair or mattress may also be the cause.

TREATMENT
Immediate Relief

Apply the home ice program (see Section A.1). Resist movements that produce the pain. Aspirin or other over-the-counter pain relievers may help. Massage to the tight areas and trigger points will reduce the pain and spasm (see Sections A.2 and C.8).

PREVENTION
Technique

Change seat height, set instruments up within easy reach, and use good playing posture. Drink plenty of water, rest periodically during playing, and take one day a week to let the body rejuvenate. Proper lifting techniques help prevent this injury (see Section A.3).

Stretches

Massage the sore muscles, and then gently stretch the area (see Stretch 4.2, Stretch 6.2, and Stretch 11.1). Change positions when you feel tight.

Exercises

Repeat the movements that caused the pain but at a lower intensity and for shorter periods of time (about half as long). Gradually increase the time and intensity over a period of weeks, stopping when the pain begins (see Exercise B.20). Swimming is also a good exercise for conditioning the mid-back (see Exercise B.8).

IF NO RELIEF

If no improvement occurs within one to two weeks, consult your doctor.

PROGNOSIS

This is easy to treat and resolves well. However, it can become chronic (needing treatment) and serious. It will affect your endurance, strength, and coordination.

OTHER POSSIBILITIES

Contusion or bruise (usually from a direct hit to the painful area, and it leaves a red or purple mark on the skin) or rib fracture (almost always from a trauma).

DIGGING A LITTLE DEEPER

What are muscle spasms? What are trigger points? See Sections C.1 and C.8, respectively.

SIGNS AND SYMPTOMS

Hunchback, shoulders rolled forward—more common with older age.

NAME OF INJURY

Hyperkyphosis (aka hunchback)

DESCRIPTION

Tight pectoralis muscles (chest) pull shoulders forward. Tight sternocleido-mastoid muscles (front of the neck) pull the neck forward. Weak back muscles are unable to prevent the back from rolling forward, and weak lower back muscles allow loss of the lower back curve.

CAUSE

Having a lack of muscle conditioning, playing while fatigued, and not focusing on proper posture all add to the possibility of this ailment. Most important, it could be a result of bone deformation, which should be investigated by your primary care doctor.

TREATMENT

Immediate Relief

Lie on your back with a cervical (neck) pillow or rolled up towel (three to five inches high) placed under your neck (collar area) every morning and evening and when in pain, for up to one hour. I do not recommend sleeping at night in this position. Massage to the pectoralis muscles and midback muscles is usually helpful (see Section A.1).

PREVENTION

Technique

Raise your drums up (if applicable), and perhaps sit a little lower and closer to the drums. A drum throne with a strong sacral support would also help.

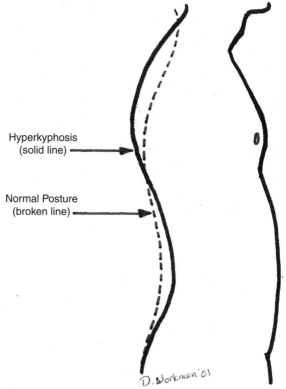

Hyperkyphosis (solid line)

Normal Posture (broken line)

D. Workman '01

Figure 11.2 Hyperkyphosis, as illustrated in this figure, can be caused by something as simple as muscles adapting to poor posture or as complex as a vertebral bone fracture.

Stretches

Pectoralis stretches against a corner or a door opening (see Stretch 6.2).

Exercises

Various back exercises are good for this ailment. When lifting weights, you can try cable rows, pull downs, and other pulling-to-the-chest exercises. You can also do pull-ups on a bar. It may also help to do some neck exercises (ask one of the personal trainers at the gym).

IF NO RELIEF

You should feel and see some changes occurring within two to four weeks. If you don't (even if you do) it is a good idea to see your medical or chiropractic doctor to investigate any bone deformity possibly causing or contributing to the problem.

PROGNOSIS

This ailment is difficult to change or reverse if it is due to bone deformity or if it goes untreated for too long. However, the chances of improvement are good if there is no bone deformity.

OTHER POSSIBILITIES

Gibbous deformity, fracture of the thoracic vertebrae (especially in older people), infection, or cancer (more rare).

SIGNS AND SYMPTOMS

Occasional (off and on) burning or constricting feeling in the chest, moving up to the throat, where you may have an acid taste.

NAME OF INJURY

Gastroesophageal reflux (aka heartburn)

DESCRIPTION

Inability of gastric sphincter muscle (see Figure 11.3) to hold contents of stomach, allowing stomach acids to go up the esophagus to the mouth, burning it.

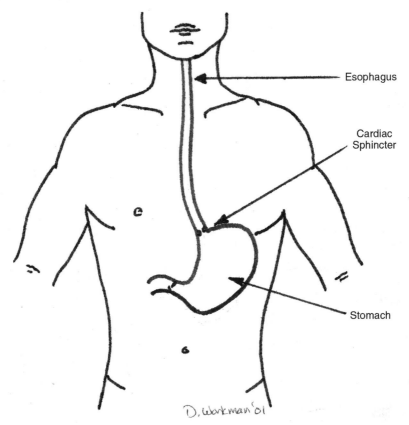

Figure 11.3   Once food or liquid travels from the mouth down the throat (esophagus) to the stomach, a sphincter closes to keep it there. In the stomach, strong acids are released into the food to break it down. The lining of the stomach has a coating to protect it from the acids. If the sphincter is not operating properly, the acids may go back up to the esophagus and burn it.

CAUSE

Pressure in the stomach or weakness in the sphincter sometimes allows the stomach contents to go back up the throat—even to the mouth—causing a burning sensation (thus the term *heartburn*).

TREATMENT

Immediate Relief

Antacids (found over the counter at your neighborhood drugstore).

PREVENTION

Technique

Good posture will assist in curing heartburn. Diet is also very important—find out which foods and drinks give you heartburn (commonly those high in carbohydrates and fats, etc.) and stop ingesting them. Do not recline after meals, stop smoking, and don't force burps. Stress reduction is another recommendation for reducing heartburn.

IF NO RELIEF

If no change occurs after a few days of following these suggestions, see your medical doctor or gastroenterologist for an examination. If accompanied by pain rather than just irritation, see your medical doctor immediately.

PROGNOSIS

Simple heartburn can be prevented and cured through diet, stress control, and antacids, with little chance of return.

OTHER POSSIBILITIES

Stomach ulcer, gastritis, gallbladder disease, cancer, and so forth.

SIGNS AND SYMPTOMS

Pressure or pain in the front chest after effort, emotion, or other stress. Pain may radiate to jaw or left shoulder or arm, or all three. It usually lasts one to twenty minutes and is relieved by rest.

NAME OF INJURY

Angina pectoris

DESCRIPTION

Reduced blood flow through partially obstructed coronary arteries. Pain results from *temporary* oxygen deficit in the myocardium (heart muscle).

177

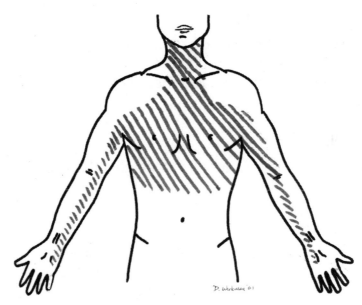

Figure 11.4   This figure shows the common areas of pain for angina pectoris (shaded). However, *you should always have a doctor rule out heart problems when you feel symptoms similar to these.*

CAUSE

High stress, fast lifestyle, drugs, alcohol, fatigue, or lack of sleep.

TREATMENT

Immediate Relief

Rest. *See your medical doctor or cardiologist immediately to rule out any heart problems.*

PREVENTION

Technique

Begin now to change your lifestyle and eliminate the symptoms (see list of causes). Learn to handle your stresses more effectively, avoid alcohol and drugs, and get plenty of sleep at night (about eight hours).

Stretches

General full body stretching program such as yoga is encouraged.

Exercises

Strengthen your heart through gradual increase in exercise (*see your doctor for approval of your exercise program before starting*). Keep your heart rate within your proper range (check with your doctor or cardiologist).

IF NO RELIEF

See your medical doctor or cardiologist immediately—don't procrastinate on this one. If you check out with them and nothing is wrong, see the description of muscle spasms of the midback in this chapter.

PROGNOSIS

The prognosis of this problem depends on the reason for the pain. It is best given by your personal doctor after a thorough evaluation.

OTHER POSSIBILITIES

Myocardial infarction, aneurysm, embolism, neoplasm, hiatal hernia (all usually cause pain for longer than twenty minutes), muscle spasms (see the description of muscle spasms in this chapter), or pericarditis (irritation of the membrane around the heart).

RELATED AREAS

Many injuries can be related to areas of the body other than where you feel the pain. For example, pain in the shoulder may be the result of a problem with the neck or elbow area. If you cannot find the injury that fits your complaints in this chapter, please look in the chapters of the related areas indicated in Figure 11.5.

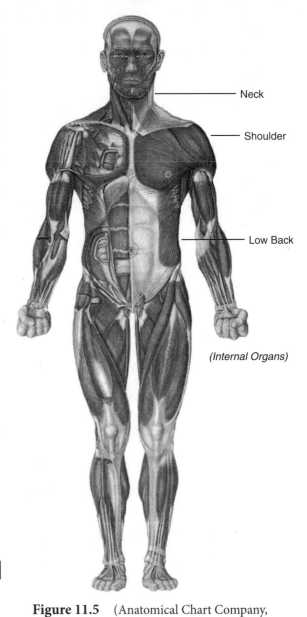

— Neck

— Shoulder

— Low Back

(Internal Organs)

Figure 11.5 (Anatomical Chart Company, Lippincott Williams & Wilkins 2003)

STRETCHES

THE PHILOSOPHY OF STRETCHING

Stretching is not something you do *to* the body; it is something you *allow* the body to do. All stretches must be done by relaxing and allowing the muscles to stretch. If you try to force the muscles to stretch, their immediate reaction is to protect themselves from tearing by pulling back. This can quickly turn into a tug-of-war of you against your muscles, and nothing good can happen. This is why many people stretch and stretch without any positive results, and sometimes they even injure themselves.

GENERAL RULES FOR STRETCHING

Stretches are most effective when the body is warmed up first. This means you should do some mild exercise of the area to be stretched prior to beginning. For example, if you are stretching the legs, do some walking or running until the muscles get warm and loose (usually just before you begin to perspire). With the hands, try some basic rudiments—singles and doubles are best. If you are paying attention to your body, you will notice the area warming up as the blood is pumped into it. Or you can take a shower or sit in hot water prior to stretching—which is not as effective, but still good.

Do not

- pop your knuckles
- stretch when that part of the body is cold
- use bouncing or jerking motions while stretching
- force the stretch to the point you cannot let the area relax

BASIC STRETCHES FOR UPPER BACK AND CHEST

STRETCH 11.1: UPPER BACK STRETCHES

These stretches were specially designed to stretch the difficult areas of the upper back and neck and unlock the back and shoulder blades. As you move into the stretch, you must relax the muscles and allow them to lengthen. While holding the stretch, breathe deep and relaxed, allowing the stretch to go further with each exhale. Do not force the stretch; just allow it to happen.

11.1.1: Overhead Tilt Stretch

This stretch works the lower muscles of the midback and upper back.

Figure 11.6 Sit straight, with both feet flat on floor, right hand draped over the head to the left, and left hand holding right wrist.

Figure 11.7 Slowly tilt the upper body to the left while pulling the right arm with the left until you feel the stretch. Hold for twenty seconds. Repeat with left side.

Figure 11.8 After the stretch, put the arms out to the side as shown in this figure, and rotate to the right and left, slow and relaxed. Repeat the stretch five to ten times.

11.1.2: Recline Pull Stretch

By dropping the shoulders, you stretch the midback and upper back muscles.

Figure 11.9 Sit straight, with both feet flat on floor and hands crossed in front of you holding throne, as shown in this figure.

Figure 11.10 Slowly tilt the upper body back at the waist with back straight and shoulders rolled forward until you feel the stretch. Relax and hold for twenty seconds.

Figure 11.11 After the stretch, position the arms out to the side, as shown in this figure, and rotate right to left slowly and while relaxed. Repeat the stretch five to ten times.

11.1.3: Side Rotate Stretch

This stretches the muscles that lock the shoulder blades back. As they release their pull, you will feel greater movement, strength, and endurance in the upper back and shoulders.

Figure 11.12   Sit straight, with both feet flat on floor and right hand wrapped around the left shoulder, as shown in this figure.

Figure 11.13   Slowly rotate the upper body to the left while pulling the right arm with the left until you feel the stretch. Hold for twenty seconds. Repeat with the left side.

Figure 11.14   After the stretch, position arms out to the side as shown in this figure, and rotate right to left slowly and while relaxed. Repeat the stretch five to ten times.

11.1.4: Drop and Rotate Stretch

This stretches muscles around the lower shoulder blades, allowing greater movement of the chest cavity, shoulders, and upper back.

Figure 11.15   Sit straight, with both feet flat on floor, right hand draped over the left hip, and left hand holding the right shoulder, as shown in this figure.

Figure 11.16   Slowly rotate the upper body to the left and down while pulling the right shoulder with the left hand until you feel the stretch. Hold for 20 seconds. Repeat with the left side.

Figure 11.17   After the stretch, position the arms out to the side as shown in this figure, and rotate right to left slowly and while relaxed. Repeat the stretch five to ten times.

For those who play more than four times a week (or ten hours a week), all of these stretches should be done on a daily basis for warm-up and stress reduction.

STRETCH 11.2: SHOULDER SHRUG STRETCHES

This stretch focuses on the muscles that support the shoulders and neck. These muscles are commonly tight, which can interfere with the strength, endurance, and coordination of the upper limbs and can cause headaches and stress. When doing them, remember to relax and move slowly and smoothly, especially at the end when you drop the shoulders. You can do as many sets of these as you like, but it is recommended to do five sets of twenty.

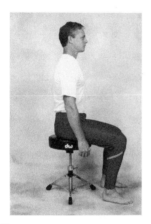 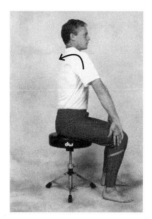 

Figure 11.18 Begin in the relaxed position, either standing or sitting, with the shoulders completely dropped and the arms relaxed.

Figure 11.19 Begin rolling the shoulders forward and up in a counterclockwise motion. Roll them smoothly and only forward (never clockwise).

Figure 11.20 Continue the position to the backside, and let shoulders drop at the end in the same relaxed position as in the beginning. Slowly repeat ten to twenty times.

CHAPTER 12

NECK PROBLEMS

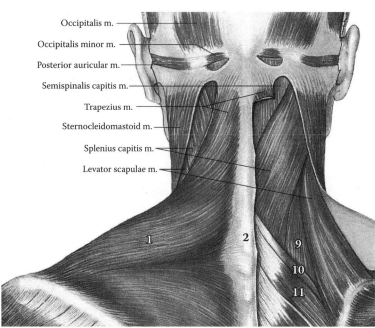

Occipitalis m.

Occipitalis minor m.

Posterior auricular m.

Semispinalis capitis m.

Trapezius m.

Sternocleidomastoid m.

Splenius capitis m.

Levator scapulae m.

1

2

9

10

11

1. Trapezuis m.
2. Spine of C7
9. Splenius cervicis m.

10. Serratus poseterior superior m.
11. Rhomboid minor m.

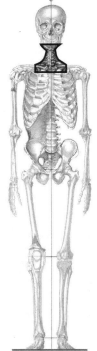

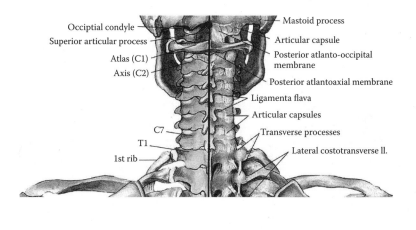

Occiptial condyle

Superior articular process

Atlas (C1)

Axis (C2)

C7

T1

1st rib

Mastoid process

Articular capsule

Posterior atlanto-occipital membrane

Posterior atlantoaxial membrane

Ligamenta flava

Articular capsules

Transverse processes

Lateral costotransverse ll.

SIGNS AND SYMPTOMS

Knifelike pain and spasm in the neck muscles. Worse in morning or from stress. Neck may be tender to the touch if severe (no bruise), and may be hot.

NAME OF INJURY

Muscle spasm (neck)

DESCRIPTION

Muscle overuse or trauma causes damage to muscle or depletion of the muscle's energy and cramps.

CAUSE

Doing too much too soon or too often, or both. Overuse or improper use of the neck or shoulders may cause it (e.g., large increase in practice time, poor technique, or improper posture, especially with marching harnesses).

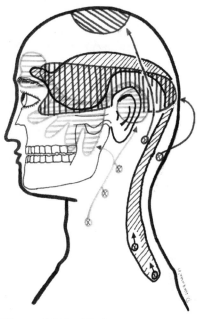

Figure 12.1 Neck pain is commonly caused by muscle spasms and trigger points (X). When they are pressed, they give a referred pain to other areas (shaded lines). Your neck pain may actually be caused by problems in another area.

TREATMENT

Immediate Relief

Rest, ice the area of pain, and resist moving the neck. Aspirin or other over-the-counter pain relievers may relieve some of the pain. Massage to the tight areas and trigger points will reduce the pain and spasm (see Sections A.2 and C.8).

PREVENTION

Technique

Change your seat height (usually the drummer is sitting too low, causing the arms to constantly be reaching up when playing). If pain is caused when marching, a properly fitting harness is important. Drink plenty of water to flush out the muscles. While playing, change positions and rest ten minutes each hour, and don't play one day a week to let the body rejuvenate. If marching, wear harness only when necessary. Proper lifting techniques will also help prevent this injury (see Section A.3).

STRETCHES

Try some mild massage to the sore muscles followed by gentle stretching of the area—no pain (see Stretch 12.1).

Exercises

Repeat the exercises that caused the pain, but at a lower intensity for shorter periods of time (about half as long). Gradually increase the time and intensity over a period of weeks, stopping when the pain begins, to strengthen the injured muscles and prevent repeated injury in the future.

IF NO RELIEF

If no improvement occurs within one or two weeks, consult your doctor.

PROGNOSIS

This should never become a big problem because it is so easy to treat and resolves so well. However, if you let it continue too long, it can become chronic (requiring extensive treatment) and lead to serious injuries. Not to mention that it decreases your endurance.

OTHER POSSIBILITIES

Contusion or bruise (usually caused by a direct hit to the painful area and accompanied by a red or purple mark on the skin).

DIGGING A LITTLE DEEPER

What are muscle spasms? What are trigger points? See Sections C.1 and C.8, respectively.

SIGNS AND SYMPTOMS

Sore neck (especially in the morning and evening), pain in all neck motions, possible tingling feeling, or numbness or burning feeling in one or both arms.

NAME OF INJURY

Torticollis (spasmodic)

DESCRIPTION

Tightening of all of the neck muscles, causing neck rigidity, pain, and possible symptoms in one or both arms.

CAUSE

Stress, trauma (one large one or repetitive small ones), cool breeze on the neck while sleeping, or wrong position when sleeping.

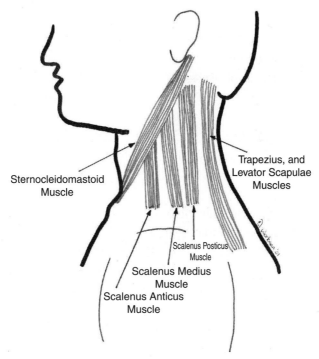

Figure 12.2 The head is about the same weight as a bowling ball. Many muscles are needed to balance and move it on top of the neck. This illustration shows just a few of the larger muscles used to do so. When they are irritated, movement becomes painful and difficult.

TREATMENT

Immediate Relief

Relaxation techniques (conscious and subconscious) are most effective in handling the stress that usually causes the problem. Anti-inflammatories (aspirin, ibuprofen, etc.), mild soft tissue techniques, and very light slow stretch are very effective in dealing with the problem (see Section A.2 and Stretch 12.3).

PREVENTION

Technique

Most of the problem can be solved by learning to better handle stress. Proper lifting techniques will also help prevent this injury (see Section A.3).

Stretches

Contraction–relaxation–contraction (CRC) stretches are very effective (see Stretch 12.3). Once the acute pain has subsided (usually one to four days), begin stretches in the various ranges of motion (see Stretch 12.1).

Exercises

Shoulder rolls and isometrics (see Stretch 11.2). When you can do these without discomfort, begin low impact exercises such as swimming, walking, biking (reclined position is best), and so forth.

IF NO RELIEF

Your primary care physician should be contacted if the pain doesn't begin to fade in two or three days or continues for more than a week.

PROGNOSIS

Chances of recovery without lingering pain are excellent in most cases. Relapse of the condition is greatly reduced if you learn to manage your stress more effectively and continue a regular stretching program for the neck and shoulder areas.

OTHER POSSIBILITIES

Thoracic outlet syndrome or cervical intervertebral disc syndrome (usually is caused by trauma at some point and doesn't get relief as fast).

DIGGING A LITTLE DEEPER

What are muscle spasms? What is a trigger point? See Sections C.1 and C.8, respectively.

SIGNS AND SYMPTOMS

Ongoing or recurring neck pain, with pain, burning or tingling feeling, numbness, weakness, and so on, down one or both arms (possibly to the fingers).

NAME OF INJURY

Cervical intervertebral disc herniation or degeneration

DESCRIPTION

The disc between the vertebral bodies deteriorates (aging faster than typical or faster than the rest of the discs) or herniates (Figure 12.3). This can include decrease in disc height (distance between the vertebrae), which puts pressure on the nerves or spinal cord, or both. This can cause symptoms in that area and farther down the arm.

CAUSE

Micro- or macrotrauma to the neck. Can be caused by years of improper movement or posture.

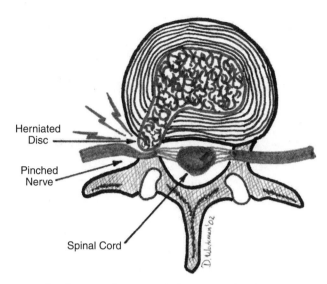

Herniated Disc

Pinched Nerve

Spinal Cord

Figure 12.3 Shown in this figure is the view of a herniated disc from the top. Note how the disc material (arrow) pushes out, squashing the nerve against the bone and causing pain down the shoulder and arm.

TREATMENT

Immediate Relief

Ice the area, take Ibuprofen, and rest in a reclined or back-lying position with a neck roll right where a collar would be.

PREVENTION

Technique

Heavy work with the arms, prolonged use of the arms, or stress can all cause increased pressure and swelling around the neck area, leading to increased symptoms. Proper lifting techniques will help prevent this injury (see Section A.3).

Stretches

Stretches should be done only after the initial swelling has somewhat subsided and the symptoms have almost gone. They should be done lightly and without pain. First concentrate on restoring your neck motion (see Stretch 12.1). When that has happened (usually a few days), then work on more aggressive stretches (see Stretch 12.2).

Exercises

General exercises such as swimming and walking loosen and strengthen the neck muscles without irritating them. Once the pain is almost gone and the range of motion is restored, then begin light exercise (see Exercise B.21).

IF NO RELIEF

See your doctor (medical or chiropractic) if no relief occurs within a week.

PROGNOSIS

A degenerative intervertebral disc will not reverse and become new again. Your best bet is to take good care of your neck by avoiding the activities that inflame it. In this way, you can stop it from aging quicker than it should. Pain will tell you when you are doing something wrong.

OTHER POSSIBILITIES

Thoracic outlet syndrome or neural disorders.

DIGGING A LITTLE DEEPER

What is nerve impingement? See Section C.4.

SIGNS AND SYMPTOMS

Neck pain, headaches, and possible symptoms down one or both arms following a trauma (e.g., car accident, slip or fall, sports injury, etc.).

NAME OF INJURY

Cervical spine sprain or strain

DESCRIPTION

Sudden whip of the neck in any direction, causing microtears in the soft tissues (muscles, tendons, or ligaments). This causes swelling that puts pressure on the nerves, decreasing circulation and causing pain to the affected area.

CAUSE

Jarring, jerking, or whipping of the neck, often unexpected.

TREATMENT

Immediate Relief

See your doctor immediately to rule out serious damage (e.g., fracture, dislocation, etc.). Apply ice, compression, and rest (see Section A.1).

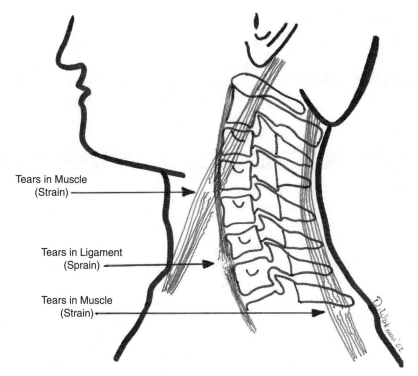

Tears in Muscle
(Strain)

Tears in Ligament
(Sprain)

Tears in Muscle
(Strain)

Figure 12.4 A sprain typically means tears in tendons or ligaments, whereas a strain is tears in the muscle fiber. Muscles typically heal quicker than tendons or ligaments because they have greater circulation (among other reasons).

PREVENTION

Technique

Do not lift or carry instruments until the doctor indicates you can. Even then, let pain be your guide. Proper lifting techniques will also help prevent this injury (see Section A.3).

Stretches

Do these when your doctor says you can (usually two to four weeks into care).

Exercises

Do these when your doctor says you can (usually four to eight weeks into care). *Important: See your doctor immediately for proper treatment of this injury.*

PROGNOSIS

Good healing is expected within one to three months with quick care and good rehabilitation. Most people have mild residual pain and symptoms from this injury.

OTHER POSSIBILITIES

Cervical spine intervertebral disc syndrome or vertebral fracture.

DIGGING A LITTLE DEEPER

What is a strain? What is a sprain? See Sections C.5 and C.6.

SIGNS AND SYMPTOMS

Pain in the neck and upper back, achy in nature. Pain on motion of the joint, worse in the morning and after activity, decreases during the day or during activity.

NAME OF INJURY

Osteoarthritis (spine–neck)

DESCRIPTION

Pain in a joint of the body, with swelling and pain (usually is worse in the morning and improves with movement during the day). Not much pain during activity but increased pain after. It usually has tenderness, grinding feeling, and painful loss of range of motion.

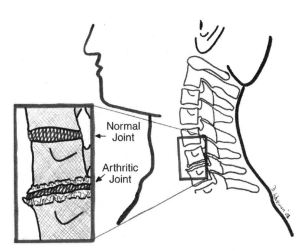

Figure 12.5 Note that the normal joint in this figure has smooth, rounded, clean corners and edges, while the arthritic one shows rough, thick edges, bone spurs, and decreased space between the bones. This indicates a degenerative disc (degenerative arthritis, wearing down of the joint from improper use). The spurs are believed to be the bone's attempt to heal.

CAUSE

Repetitive inefficient movements or macrotrauma, causing the joint or joints to be dysfunctional (gradual onset). Also called "getting old before your time." This may affect those using mostly the upper body.

TREATMENT

Immediate Relief

Prevention is really the key in this injury. If you feel pain, it's been there too long. You can slow the process, but there is no proven way to reverse it. Ice (see Section A.1), rest, and use firm and supportive furniture. Aspirin or muscle relaxants may help control the pain.

PREVENTION

Technique

Low back and neck pain usually stems from poor sitting or standing posture, sitting on a poor throne, or playing while fatigued. Proper lifting techniques will help prevent this injury (see Section A.3).

Stretches

Stretch the major muscle groups around the spine and muscles surrounding the affected joint. The main idea is to relieve pressure on the joint from opposing muscle pull. A few stretches are provided in Stretches 8.1, 8.2, 9.1, 9.2, and 10.1.

Exercises

Postural exercises (see Appendix B) will help strengthen the muscles. Strong muscles greatly aid the joint in its motion and protect its ligaments and intricate parts from unnecessary wear that leads to osteoarthritis.

IF NO RELIEF

Give treatment for two weeks, then see your doctor for his or her opinion and professional diagnosis to rule out (among other things) other arthropathies.

PROGNOSIS

The damage done cannot be undone. The sooner you treat it, the better.

OTHER POSSIBILITIES

Other types of arthritis (see your doctor).

DIGGING A LITTLE DEEPER

Rheumatoid Arthritis versus Degenerative Arthritis. See Section C.9.

SIGNS AND SYMPTOMS

Burning, scratchy sore throat with pain, swelling, loss of voice, and so on.

NAME OF INJURY

Sore throat

DESCRIPTION

Irritation of the throat lining due to inflammation of tissue (or infection).

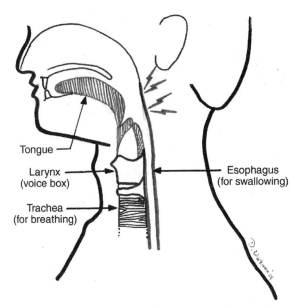

Figure 12.6 Infections of the mouth or upper throat commonly pass down the throat during swallowing, infecting other areas, including the vocal cords.

CAUSE

Using the voice loudly for prolonged amount of time, coughing, burning from liquids, smoking, and breathing cold dry air, among other things.

TREATMENT

Immediate Relief

Try sitting in a steam room (about ten minutes), using a humidifier (especially at night), gargling with salt water (for shallow sore throats), sucking on lozenges with phenol or zinc, using a decongestant, clearing your nose, eating plenty of carrots, and throwing your old toothbrush away. *Do not cough.*

PREVENTION

Technique

Performing in cold weather is always hard on the throat, so bundle up (especially around the neck). If you use your voice in conjunction with your playing (e.g., singing, coaching, or teaching), get proper instruction on using the voice.

Stretches

General neck stretches (see Stretches 12.2) to relieve tightness around the vocal cords and improve drainage.

Exercises

Vocal exercises are most important for this area. It is important to get proper training from a vocal coach or teacher. It is best to get a doctor's approval prior to beginning any exercises.

IF NO RELIEF

If you have followed these suggestions and there is no sign of relief within a few days, contact your medical doctor or throat specialist. See your medical doctor immediately if you have severe, prolonged, or recurrent pain (longer than four days); have a fever; feel a lump in the throat; or cough up blood.

PROGNOSIS

A mild, irritated throat is a fairly easy thing to get over; however, the reason or cause of your sore throat will determine how well it will heal and if it will return. Be aware that minor sore throats will return over and over again if you do not stop doing what caused them in the first place. The more they recur, the greater the damage to the throat and vocal cords, increasing the risk of recurrence and permanent damage to the voice.

OTHER POSSIBILITIES

Infection, tumor, throat-lining tears, or reflux esophagitis (all should be examined by your medical doctor or throat specialist).

RELATED AREAS

Many injuries can be related to areas of the body other than where you feel the pain. For example, pain in the shoulder may be the result of a problem with the neck or elbow area. If you cannot find the injury that fits your complaints in this chapter, please look in the chapters of the related areas indicated in Figure 12.7.

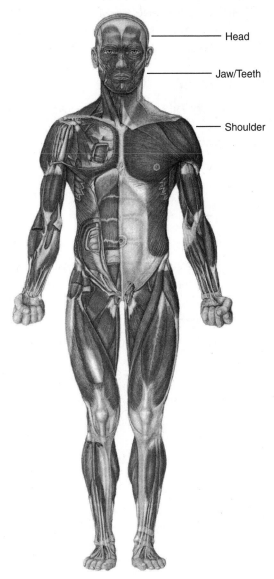

Head

Jaw/Teeth

Shoulder

STRETCHES

THE PHILOSOPHY OF STRETCHING

Figure 12.7   (Anatomical Chart Company, Lippincott Williams & Wilkins 2003)

Stretching is not something you do *to* the body; it is something you *allow* the body to do. All stretches must be done by relaxing and allowing the muscles to stretch. If you try to force the muscles to stretch, their immediate reaction is to protect themselves from tearing by pulling back. This can quickly turn into a tug-of-war of you against your muscles, and nothing good can happen. This is why many people stretch and stretch without any positive results, and sometimes they even injure themselves.

GENERAL RULES FOR STRETCHING

Stretches are most effective when the body is warmed up first. This means you should do some mild exercise of the area to be stretched prior to beginning. For example, if you are stretching the legs, do some walking or running until the muscles get warm and loose (usually just before you begin to perspire). With the hands, try some basic rudiments—singles and doubles are best. If you are paying attention to your body, you will notice the area warming up as the blood is pumped into it. Or you can take a shower or sit in hot water prior to stretching—which is not as effective, but still good.

Do not

- pop your knuckles
- stretch when that part of the body is cold
- use bouncing or jerking motions while stretching
- force the stretch to the point where you cannot let the area relax

BASIC STRETCHES FOR THE NECK

STRETCH 12.1: GENERAL NECK STRETCHES (FOR ACUTE INJURIES)

These stretches are a first step to loosening the neck muscles after an acute injury. They should be done only with your doctor's approval and must be done slowly and without pain. The arms should be used only to support the head in case its weight causes pain. The arms anchor to the neck, so the less you use them, the better stretch your neck will get. *Do not force these stretches*.

12.1.1: Neck Flexion Stretches

Allow the chin to drop first, and then curl up the rest of the neck from the top down while completely relaxing as if you are falling asleep in a sitting position.

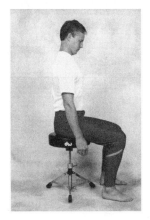

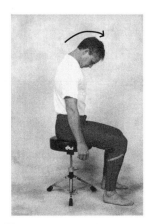

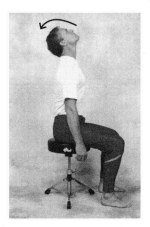

Figure 12.8 While sitting, allow the chin to drop and tuck to the chest.

Figure 12.9 Allow the rest of the neck to roll up like a piece of paper until you feel the stretch. Relax, and hold for twenty seconds.

Figure 12.10 When the stretch is done, roll the head up slowly, and lean it back, relaxed (thirty seconds). Do stretch five times.

12.1.2: Neck Extension, Rotation, and Lateral Flexion Stretches

Both of these are to be done exactly like those in the previous section, only in a different direction.

Figure 12.11 This stretch is just like the previous one, but the head is tilted back until the stretch is felt. Hold, and relax.

Figure 12.12 This stretch is just like the previous one, but the head is rotated to one side, relaxed, then rotated to the other side, and relaxed.

Figure 12.13 This stretch is just like the previous one, but the head is tilted to one side, relaxed, then tilted to the other side, and relaxed.

Shoulder shrugs (Stretch 11.2) should be included in the acute stretches but should be done very lightly and without pain.

STRETCH 12.2: GENERAL NECK STRETCHES—MORE AGGRESSIVE (FOR CHRONIC INJURIES)

These stretches are standard for those without recent neck injury. Do them until you can feel the stretch. If you cannot feel it, you are not allowing the neck muscles to relax. The arms anchor to the neck, tightening the neck muscles, so the less you use the arms, the better neck stretch you will get.

12.2.1: Aggressive Neck Flexion Stretches

Allow the chin to drop first, and then curl up the rest of the neck from the top down while completely relaxing as if you are falling asleep in a sitting position. The hands are just for extra weight; do not pull the neck with them.

Figure 12.14   While sitting, allow the chin to drop and tuck into the chest.

Figure 12.15   Allow the rest of the neck to roll up, as shown in this figure, until you feel the stretch. Relax and hold for twenty seconds.

Figure 12.16   When the stretch is complete, roll the head up slowly, and lean it back to relax (thirty seconds).

12.2.2: Aggressive Neck Extension, Rotation, and Lateral Flexion Stretches

Both of these are to be done exactly like those in the previous section, only in a different direction. Again, the hands are just for extra weight; *do not pull the neck with them*.

Figure 12.17 This stretch is just like Figure 12.13, but the head is tilted back until the stretch is felt. Hold, and relax.

Figure 12.18 This stretch is just like the previous one, but the head is rotated to one side, relaxed, then rotated to the other side, and relaxed.

Figure 12.19 This stretch is just like the previous one, but the head is tilted to one side, relaxed, then tilted to the other side, and relaxed.

Shoulder shrugs (Stretch 11.2) should be included in the aggressive stretches. If you do not feel the stretch, you are not relaxing enough.

STRETCH 12.3: CRC STRETCHES FOR THE NECK

Contraction–relaxation–contraction (CRC) stretches are not traditional stretches, so *you must follow the directions carefully*. They reprogram the brain and muscles as to when muscles are tight (during the contraction) and when they are relaxed (during relaxation). You can push against the arms, but they anchor to the neck, causing those muscles to tighten up, so the less you use them, the better stretch you will get.

12.3.1: CRC Neck Extension Stretches

Gradually increase the neck muscle contraction, and then hold for ten seconds. Allow the head to relax against the wall as if you are falling asleep. This makes neck muscles work without moving (isometric contraction).

Figure 12.20 While sitting, allow the head to rest against a wall behind you.

Figure 12.21 Gradually try to tilt the head back against the wall. Without moving the head, hold the contraction for ten seconds.

Figure 12.22 Allow the head to relax, leaning against the wall for ten seconds. Repeat contraction and relax steps until you are loose.

12.3.2: CRC Neck Flexion, Rotation, and Lateral Flexion Stretches

Both of these are to be done exactly like those in the previous section, only in a different direction. Again, use the hands as little as possible.

Figure 12.23 This stretch is just like Figure 12.20, but the head is pressed against wall by a fist held and relaxed as shown in this figure.

Figure 12.24 This stretch is just like Figure 12.18, but the head is rotated to one side, relaxed, then rotated to the other side, and relaxed.

Figure 12.25 This stretch is just like the previous one, but the head is tilted to one side, relaxed, then tilted to the other side, and relaxed.

These stretches can help neighboring muscles by stretching the areas in between those mentioned previously, and even more by adding rotation of the head while in any direction.

CHAPTER 13

HEAD PROBLEMS

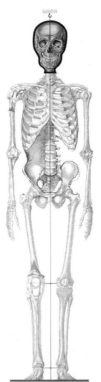

Anterior View

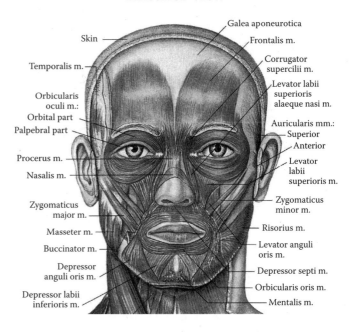

Skin

Temporalis m.

Orbicularis
oculi m.:
Orbital part
Palpebral part

Procerus m.

Nasalis m.

Zygomaticus
major m.

Masseter m.

Buccinator m.

Depressor
anguli oris m.

Depressor labii
inferioris m.

Galea aponeurotica

Frontalis m.

Corrugator
supercilii m.

Levator labii
superioris
alaeque nasi m.

Auricularis mm.:
Superior
Anterior

Levator
labii
superioris m.

Zygomaticus
minor m.

Risorius m.

Levator anguli
oris m.

Depressor septi m.

Orbicularis oris m.

Mentalis m.

Anterior View

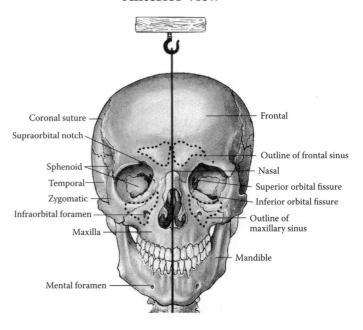

Coronal suture

Supraorbital notch

Sphenoid

Temporal

Zygomatic

Infraorbital foramen

Maxilla

Mental foramen

Frontal

Outline of frontal sinus

Nasal

Superior orbital fissure

Inferior orbital fissure

Outline of
maxillary sinus

Mandible

SIGNS AND SYMPTOMS

Headaches in various areas, especially behind the eyes and in the temples. Worse at the end of a stressful day. Tender to pushing under the back of the skull (occiput) and around the shoulder blades (scapulae).

NAME OF INJURY

Tension headaches

DESCRIPTION

Muscle spasms tend to increase pressure on the nerves that trigger headache pain.

CAUSE

Referred pain from other areas (neck, upper back, temples, etc.).

TREATMENT

Immediate Relief

Try heat, stretches for neck muscles, and deep massage to the shoulders, neck, and head (see Section A.2). It is important to decrease your anxiety and stress because they cause you to tense the muscles, producing headaches. Aspirin or acetaminophen usually helps erase the pain but will not reduce all of the muscle tension. Chiropractic treatment, massage, and physical therapy are proven to successfully relieve headaches.

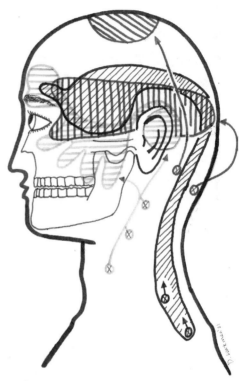

Figure 13.1 Neck pain is commonly caused by muscle spasms and trigger points (X). When they are pressed, they refer pain to other areas (shaded lines). Your neck pain may actually be caused by problems in another area.

PREVENTION

Technique

Try not to concentrate too hard on small areas (reading music), make rapid head movements, and hold specific positions for long periods.

Stretches

Neck, shoulder, and upper back stretches to decrease muscle tension and lengthen the muscles (see Stretches 11.2 and 12.2). Try relaxation techniques such as yoga, Alexander Technique, and so forth.

Exercises

Regular aerobic activities (hiking, walking, running, swimming, etc.) regularly will decrease the stress and flush or loosen the muscles.

IF NO RELIEF

Your chiropractor or medical doctor can refer you to the proper specialist.

PROGNOSIS

The chance of curing tension headaches is excellent if you treat them quickly and change the behaviors that caused them. The longer you have them, the slower they heal.

OTHER POSSIBILITIES

There are many kinds of headaches. Tension headaches are the most common. Other types to rule out are sinus headaches (associated with sinus problems), migraine headaches, and cluster headaches.

DIGGING A LITTLE DEEPER

What are muscle spasms? What is a trigger point? See Sections C.1 and C.8, respectively.

<hr>

SIGNS AND SYMPTOMS

Ringing, buzzing, or roaring in the ears, most notable after loud noise exposure (especially noise of long duration) or at very quiet times.

NAME OF INJURY

Tinnitus

DESCRIPTION

Ringing in the ears, making it difficult to hear.

CAUSE

Noises loud enough or for long enough periods of time to cause damage to the hearing system.

TREATMENT

Immediate Relief

Get to a quiet place, and avoid prolonged loud noises. Tinnitus is a warning sign that damage is being done to the hearing. If you persist in spite of it, the damage will increase, and it is permanent for the most part.

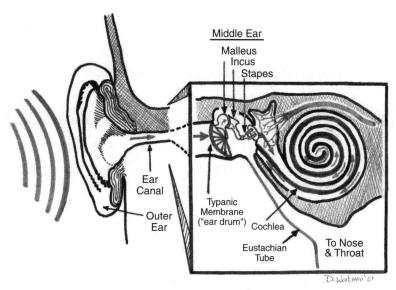

Figure 13.2 Notice the path that sound takes as it hits the external ear and eardrum. It even vibrates the body to allow the brain to decipher what is being heard. This is a fragile and important system.

PREVENTION

Technique

The best way to deal with hearing problems is to prevent them from happening because the damage is not reversible. As a rule, louder noises can do damage in shorter periods of time, and not-so-loud noises can do the same damage if continued for long enough. So, intensity and duration of sound are a function of hearing damage. When possible, play on a pad or other quiet practice surface. Reserve the loud playing for when it is absolutely necessary, and then use the proper hearing protection of your choice (i.e., various ear plugs). Headphones are just as damaging, if not more so, because of their nearness to the eardrum. As a rule, the louder you hear it, the more damage it is doing.

IF NO RELIEF

If the ringing persists for twenty-four hours, see your medical doctor for an exam or referral to a hearing specialist.

PROGNOSIS

The longer your tinnitus (ringing) stays and the slower it fades, the more progressed and irreversible it is.

OTHER POSSIBILITIES

Tinnitus is often a symptom of other diseases, so if it is accompanied by any symptoms other than ringing in the ears (e.g., increased temperature, nausea, dizziness, headache, etc.), see your medical doctor immediately.

SIGNS AND SYMPTOMS

Hearing loss that is temporary or permanent after exposure to a loud sound of either short-term or long-term duration. Sounds typically seem muffled, or speech is difficult to hear and understand.

NAME OF INJURY

Hearing loss (temporary or permanent)

DESCRIPTION

Music-induced hearing loss makes sounds seem muffled. Permanent inner-ear (nerve) hearing loss makes speech difficult to hear and understand.

CAUSE

Loud sounds damage the delicate hair cells of the cochlea (inner ear). Hair cell damage leads to permanent hearing loss.

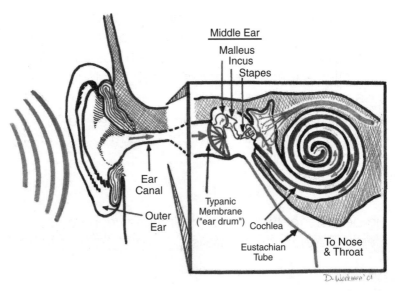

Figure 13.3   Notice the path that sound takes as it hits the external ear and eardrum. It even vibrates the body to allow the brain to decipher what is being heard. This is a fragile and important system.

TREATMENT

Immediate Relief

Get to a quiet place and avoid prolonged loud noises. Some loss of hearing is a warning sign that damage is being done to the hearing. If you persist in spite of it, the damage will increase, and it is permanent for the most part.

PREVENTION

Technique

Reduce the loudness of music at both practice sessions and performances. Reduce the amount of time you are exposed to intense sounds. Use musician-quality earplugs to reduce the loudness of sound that reaches your inner ear. The best choice is custom-made earplugs made from impressions of your ears. Have a complete audiologic evaluation with an annual reevaluation. Avoid other sources of noise exposure (power tools, firearms, power mower, etc.) unless you use earplugs. (See discussion of tinnitus in this chapter.)

IF NO RELIEF

Exposure to loud music can cause sound to seem muffled and cause your ears to ring for hours or days after the exposure. This is called *temporary (hearing) threshold shift* (TTS). TTS can become a *permanent (hearing) threshold shift* (PTS) over time. Any amount of TTS is to be avoided. If ringing or hearing loss persists beyond twenty-four hours, have a thorough audiologic evaluation by an audiologist or otologist as soon as possible.

PROGNOSIS

The inner-ear hair-cell damage is permanent. This leads to high-pitched hearing loss in both ears. This is commonly called *nerve deafness*. The usual treatment of nerve deafness is properly fitted hearing aids.

OTHER POSSIBILITIES

Hearing loss and tinnitus can be caused by diseases and other types of injury to the ears. Don't assume that loud sound is the only cause of your hearing loss. Only a complete audiologic evaluation or an examination by an audiologist or otologist can determine the exact cause.

SIGNS AND SYMPTOMS

Wearing down of the tops of the teeth. Grinding teeth, especially at night.

NAME OF INJURY

Bruxism

DESCRIPTION

Biting or grinding the teeth together, wearing down of the surface.

CAUSE

Bruxism is often a response to stress. The best way to prevent it is to control the way you respond to stress. Don't let the teeth touch unless you are eating or swallowing.

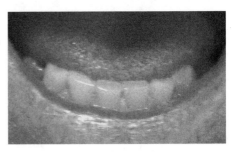

Figure 13.4 After years of grinding the teeth (bruxism), the wearing down of the teeth becomes very obvious.

TREATMENT

Immediate Relief

Make a conscious effort to stop grinding the teeth together. If you are doing the following, *stop*: pushing your tongue to the roof of your mouth, clicking or grinding your teeth, holding your teeth together, or chewing your food so hard that your teeth grind together.

The best help is to try to keep the jaw relaxed. Apply a hot pack to the jaw muscles, and massage the muscles just below the cheek. Chewing gum is not a good idea.

PREVENTION

Technique

When you are under stress (whether you are aware of it) you may be grinding your teeth. It is helpful to remind yourself to keep your lips together and teeth apart. See the description of temporomandibular joint dysfunction in this chapter for additional help.

Stretches

If you grind your teeth at night, you may try avoiding caffeine and candy, learning relaxation techniques, or having a meditation routine. In addition, you can have a guard made to protect the teeth at night (these are usually made by a dentist or temporomandibular joint specialist). Some people choose to use sports mouth guards as a substitute, but they make it harder to breathe, and soft mouth guards tend to make you chew during sleep, making the jaw sore. Temporomandibular joint stretches can relieve tension (see Stretches 13.1–13.3) but will not solve the problem.

Exercises

You need to remind yourself not to grind. Tie a string around your finger (some set a timer for each hour), and each time you see the string, put your lips together, and teeth apart. Find your own way of being reminded, but you will need to make a conscious effort to overcome this bad habit.

IF NO RELIEF

If this problem continues, it may lead to temporomandibular joint dysfunction problems and teeth problems (including having the teeth capped). This could become very expensive, so see your dentist if you are unable to stop the grinding within a month or so.

PROGNOSIS

The sooner you stop grinding, the more teeth and jaw problems you are going to avoid. Remember, there is no evidence of the teeth being able to rebuild from the grinding. It is much like the tires on a car, once the tread wears down, you cannot put it back on.

OTHER POSSIBILITIES

This could be accompanied by temporomandibular joint problems.

SIGNS AND SYMPTOMS

Clicking or pain in the jaw at the ears (temporomandibular joint). It is usually accompanied by headaches.

NAME OF INJURY

Temporomandibular joint (TMJ) dysfunction

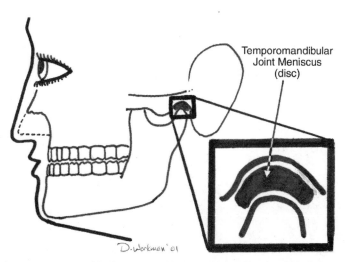

Figure 13.5   The temporomandibular joint is the joint between the temporalis bone and the mandible bone (jaw). Through misuse, the joint and disc become worn and painful to use.

DESCRIPTION

The disc or joint in the temporomandibular joint becomes worn from macro- or microtrauma or malalignment of both joints, producing wear and tear to the joint. When this happens, degenerative arthritis begins to set in. The longer it persists, the more likely it will produce increased clicking and pain.

CAUSE

Macrotrauma: A blunt and very obvious hit or pull to the jaw that usually causes immediate and lasting pain. Microtrauma: Most common cause of temporomandibular joint problems. This is usually in the form of constant tightening of the jaw or grinding of the teeth (even in your sleep) from nervous habit or stress response.

TREATMENT

Immediate Relief

If you are doing the following, *stop*: pushing your tongue to the roof of your mouth, clicking or grinding your teeth, holding your teeth together, or chewing your food so hard that your teeth grind together.

The best help is to try to keep the jaw relaxed (keep the teeth from touching—do not clench them), massage the muscles just below the temporomandibular joint, and apply ice (cold drink, cold pack, sucking on ice). Avoid opening the jaw to its maximum (yawning), especially for extended periods of time. Chewing gum also irritates the temporomandibular joint problem. Keep good neck posture.

PREVENTION

Technique

Be aware of your stress reaction to playing situations. Try to relax during playing and practicing (see if you are doing any of the things mentioned previously).

Stretches

See Stretches 13.1–13.3.

Exercises

See Exercise B.22.

IF NO RELIEF

If no relief occurs within one or two weeks, have your dentist refer you to a temporomandibular joint specialist.

216

OTHER POSSIBILITIES

The temporomandibular joint is a very intricate joint with constant use, and when it is injured, full recovery is rare. With proper splinting in severe cases, you can reduce the pain, but this most likely will not erase all of it. As with most injuries, the earlier you catch and treat it, the better you will heal. However, by the time the pain sets in from microtrauma, the jaw's biomechanics have changed and are difficult to restore.

RELATED AREAS

Many injuries can be related to areas of the body other than where you feel the pain. For example, pain in the shoulder may be the result of a problem with the neck or elbow area. If you cannot find the injury that fits your complaints in this chapter, please look in the chapters of the related areas indicated in Figure 13.6.

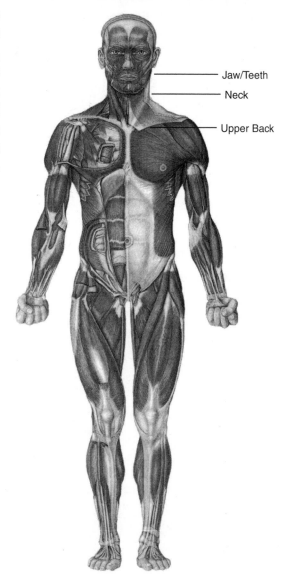

Jaw/Teeth

Neck

Upper Back

Figure 13.6 (Anatomical Chart Company, Lippincott Williams & Wilkins 2003)

STRETCHES

THE PHILOSOPHY OF STRETCHING

Stretching is not something you do *to* the body; it is something you *allow* the body to do. All stretches must be done by relaxing and allowing the muscles to stretch. If you try to force the muscles to stretch, their immediate reaction is to protect themselves from tearing by pulling back. This can quickly turn into a tug-of-war of you against your muscles, and nothing good can happen. This is why many people stretch and stretch without any positive results, and sometimes they even injure themselves.

GENERAL RULES FOR STRETCHING

Stretches are most effective when the body is warmed up first. This means you should do some mild exercise of the area to be stretched prior to beginning. For example, if you are stretching the legs, do some walking or running until the muscles get warm and loose (usually just before you begin to perspire). With the hands, try some basic rudiments—singles and doubles are best. If you are paying attention to your body, you will notice the area warming up as the blood is pumped into it. Or you can take a shower or sit in hot water prior to stretching—which is not as effective, but still good.

Do not

- pop your knuckles
- stretch when that part of the body is cold
- use bouncing or jerking motions while stretching
- force the stretch to the point where you cannot let the area relax

BASIC STRETCHES FOR THE JAW AREA

STRETCH 13.1: TEMPOROMANDIBULAR JOINT STRETCHES

The temporomandibular joint is a delicate joint and can be damaged if pushed too hard or in the wrong way, so do these stretches carefully.

Figure 13.7 This figure shows the standard amount the jaw should open comfortably (three fingers).

Figure 13.8 Slowly roll a spacer back on both sides until you feel a slight stretch in the jaw area.

Figure 13.9 Allow the jaw to relax and stretch without any effort (for twenty to thirty seconds). Roll the spacers back slightly until stretch is felt again, relax, and repeat until jaw opens to normal amount.

STRETCH 13.2: CRC STRETCHES FOR THE JAW

Contraction–relaxation–contraction (CRC) stretches for the jaw are not traditional stretches, so you must follow the directions carefully. They reprogram the brain and muscles as to when muscles are tight (during contraction) and when they are relaxed (during relaxation). Bite down lightly, do not bite down in an attempt to strengthen the muscles—we are not trying to do that.

Figure 13.10 Place a spacer between top and bottom teeth on both sides until you feel a slight stretch in the jaw area.

Figure 13.11 Bite down slightly on the spacer (like a candy bar, for twenty to thirty seconds). Relax completely, letting the jaw hang open.

Figure 13.12 Roll the spacers back slightly until stretch is felt again, relax, and repeat steps 2 and 3 until jaw opens to normal amount.

STRETCH 13.3: OPEN AND CLOSED JAW STRETCHES

While lightly pushing your tongue against the top of your mouth, open and close the jaw as if chewing slowly. Concentrate on opening and closing smoothly. It might help to put a finger of each hand just in front of the ears on each side to feel the joint move. If it moves forward, keep the chin in during the movement to prevent this.

Figure 13.13 Begin with the mouth closed and relaxed, and a finger on the right temporomandibular joint and one on the left joint.

Figure 13.14 Open and close the mouth, making sure that the temporomandibular joint is not moving forward by feeling with the hands.

Figure 13.15 If the jaw is slipping forward, lightly touch it to train it to stay back during the uninterrupted opening and closing movement (thirty to sixty seconds).

CHAPTER 14

MISCELLANEOUS PROBLEMS

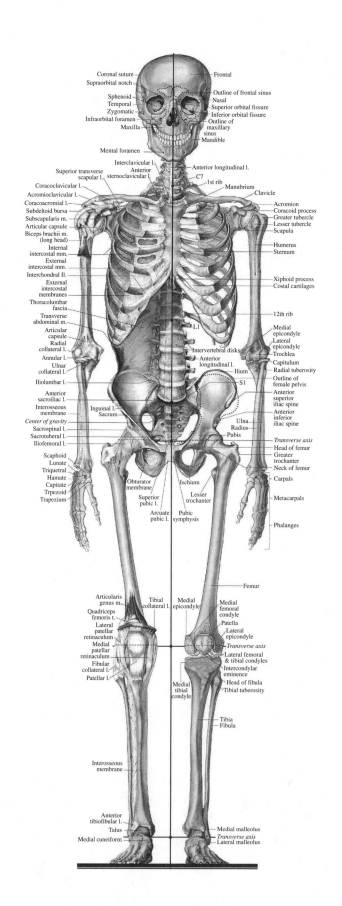

Coronal suture
Supraorbital notch
Sphenoid
Temporal
Zygomatic
Infraorbital foramen
Maxilla
Mental foramen
Frontal
Outline of frontal sinus
Nasal
Superior orbital fissure
Inferior orbital fissure
Outline of maxillary sinus
Mandible

Interclavicular l.
Superior transverse scapular l.
Anterior sternoclavicular l.
Coracoclavicular l.
Acromioclavicular l.
Coracoacromial l.
Subdeltoid bursa
Subscapularis m.
Articular capsule
Biceps brachii m. (long head)
Internal intercostal mm.
External intercostal mm.
Interchondral ll.
External intercostal membranes
Thoracolumbar fascia
Transverse abdominal m.
Articular capsule
Radial collateral l.
Annular l.
Ulnar collateral l.
Iliolumbar l.
Anterior sacroiliac l.
Interosseous membrane
Center of gravity
Sacrospinal l.
Sacrotuberal l.
Iliofemoral l.
Scaphoid
Lunate
Triquetral
Hamate
Capitate
Trpezoid
Trapezium

Anterior longitudinal l.
C7
1st rib
Manubrium
Clavicle
Acromion
Coracoid process
Greater tubercle
Lesser tubercle
Scapula
Humerus
Sternum
Xiphoid process
Costal cartilages
12th rib
Medial epicondyle
Lateral epicondyle
Trochlea
Capitulum
Radial tuberosity
Outline of female pelvis
Anterior superior iliac spine
Anterior inferior iliac spine
Transverse axis
Head of femur
Greater trochanter
Neck of femur
Carpals
Metacarpals
Phalanges

L1
Intervertebral disks
Anterior longitudinal l.
Ilium
S1
Ulna
Radius
Pubis

Inguinal l.
Sacrum
Obturator membrane
Superior pubic l.
Arcuate pubic l.
Ischium
Lesser trochanter
Pubic symphysis

Femur

Articularis genus m.
Quadriceps femoris t.
Lateral patellar retinaculum
Medial patellar retinaculum
Fibular collateral l.
Patellar l.
Tibial collateral l.
Medial epicondyle
Medial tibial condyle
Medial femoral condyle
Patella
Lateral epicondyle
Transverse axis
Lateral femoral & tibial condyles
Intercondylar eminence
Head of fibula
Tibial tuberosity
Tibia
Fibula

Interosseous membrane

Anterior tibiofibular l.
Talus
Medial cuneiform
Medial malleolus
Transverse axis
Lateral malleolus

224

Anterior View

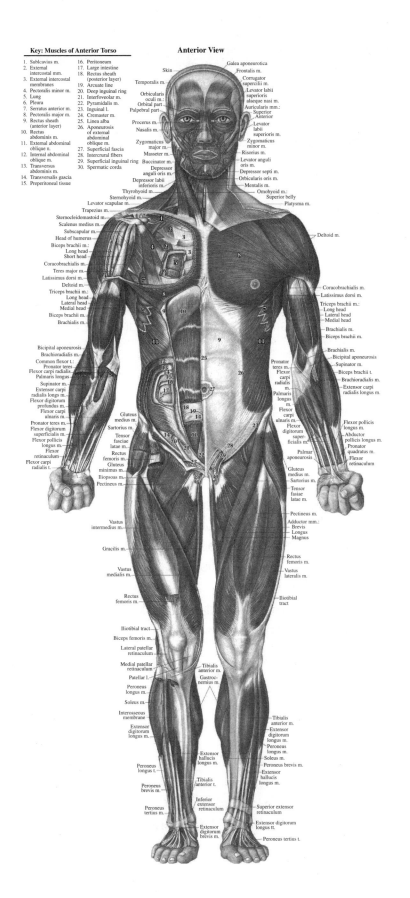

225

SIGNS AND SYMPTOMS

Headache, teeth grinding, sore jaw, anxious, irritability, poor sleep, digestive problems, or personality changes.

NAME OF INJURY

Stress

DESCRIPTION

The way your body responds to the physical, emotional, and mental demands put on it.

CAUSE

The way you handle any situation—keeping your body in crisis mode (high gear) for too long.

TREATMENT

Immediate Relief

1. *Stop!* Take time out to relax and clear your mind. (Write down your commitments or problems and solve them. If you can't solve them, forget them.)
2. *Distract* yourself: Take a minivacation in your mind to your favorite place for fifteen to thirty minutes, ponder your past successes, meditate, go to a movie, go shopping, read a book, and so forth. These activities tend to take most people's mind off of whatever is bothering them at the time.
3. *Distance* yourself from the problem for just a short time; it will become smaller to you and more solvable.

PREVENTION

Technique

Relax by taking a hot bath, listening to or playing music, taking a vacation, and so on.

Stretches

Deep breathing exercises are very helpful while you are relaxing: Stretch your jaw, roll your shoulders forward, and open your chest and stretch (see Tip 14.2).

Exercises

Pick any exercise you enjoy enough to stick with, and make it part of your routine at least three times per week. I suggest you do some sort of low-impact aerobic-type exercises.

IF NO RELIEF

If your symptoms are new and have no obvious cause (especially if you have entertained thoughts of self-injury or suicide), see a psychologist immediately.

PROGNOSIS

Our day and age is filled with such activity and expectation that we tend to put great pressure on ourselves. In this way, we cause our own stress. Just like no amount of water can sink the smallest boat unless it gets in, the greatest pressures of the world cannot stress you unless you let them.

SIGNS AND SYMPTOMS

Loss or decrease in volume or tonal quality of voice.

NAME OF INJURY

Laryngitis

DESCRIPTION

Swollen or scarred vocal cords form the wrong-shaped container for air to pass through to create the desired sound.

CAUSE

Swollen or scarred vocal cords caused by misuse (e.g., yelling), upper respiratory infection, allergic reaction, dry air (change in environment, airplane air, etc.), cigarettes, some prescription drugs (e.g., blood pressure medications, thyroid medications, antihistamines, etc.), and use of non-trained vocal muscles.

TREATMENT

Immediate Relief

Rest. Don't talk or whisper for at least one or two days; it bangs the vocal chords against each other. Hang your head over a steaming bowl of water for five minutes in the morning and the afternoon. Cold air humidifiers are also helpful in restoring the voice.

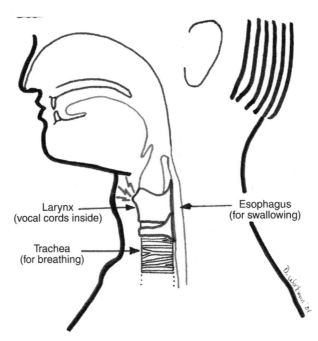

Figure 14.1 Infections commonly pass down the throat during swallowing, infecting the vocal cords, often causing laryngitis. Other causes are cold weather, smoke, and overuse and misuse of the voice.

PREVENTION

Technique

Get proper vocal training, don't shout, and keep vocal chords moist by breathing through the nose, drinking plenty of water (eight to ten glasses per day), warming up properly (see Tip 14.1), and sipping juices with honey or lemon. When you want to clear your throat, swallow—*don't cough*.

Exercises

Vocal exercises are most important for this area. It is important to get proper training from a vocal coach or teacher. It is best to get a doctor's approval prior to beginning any exercises if you currently have laryngitis.

IF NO RELIEF

If your voice doesn't begin to return within three to five days, see a throat specialist (otolaryngologist).

PROGNOSIS

Standard laryngitis has an excellent recovery if you treat it as suggested. However, your chances of doing permanent damage increase the more you use the voice while it is not working properly. If you continue to push your voice while it is sick, you can do permanent damage.

OTHER POSSIBILITIES

Possible tumor in the throat (symptoms usually include coughed-up blood and noises in the throat when breathing, and constant rest does not relieve the hoarseness).

SIGNS AND SYMPTOMS

Hot environment with normal body temperature; cool, pale, or moist skin; heavy sweat; rapid pulse and breathing; headache; nausea; dizziness; vomiting; or faintness.

NAME OF INJURY

Heat exhaustion

DESCRIPTION

Body becomes unable to adequately cool itself in a hot environment or while under heavy physical exertion.

CAUSE

Excessive sweating from playing in a very hot venue without proper hydration or breaks to cool off. Outdoor playing commonly carries this risk; the most common cause is marching in the hot sun for hours with hot uniforms. Heavy equipment puts an extra load on the body and doesn't allow the skin to breathe and cool.

TREATMENT

Immediate Relief

Get to a cool place immediately, lie on back with feet elevated, loosen clothing, suck on ice, wipe the skin with a wet rag and fan it off, drink

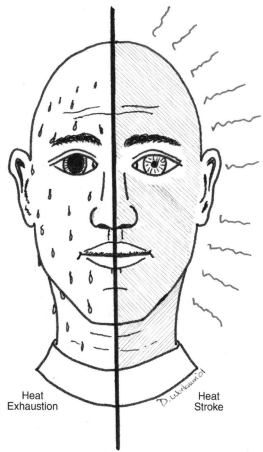

Heat
Exhaustion

Heat
Stroke

Figure 14.2 Symptoms of heat exhaustion include cool, pale, moist skin; heavy sweat; headaches; nausea; dizziness; vomiting; and faintness. Heat exhaustion is illustrated on the left side, and heatstroke is on the right.

both cool (not cold) water and electrolyte drinks if conscious—one glass every fifteen minutes. The person with heat exhaustion should begin feeling better within thirty minutes.

PREVENTION

Technique

To prevent the chance of heat exhaustion or heatstroke, try the following: Have fans running on the performers; wear cool clothes and a hat that will shade your face but allow cooling of the head; drink plenty of water and electrolyte drinks (Gatorade, POWERade, etc.); intake plenty of salt (perhaps even salt tablets); and wet the skin constantly with a cool, wet cloth until temperature returns to normal. For suggestions for first-aid care of heat exhaustion, see Tip 14.3.

IF NO RELIEF

If the person doesn't begin feeling better within thirty minutes, or is getting worse, *get medical care immediately*—have someone take the person to the hospital emergency room.

PROGNOSIS

Heatstroke can cause severe damage and death. The longer the body stays at high temperatures, the more severe and irreversible the damage can become. Signs of heat exhaustion appear first to warn you to act quickly to cool the body before heatstroke happens.

OTHER POSSIBILITIES

Heatstroke (hot, red skin; constricted pupils).

SIGNS AND SYMPTOMS

From hot environment, person has hot, red, dry skin; has very high body temperature (104°F or higher); is disoriented; and has possibly passed out.

NAME OF INJURY

Heatstroke

DESCRIPTION

Body becomes unable to cool itself, and the temperature reaches deadly levels (104°F/40°C and higher).

CAUSE

Extended time in very hot places causes the brain's temperature gauge to stop and the temperature to rise. Playing in a very hot venue or outside without proper hydration or breaks to cool off increases this risk. The most common cause is marching in the hot sun for hours in hot uniforms or with heavy equipment that puts an extra load on the body and doesn't allow the skin to cool.

TREATMENT

Immediate Relief

Act quickly! Call 911 or an ambulance, and get the person to a cool place immediately. Begin cooling the body by wiping a wet cloth all over it—remove clothing to wet the skin. *Don't give anything to the person by mouth, as the person may not be conscious and may choke.*

PREVENTION

Technique

To prevent the chance of heat exhaustion or heatstroke, you can do a few things: Have fans running on the performers; wear cool clothes and a hat that will shade your face but allow cooling of the head; drink plenty of water or sports drinks (Gatorade, POWERade, etc.); intake plenty of salt (perhaps even salt tablets); and wet your skin with a cool, wet cloth constantly until temperature returns to normal. For first-aid care of heatstroke, see Tip 14.4.

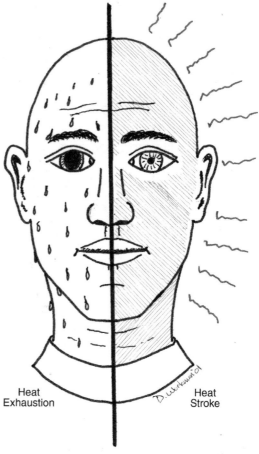

Heat
Exhaustion

Heat
Stroke

Figure 14.3   Symptoms of heatstroke include hot, red, dry skin; very high temperature (usually higher than 104°F/40°C degrees); disorientation; and unconsciousness. Heat exhaustion is illustrated on the left side, and heatstroke is on the right.

IF NO RELIEF

Get medical care immediately—go to the hospital emergency room.

PROGNOSIS:

Heatstroke can cause severe damage and death. The longer the body stays at high temperatures, the more severe and irreversible the damage can become. Signs of heat exhaustion appear first to warn you to act quickly to cool the body before heatstroke happens.

OTHER POSSIBILITIES

Heat exhaustion (cool, pale, moist skin; dilated pupils).

STRETCHES

THE PHILOSOPHY OF STRETCHING

Stretching is not something you do *to* the body; it is something you *allow* the body to do. All stretches must be done by relaxing and allowing the muscles to stretch. If you try to force the muscles to stretch, their immediate reaction is to protect themselves from tearing by pulling back. This can quickly turn into a tug-of-war of you against your muscles, and nothing good can happen. This is why many people stretch and stretch without any positive results, and sometimes they even injure themselves.

GENERAL RULES FOR STRETCHING

Stretches are most effective when the body is warmed up first. This means you should do some mild exercise of the area to be stretched prior to beginning. For example, if you are stretching the legs, do some walking or running until the muscles get warm and loose (usually just before you begin to perspire). With the hands, try some basic rudiments—singles and doubles are best. If you are paying attention to your body, you will notice the area warming up as the blood is pumped into it. Or you can take a shower or sit in hot water prior to stretching—which is not as effective, but still good.

Do not

- pop your knuckles
- stretch when that part of the body is cold
- use bouncing or jerking motions while stretching
- force the stretch to the point where you cannot let the area relax

BASIC TIPS FOR MISCELLANEOUS PROBLEMS

TIP 14.1: WARM-UPS FOR VOICE

Before beginning these vocal warm-ups, do Stretches 12.2 and 12.3. After your neck is loose, begin the following warm-ups. To get a more thorough warm-up, do up-and-down scales with the lips closed (humming) prior to doing the "Ahh" scales and "Mah" scales. *Note:* If time is limited, do just the humming scales. This is basic advice; consult a vocal coach for a more thorough warm-up and other advice.

Figure 14.4   In the position shown in this figure, take a deep breath and begin singing one note in your comfortable range until fully exhaled. Repeat three times, holding the note longer each time.

Figure 14.5   Beginning at your comfortable midrange note, sing "Ahh" up and down a comfortable three-note scale (e.g., C, D, E). Repeat, starting one-half step higher each time, to the top of your comfort zone.

Figure 14.6   Beginning at your comfortable upper-range note, sing "Mah" down a comfortable five-note scale (e.g., G, F, E, D, C). Repeat, starting one-half step lower each time, to the bottom of your comfort zone.

TIP 14.2: STRESS REDUCTION ROUTINE

This is an overall relaxation routine. With each breath, relax a part of the body, beginning with the feet and working up to the legs, pelvis, chest, hands, arms, shoulders, neck, head, face, and mouth. Each time you exhale, release stress from the area you are focusing on. If you feel a particularly tight area, continue to focus on that area while breathing. In addition, you should stretch your jaw (Stretches 13.1–13.3), roll your shoulders (Stretch 11.2), and open your chest and stretch (Stretch 6.2).

Figure 14.7   Lie flat on your back on a soft, firm surface, as shown in this figure. Completely relax.

Figure 14.8   Slowly inhale, allowing the tummy to come up like a balloon.

Figure 14.9   Exhale slowly and completely, blowing the stress out.

TIP 14.3: FIRST-AID CARE FOR HEAT EXHAUSTION

Follow these directions: Constantly talk to the person to assess his or her mental state, and give the person fluids only when he or she is able to take them safely without choking. Give the person straight water or water with a salt mixture (one teaspoon of salt dissolved in one quart of water). When the person is able to sit, allow him or her to do so with assistance. He or she may need medical care.

Figure 14.10   Lay patient on his or her back and remove as much clothing as possible to allow cooling of the skin.

Figure 14.11   Begin wetting down the body with water or fanning the skin, or both, to cause evaporative cooling.

Figure 14.12   Let the patient sit and drink water or sports drink until he or she feels up to standing or walking. Monitor the patient until he or she feels back to normal.

TIP 14.4: FIRST-AID CARE FOR HEATSTROKE

First, call emergency medical personnel (911). Follow these directions: Constantly talk to the person to assess his or her mental state. When the person is able to sit, allow him or her to do so with assistance, and give fluids only when he or she is conscious and able to take them safely without choking. *Get the person medical care as soon as possible to check the vital organs for damage*.

Figure 14.13 *Call 911 immediately* for an emergency health care crew. Lay patient on his or her back, and remove as much clothing as possible to allow cooling of the skin.

Figure 14.14 Begin wetting down the body with water or fanning the skin, or both, to cause evaporative cooling.

Figure 14.15 When the patient's temperature drops below 101°F/38°C, put him or her in recovery position (as shown in this figure). This allows the patient to breathe freely and allows liquids to drain from the mouth.

APPENDIX A

CARE PROGRAMS

A.1: HOME ICE PROGRAM

If done correctly, ice is a very effective way of reducing swelling to an injured area. However, I have seen many occasions where such a simple and harmless therapy can cause considerable damage when used incorrectly.

The most common problem occurs when people use it too much. Many seem to think that if a little is good, a lot is better. Remember that ice can cause damage to the skin if it is applied for too long a period of time. I am sure that many of you have heard of frostbite, for example.

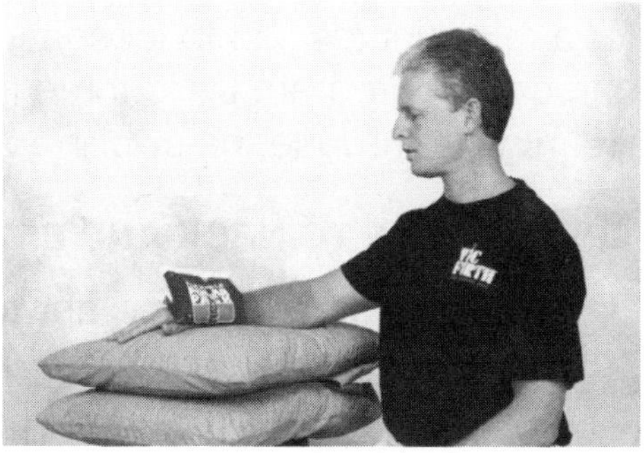

If you choose not to put the ice directly on the skin, then the ice will just

Figure A.1 The correct application of ice is, after elevating the injured area, to apply the ice directly to the skin and leave it there for a maximum of fifteen minutes. You can alternate ice for fifteen minutes and no ice for fifteen minutes, for up to two hours if needed.

cool the blood and carry it to the rest of the body. This will have no great effect on the injured area but will make your body feel generally colder.

APPLYING THE ICE

Ice is used to cool the surface of the skin. Apply it directly to the skin for fifteen to twenty minutes. During this time, the ice slows the circulation of fluids to the area and allows excess fluid to leave. With this decrease in fluid volume comes a decrease in both pressure and pain. However, if you stop the flow of blood to and from an area for too long, or put it into a deep, prolonged freeze, it will be damaged and perhaps leave a scar.

The most effective way to reduce the swelling of an injury is to follow the rules of "RICE." This is an acronym for *rest, ice, compression* (mild to moderate pressure on the pain area), and *elevation* (above the heart if possible). Together, these are much more effective than just applying ice in reducing swelling and healing injury. Like any program, its effect is proportional to your accuracy in following it. You cannot cut corners and expect it to work as well.

R = Rest—get in a comfortable position.
I = Ice—use gel ice pack, ice (crushed), frozen vegetables, and so forth.
C = Compression—apply gentle pressure to the area.
E = Elevation—raise the injury, above the heart if possible.

When you are finished, you may find it helpful to move the area lightly for a few minutes just to loosen it up, then rest for a while without ice. You can do this program up to three times per day if necessary. It is best to do it at night to reduce the swelling of the day's activities.

APPLYING ICE TO NECK AND BACK AREAS

Begin this program by lying down on your back on the floor (lie on top of a couple of layers of quilting to prevent soreness). It is best to be on a firm, comfortable surface that gives adequate support. I encourage patients to have the *remote phone, remote control,* and something to *drink* within reach so they can ice without being forced to get up.

The drink should be water; any clear, pure fruit juice; or sports drink. This is to help flush out the garbage and bring nutrition to the injured area. It is important that you ice without interruption, so the remote phone is to answer or make calls without getting up, and the remote control is to watch a movie or television without having to move. You are going to be icing fifteen minutes on and fifteen minutes off for two hours, so I suggest a good movie.

Lying on your back, apply the ice directly to the skin over the injured area, drink, and relax for fifteen minutes. On first contact, the ice will feel cold (ice does that), then the area will feel tingly, then a burning, dull throb, and finally numb (after about eight to ten minutes). The numbness means that the therapy is working. *Do not* leave the ice on for longer than fifteen minutes, regardless of the sensations you are feeling.

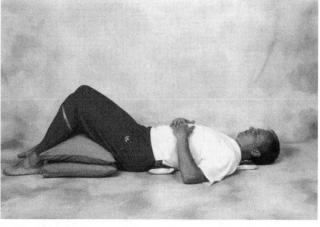

Figure A.2 The correct application of ice to the spine areas is to lie in the position shown in the figure and apply the ice directly to the skin. Rotate ice and no ice to the painful area every fifteen minutes as needed for up to two hours. I suggest having the remote control and remote phone handy to avoid getting up unnecessarily.

When time is up, take your ice to the freezer, get some more to drink, go to the restroom, and go lie down for fifteen minutes without ice. When time is up, repeat the same routine with the ice, continuing fifteen minutes with ice and fifteen minutes without ice for up to two hours.

KEY POINTS

1. Ice should be used for up to three days following an injury.
2. Ice should be applied directly to the area of pain.
3. Serious injuries or constant, recurring pain should be reported to your doctor.

A.2: HOW TO DO BASIC MASSAGE

This section is designed to teach the reader how to do a *basic* massage. It in no way gives the reader enough information to have the skills or knowledge of a professional. It gives beginner information that will enable one to do useful soft tissue work in a relatively safe way. Massage and soft tissue work is best done by an experienced professional: certified massage therapist (CMT) or doctor of chiropractic (DC) with soft tissue work experience.

The benefits to the body of a good massage are not very well known to the general public. Likewise, the ability to give an effective soft tissue massage is highly underestimated. Massage is an art form requiring talent and practice, not to mention a good knowledge of the anatomy beneath the skin. It is important to know where the muscles are and the direction their fibers go. In addition, knowing which muscles perform the various functions that are causing pain allows one to more effectively relieve that pain. Massage is a very simple thing to physically do, but at the same time it is difficult to be effective at. It involves all of the senses. In particular, being able to feel what is under the skin is of great importance. The subtle changes that happen during the massage indicate what should be done next. They also show where and how hard to push. Only through focus and constant practice can one become a great masseuse.

Important: If the area to be massaged has been injured, consult your physician before working on it.

Begin by finding the area of pain. Lightly rub the areas around it to feel all of the spots that might be involved. Once you have found them, begin doing a general massage of the area by rubbing lengthwise along the muscle fibers, starting at one end of the muscle and moving

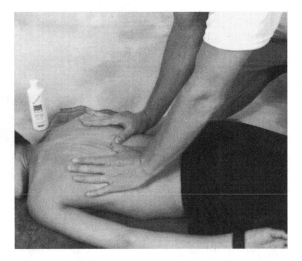

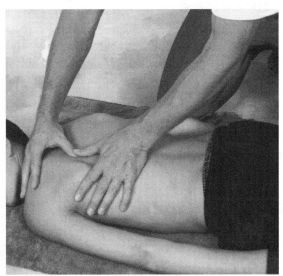

Figure A.3 and A.4 For larger muscle areas such as the legs and back, use the palms and outer edge of the hands (top). For smaller areas, it is convenient to use the thumbs to massage the muscles (bottom). It is important to move along the skin slowly and smoothly (using lotion helps), ironing out the painful bumps of muscle spasm.

to the other end slowly (one inch per second, moving toward the heart in most cases), with moderate pressure. It is best to use some kind of lotion to guide along the skin smoothly to "iron out" the muscle fibers.

While working the muscle, try to determine if the knots and sore spots smooth out. If they do, continue massaging along the muscle fibers, starting at the left side and moving to the right approximately one-quarter inch after each stroke. Once you have moved to the right edge of the muscle, go back to the left side and start again, doing the same thing. Repeat this three to five times. Each time you make a sweep over the muscle, the pain should decrease slightly, and the bumps should smooth out and flatten.

If the bumps are too hard and refuse to give way after doing this each day for two to three days, you can use a more aggressive technique that specifically works on the trigger points and spasms. Here's how it works: Massage along the muscle area as described previously. If you hit a trigger point, immediate pain will cause the patient to jump. The trigger point will be round shaped, about the size of a marble (they are various sizes). Spasms are very different. They usually feel like a rope or cable within the muscle going with the fibers. They are usually not painful unless you apply hard pressure to them.

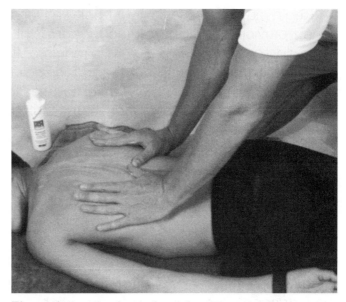

Figure A.5 This figure shows the pattern and direction you should massage. Note the strokes should be along the muscle fiber toward the heart in most instances. You should start at your left, and with each stroke move to the right one-quarter inch until you reach the edge of the muscle. Repeat this three to five times to smooth out the bumps (trigger points and spasms).

If it is a *spasm,* single it out and work on it as described earlier, going along the fiber, bottom to top and left to right. However, you will need to apply more pressure than usual on this area to get it to release or relax.

While you are doing this, the hands will probably slide off of the spasm—usually causing pain. It is important that you stay on top of it as you move along the fibers. I call this "surfing out the spasm." Repeat the left-to-right process three to five times—it should begin releasing within three to five treatments if you are doing it each day. As it releases, the patient will feel less pain during the massage, and the spasm will slowly melt, becoming softer each time. If you are really paying attention to your body, you will probably notice more strength, coordination, and endurance in that muscle.

When you find a *trigger point,* the pain will make the person jump (thus the term *trigger point*). Massage around it, and mark in your mind its boundaries. It will feel like a marble (of various sizes) within the muscle.

Begin moving in a left-to-right pattern along the muscle fibers as mentioned previously, staying on the trigger point only. This is usually a very painful process, so less pressure is required. It is important that you move very slowly while working out the trigger point—one-quarter inch or less per second. This gives it a chance to release while you are working it. Gradually, the area will become less painful, and the trigger point should deflate over three to five treatments.

Stubborn trigger points respond well to static pressure. This technique requires more training to be really effective, so it may take a while for you to become good at it. Find the trigger point, and place both thumbs on top of it. Slowly increase pressure on the area, being careful not to roll off. It will usually be painful, but the pain should reach only a level that the patient can tolerate without fighting back (tightening up). The patient should allow the muscle to relax during this process, or the massage will not be as effective. If the patient is tightening up, you will need to reduce pressure to the trigger point until the muscle stops fighting back.

Hold the pressure on the trigger point for twenty to thirty seconds. During this time, it will usually deflate, and, at the same time, the pain will fade. The key to this technique is being able to put the right amount of pressure on the trigger point. If too much pressure, it will just fight you back to protect itself. If too little pressure, it will just laugh at you without releasing. As it starts to deflate, you can increase the pressure slightly to accelerate the process.

This technique can be repeated two or three times if needed, but if it is not responding, you will need to do general massage as described previously for a day or two, and then try it again. If you cannot get it to release, or if the soreness doesn't go away after a day or two, see your chiropractor or massage therapist.

Remember that the muscle spasms and trigger points appeared because you are doing something that irritates the body—something that it wasn't designed to do or

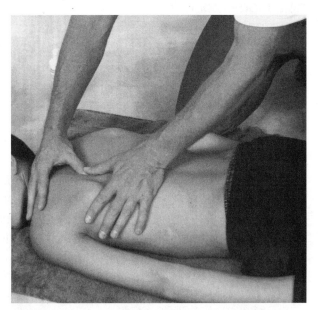

Figure A.6   The longer a trigger point or spasm has been there, the more difficult it is to remove it. Static pressure on a specific knot is one way of singling out the problem area and focusing on its removal. Once it is gone, you can do general massage to relax the entire muscle.

wasn't ready to do as much of. Unless you change the thing you are doing that causes the problem, it will constantly return, and you will be chasing muscle spasms and trigger points the rest of your life. Fix the problem, and remove the spasms and trigger points. If they return, call a doctor who works with musicians, and have the problem corrected properly.

KEY POINTS

1. Move in long, smooth strokes, very slowly, keeping the hands on the body.
2. Find the trigger points and spasms, and work them out.
3. Try to feel what the body is doing, and respond to it.
4. Find out what is causing the tightness, and change it.

A.3: PROPER LIFTING TECHNIQUES FOR THE BODY

As percussionists, we continuously have demands placed on us for hauling equipment and, in the case of marching players, nearly sprinting at 200 beats per minute while carrying upward of thirty pounds on our bodies. We need to be informed about how these movements and instruments affect our bodies, so we can be prepared for each rehearsal and performance and can be put to the test both mentally and physically.

A COMPLEX SYSTEM FOR SIMPLE MOVEMENTS

The erector spinae muscles line the spinal column and consist of three columns: iliocostalis muscles, longissimus muscles, and spinalis muscles. Erector spinae muscles provide resistance that controls the act of bending forward at the waist and act as powerful extensors to promote the return to an erect (standing) position.

However, if you bend forward at the waist so that your fingertips are touching the ground, the erector spinae muscles cannot return you to an erect position. At this position, the erector spinae muscles are relaxed and the strain is completely on the back ligaments. This is one of the reasons this position is dangerous; standing up too abruptly or lifting a load from this position will typically result in back injury.

From this position, the hamstring muscles and gluteus maximus muscles begin bringing the body upright, and the motion is completed by the erector spinae muscles.

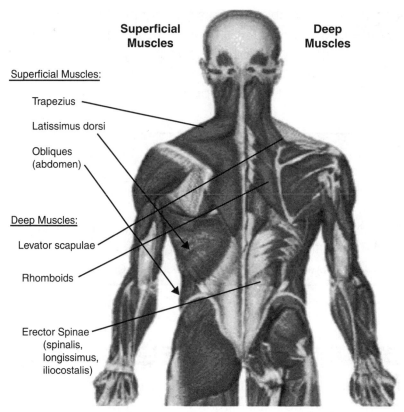

**Superficial
Muscles**

**Deep
Muscles**

Superficial Muscles:

Trapezius

Latissimus dorsi

Obliques
(abdomen)

Deep Muscles:

Levator scapulae

Rhomboids

Erector Spinae
(spinalis,
longissimus,
iliocostalis)

Figure A.7   Shown in this figure are the superficial muscles of the back and the deep muscles of the back. These are vital in supporting the torso and providing power and movement to the body. (Anatomical Chart Company, Lippincott Williams & Wilkins 2003)

The trapezius muscle is located on the upper part of the shoulder and takes much of the load when you are carrying equipment. The shoulders are held to the body by these muscles, so when you use the arms, the trapezius muscles are working hard. The rectus abdominis muscle flexes and rotates the waist and stabilizes the pelvis during walking and lifting. External oblique muscles help the rectus abdominis muscle in forward bending at the waist and aid the back muscles in rotating and side bending at the waist.

ALTERED CENTER OF GRAVITY

What does all this mean, and how does it affect you as you lift? When a person carries something, the weight hangs on the front of the body. Because of the location of the weight, the natural center of gravity changes.

Watch someone who is carrying equipment. He or she will alter the body movement to accommodate that change in his or her center of gravity. Most of the time the person will lean backward to reposition the weight to sit over the legs. Heavier loads make the change more obvious.

However, leaning backward only complicates the problem by putting the lower back in a greater swayback position (hyperlordosis). As the natural curve (lordosis) increases, the small ligaments between the vertebrae (bones in the back) stretch to their maximum and beyond, which may cause them to stretch or tear. This translates into injury and pain that can limit players' abilities. The degree of damage is usually gauged by how long the pain lasts after the occurrence and how intense it is.

When lifting or carrying something, the body becomes a seesaw. The back is the fulcrum with the weight pulling to one side. On the other side, the back muscles try to hold the body from falling forward. Greater loads are obviously more difficult for the body to lift and maneuver, because they require more muscle pull to balance and put more pressure on the spine.

To decrease pressure on the body, you can try taking smaller loads (which usually means more trips)—this is the very best idea. Another approach is to lift properly by holding the load as close to the body as possible. Still another idea is to build the strength of the involved muscles.

BUILD UP THE MUSCLES

Because of the weight of percussion instruments, the musician must build and maintain strong muscles. Doing the exercises found in Appendix B will help to build and maintain the muscles required to handle the weight of these instruments. They are specially selected to provide strength for the most difficult movements of the back, without causing risk to the back.

Special consideration should be given to players who are responsible for multiple instruments, some of which are extremely heavy and difficult to maneuver. It is good to have a pair of gloves to use while moving equipment. Some of the instruments may give splinters or slivers of fiberglass (mainly from the xylophone).

Be sure to push the instruments as opposed to pulling. There is controversy on this topic. Many people believe that pulling is better for the instruments, but pushing them is better for the players' spines. Be sure to lift the instruments (with your leg muscles, not your back) over bumps in your path. Do this by bracing your knees against the object while lifting. And remember: When loading equipment onto the truck, always lift using your leg muscles and *never* bend over at the waist to lift a load.

BODY MECHANICS

The majority of back injuries occur when we least expect them. This can come from repeated microtrauma (constant irritating movement) to specific areas from doing sports, having poor posture, carrying heavy weights for extended periods of time (marching percussion), and many other reasons. The main reason, and the last straw, is usually because of poor body mechanics. When poor body mechanics are used, it is common for a seemingly easy move (such as bending over to pick up a mallet) to cause a back injury.

There are three basic rules for proper body mechanics: the *nevers.* If you learn these and apply them to your everyday activities, they may help you avoid a disabling spinal injury.

THE NEVERS

1. *Never* bend forward at the waist to pick up an object. Instead, spread your feet to about shoulder width, place one foot in front of the other, and bend at the knees and lower yourself to the object while keeping your back straight. (See Figure A.8.)
2. *Never* carry an object with your arms extended. Carry objects as close to your body as possible. The body's center of gravity is just below the navel. Carrying items in this area usually puts the least amount of stress on the spine. (See Figure A.9.)
3. *Never* twist your trunk to reach for, move, or pick up an object. Bring the object into your center of gravity, turn with your feet, and keep your trunk straight. This may seem a bit robotic, but your spine was not built to twist or tilt while holding or lifting heavy objects.

As percussionists, we are responsible for a lot of heavy equipment. If an instrument appears too heavy, or a task seems too difficult, *get some help*. I always carry a piano mover to place my equipment on (you can get one at the local hardware store—they are inexpensive).

Figure A.8   To lift properly, position as shown in this figure, bring the object close to the body, and then lift with the legs.

Figure A.9   When carrying an object, hold it as close to the body as possible in a comfortable position. If you get tired, put the object down and allow the muscles to relax.

When moving equipment on wheels, you should push rather than pull because it is easier and safer for the spine. Push with your legs and not with your back. Even if you're running late for a gig, don't hurry while hauling equipment. Take your time, using correct body mechanics. It is better to be a bit late to a gig than to suffer a debilitating back injury and not be able to work at all.

When practicing or playing, change body positions often. Our bodies were not meant to stay in one position for hours on end. If learning a new piece at the marimba, or doing anything that requires you to remain in one position, remember your back and take a break. Try squatting once or twice to flex your spine, or extend your back if you were bent over. Walk around to get the blood flowing.

A leading cause of back injury is poor flexibility. A tight, stiff body is more prone to injury, because the required nutrients are not getting to the spine. More movement means more blood flow, and more blood flow means more nutrients reach the spine. A stiff body also works much harder and cannot adequately recover from injury. Especially bad for the spine are tight hip and hamstring muscles. It is good practice to gently stretch these muscles every day. Refer to the stretching sections in Chapters 4 through 14.

AFTER ACTIVITY

Playing drum/percussion music is very athletic and places heavy demands on our bodies. During the process of vigorous activity, joints of the spine are moved rapidly in many directions over an extended period of time. This process causes a thorough stretching in all directions of the soft tissues surrounding the joints. In addition, the fluid gel content of the spinal discs is loosened, and it seems that damage can occur if an exercised joint is subsequently placed in an extreme posture.

Many injuries occur after an activity—such is the case with musicians. After setting up, performing, and then tearing down, the body is tired. Typically all a person wants to do is drop into a fluffy chair and relax. This is one of the worst times to allow your body to drop into poor posture.

Poor posture, poor body mechanics, and bad flexibility will most likely lead to a back problem. When the spine's curves are exaggerated or decreased from what they should be normally, poor spinal posture results. Typically, poor posture will show (see Figures A.10 and A.11).

Imagine a vertical line running through your ear, shoulder, and hip. In keeping that line straight, you will maintain good posture, whether sitting or standing, which will help you avoid injury. Try putting a mirror in your practice area. Not only will you be able to critique your playing but you can monitor your posture as well. A video camera is even better, because you can look at it later instead of looking away while playing.

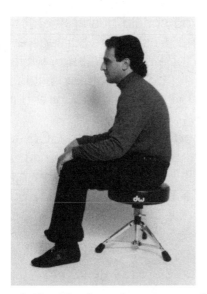

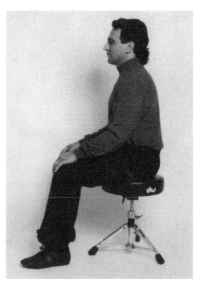

Figure A.10   This figure shows an example of *bad posture*. Note the head forward, the shoulders hunched, and the lost curve in the lower back.

Figure A.11   This figure shows an example of *good posture*. All of the curves in the neck, upper back, and lower back are present to absorb shock. Note how the head and shoulders are in line with the pelvis for balance.

Many percussion instruments require us to stand for long periods of time; therefore, every percussionist should be aware of his or her posture. Holding proper posture will help to eliminate unnecessary stress and fatigue and will enable performers to practice and perform for longer periods of time.

Percussionists should constantly be aware of sitting posture during drum set and timpani playing. When you sit slouched at the drum set, timpani, or anywhere, the ligaments and muscles in the spine become stretched and weakened and unable to do their job in supporting you. This makes you more susceptible to injury.

Traveling is another concern. For touring percussionists, many hours are spent sitting in vehicles. Out of all the positions, sitting puts the most pressure on the spine. It is a good idea to own a lumbar support pillow, or just a rolled-up towel, to place in the curve of your lumbar spine while sitting for long periods. This will cut down on the fatigue of trying to keep your muscles in control of your posture and will let you relax while maintaining the lumbar curve in your spine.

Because we spend so much time *sleeping,* good posture is also very important during downtime. When sleeping on your stomach, place a pillow underneath the top of your hips. If sleeping on your back, place a pillow under your knees. If you're in drum corps and on a gym floor, add a lumbar support pillow or towel under your lower back. This will keep the lumbar

Figure A.12 Quality sleep is vital to the body. It is important to sleep in a position that relaxes the body the most. It is best to sleep on your side in the fetal position, with your head elevated enough to keep the spine straight (as shown in this figure). If needed, place a pillow between your knees to put the pelvis in a relaxed, neutral position. If sleeping on your back, place a pillow under your knees and a flat pillow under your head and neck area.

curve and a good pelvic tilt. If sleeping on your side, bend your knees and place a pillow between them. Also, make sure the pillow under your head is thick enough to support it without bending your neck up or down. Using these techniques will help keep the back in a natural position—allowing it to rest better.

We as percussionists and as human beings are responsible for taking care of our bodies. This may be achieved by educating ourselves on basic anatomy and physiology, proper posture, good lifting techniques, body maintenance, and proper warm-up and cooldown techniques. Many injuries can be avoided if we learn these techniques and apply them to everyday living as well as to our lives as percussionists.

APPENDIX B

EXERCISES

GENERAL EXERCISE ADVICE

It is important to remember that if you have not exercised in months, if you have a heart condition or health condition, or if you are recovering from an injury, you should begin an exercise program only under your doctor's supervision.

Exercise should be done as a daily routine to keep the body in good condition. A strong body is less susceptible to illness and injury. Good daily exercises include walking, running, swimming, riding a bicycle, and so forth. If you are interested in increasing your exercise routine, do so in small increments. Make increases in either the amount of time you exercise or the intensity (speed, resistance, etc.) at which you do it.

It is normal to be slightly sore the day after exercise, but the pain should go away by the next day or so. If it doesn't, consider decreasing the routine just a bit. Work at that level for a few weeks, and then bump it up a little. It is optimal to increase your routine slowly and consistently. Pain up to three or four days after exercise is telling that you are doing more than the body can handle at that time (you bit off more than you can chew). This overload to the body is what causes injuries.

REHABILITATION OF AN INJURY

If you have been injured and have recovered sufficiently to begin exercising, it is imperative that you begin at a mild level. I have patients start at 30 percent of their regular exercise level. I progress them from that point according to their individual situation. There is no "one way is good for all." Each injury is different, and every body recovers in its own way. Once the basic strength begins to return, I feel that it is important to exercise by repeating the movements that caused the pain but at a lower intensity for shorter periods of time (about half as long).

At the initial stages, be sure to correct any flaws in technique that may have contributed to the injury. Gradually increase the time and intensity over a period of weeks, stopping each day when the pain begins. In this way you will strengthen the injured muscles and prevent repeated injury in the future.

COMMON QUESTIONS

Q: *What am I trying to accomplish?*

A: These exercises are designed to rebuild and strengthen muscles that are no longer doing the level of work that they need to. To do this, you will need to focus on making the particular muscle work. By focusing on a particular muscle, you will bring its level of performance up to par. Doing the exercises slowly and making a particular muscle do the work is going to bring you the best success.

Q: *How will I know how many repetitions and sets I should do?*

A: In this section, I have left it up to the reader to determine exactly how many repetitions and sets to do. The general rule for determining this is to do the exercise so that when you come to the end of the last set, your muscles struggle slightly to finish without aid. If you cannot finish the entire exercise, you need to decrease your repetitions or sets accordingly. Conversely, if you finish with ease, you should increase the repetitions or sets accordingly.

Q: *I know that pain is a natural part of strengthening and exercise, but how will I know if I am strengthening myself or doing damage?*

A: Strengthening the muscles is a painful process, but usually the pain is general and more of a fatiguing feeling—most likely felt at the end of a workout. If you are feeling pain in a specific area that recurs each time you exercise (and with greater intensity), then you are most likely causing or aggravating an injury. Other things that indicate injury are swelling, discoloration, and a decrease in ability to use the part.

LAST-MINUTE ADVICE

In this book, I have tried to give you stretches and exercises you can do on your own and without obtaining a lot of equipment. Unless instructed otherwise, each of these exercises must be performed in a slow, controlled, and continuous movement—without pain. Pain is your warning sign telling you that something is wrong. Unless you stop and find out what the problem is, you will end up injuring something.

Each exercise is demonstrated in a series of photographs with captions explaining what needs to be done. Many of them also give optional exercises that accomplish the same goal but may be more suited for you.

In this text, I use the terms *repetitions, times,* and *sets*. Repetitions and times refer to one complete movement from start to finish. If it says to do five repetitions (or times) for pull-ups, you are to do five pull-ups. Then, if it says to do three sets, you do the five pull-ups, rest for a period of time, and then repeat that routine three times in total—three sets.

EXERCISE B.1: THE CLOCK WARM-UP

This is a warm-up exercise. Begin with one stroke per second, and then speed up gradually to be at a comfortable speed at the twenty-five–second mark. Hold that speed relaxed and even for ten seconds, then gradually slow down over the next twenty-five seconds so that you are at one per second at the minute mark (see Figure B.1). Without stopping, do the next one. This time make your fastest ten seconds slightly faster than the previous one, but always slow down at the end and beginning to one stroke per second. Repeat continuously ten to twenty times.

If you are feeling tightness anywhere or are faltering in your technique, you must slow down (you're rushing the exercise), or it will do you no good. The exercise must be done correctly and gradually to be effective. Focus on even strokes and smooth technique. Look at a mirror to your side to be sure the sticks are reaching the same height on each stroke. Make corrections as needed. Use this exercise for any rudiment or pattern. You may also use slightly heavier sticks to build strength in the hands, but only one size heavier or you will risk causing injury (if a little is good, more is not necessarily better).

Figure B.1 Begin when the second hand is at the 12. Play one stroke per second, gradually speeding up to reach the fastest comfortable speed when the second hand is at the 5.

Figure B.2 Hold the fast speed steady and relaxed for ten seconds, and then slow down gradually to be at one per second when the second hand is at the 12.

Figure B.3 The same exercise can be done using any of the standard rudiments or using other phrases.

EXERCISE B.2: TENNIS BALL SQUEEZE

This exercise is designed to strengthen the wrist flexors and handgrip. Use this exercise to keep the hands in shape or to build strength following an injury. Do this exercise only once per day; no more times than mentioned in the figure captions.

Figure B.4   Begin in the position shown in this figure, with a relaxed grip around a punctured tennis ball or racquetball.

Figure B.5   Slowly grip the ball, then release in one smooth movement. Repeat the exercise ten times for three to five sets.

Figure B.6   At the end of each set, take the ball out of your hand and shake the hand relaxed to loosen the muscles.

EXERCISE B.3: THUMB AND PINKIE PULL

This exercise strengthens the muscles that open the hand and extend the thumb. In doing this, the hand muscles become more balanced and work together better. If you overdo this exercise, you will tighten the forearm and inhibit your playing ability.

Figure B.7   Wrap a rubber band around the pinkie (or any other finger) and the thumb, as shown in this figure.

Figure B.8   Pull the pinkie and thumb apart slowly, and return to starting position in a continuous motion.

Figure B.9   Do the exercise ten times for three sets, resting one minute between each set. Add more rubber bands until you are tired after the third repetition.

EXERCISE B.4: FINGER EXTENSION EXERCISES

These exercises will strengthen the muscles that extend the wrist and fingers. If you overdo this exercise, you will tighten the forearm and inhibit your playing ability.

  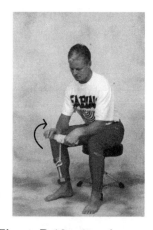

Figure B.10   Begin in the position shown in this figure, with palm down and wrist extending over the knee.

Figure B.11   Extend the wrist up and back, slowly and smoothly. Do exercise fifteen times for three to five sets, or until tired.

Figure B.12   You also can tie one end of a rope to a weight and the other end to a stick, and roll the stick to wrap the rope around it (like a motorcycle throttle), as shown in this figure.

EXERCISE B.5: FINGER FLEXION EXERCISES

These exercises will tone and strengthen the forearm muscles without creating the tension that heavy weightlifting can. With elastic tubing or dumbbells as resistance, do three sets of fifteen repetitions (more or less). As an alternate exercise, tie one end of a rope (approximately two feet long) to a weight and the other end to a stick, and roll the stick to wrap the rope around it (same action as rolling up a piece of paper with palms down). Do this until forearms are tired (about three to five times). If you overdo this exercise, you will tighten the forearm and inhibit your playing ability.

Figure B.13 Begin in the position shown in this figure, with palm up and wrist extending over the knee.

Figure B.14 Flex the wrist up, and curl slowly and smoothly. Do exercise fifteen times for three to five sets, or until tired.

Figure B.15 You also can tie one end of a rope to a weight and the other end to a stick, and roll the stick to wrap the rope around it, as shown in this figure.

EXERCISE B.6: SHOULDER RAISE EXERCISES

The lateral raises work the large muscles of the shoulder and build the muscles that support the shoulder while playing, giving you more endurance, strength, and control. This exercise should be done with light weights (five to ten pounds), three sets of ten in *forward, backward,* and *windmill* positions. Begin with the arms dropped at the sides; slowly raise the weight as high as is comfortable, then return to the original position (two seconds each direction). Repeat without stopping. The various positions are shown in Figures B.16–B.18.

Figure B.16 This figure shows the shoulder raise in the forward position at its greatest height.

Figure B.17 This figure shows the shoulder raise in the backward position at its greatest height.

Figure B.18 This figure shows the shoulder raise in the windmill position at its greatest height.

EXERCISE B.7: SHOULDER ROTATION EXERCISES

This exercise works the muscles around the shoulders, strengthening the rotation and support muscles. It is mostly used for rehabilitation of the shoulder after injury and is done under a doctor's direction. It is important to keep the arms straight and out to your sides while slowly rotating them in small circles (fifteen times). Repeat doing medium circles, and then do large circles as shown in the figure. It is important to first do them without weights for a few days, and then add weight in two- or three-pound amounts every few days if you feel no soreness. Do not rush to increase the weights, or you could cause injury to the shoulder.

Figure B.19 This figure shows the shoulder rotation at its greatest movement doing small circles.

Figure B.20 This figure shows the shoulder rotation at its greatest movement doing medium circles.

Figure B.21 This figure shows the shoulder rotation at its greatest movement doing large circles.

EXERCISE B.8: SWIMMING

Swimming is one of the best overall exercises for the body. It is used as a beginning-level rehabilitation for various injuries and is also recognized as great overall conditioning for the body. The *sidestroke, backstroke,* and *freestyle* (shown in the figure) done for fifteen to thirty minutes daily are good exercises. It is important to remember to go slowly, concentrating on proper motion and focusing on using all of the muscles involved instead of just getting from one end of the pool to the other.

Figure B.22 This figure shows the proper way to swim the sidestroke.

Figure B.23 This figure shows the proper way to swim the backstroke.

Figure B.24 This figure shows the proper way to swim the freestyle.

EXERCISE B.9: EXERCISES FOR PRONATION

B.9.1: Ankle Pronation Exercises

To strengthen the ankle muscles, attach elastic tubing around the forefoot and secure the other end to a chair leg by the inner side of the foot. Putting weight on the heel, move the foot out and curve up toward your face (as if you are trying to see the outer side of your foot). These exercises must be performed in a slow, controlled, and continuous motion. The rubber tubing is not to challenge you too much—it is only to provide some resistance as you pull the ankle around (into pronation). Continue the motion until you start to feel it (five to ten repetitions). Repeat for three to five sets.

Figure B.25   Sit in the position shown in this figure. Attach rubber tubing to the foot and the chair leg opposite to it.

Figure B.26   With a slow and continuous motion, move the foot in a "J" motion, sweeping up, as shown in this figure.

Figure B.27   Return the foot to the beginning position, and repeat without stopping until you start to feel it.

B.9.2: Foot Coordination and Strengthening

Throw some four-inch by four-inch pieces of paper on the floor, wad them into a ball with your toes, then move them with your toes to one pile or another for strength and dexterity. You can also move rocks or marbles from one pile to another with the feet. Try to relax the foot as you do them.

Figure B.28   Begin this exercise by wadding the paper into balls with your toes. Be patient—it takes time.

Figure B.29   Once this is done, move the paper balls into a pile to the left (medial).

Figure B.30   Wad another paper ball, but move this one into a pile to the right (lateral) instead.

EXERCISE B.10: WALKING PROGRAM

Walking is an excellent exercise for the entire body. The body was made to walk, and when we do, we work the muscles, circulation, and internal organs and stimulate the brain. The normal person should be able to walk ten to sixty minutes, depending on physical condition (*consult a doctor prior to beginning a walking program if you have a heart problem*). Walking should always be a part of your daily routine—especially in the morning and after dinner. Figures B.31–B.33 illustrate three phases of walking and give you an idea of some important points to remember as you walk. If the strides are too long during walking, you transfer more force to the foot on heel strike. This is hard on the body, so try to move in a smooth manner as you transfer weight from one leg to another.

Figure B.31 The stance phase is when the body's center of gravity is balanced on one leg.

Figure B.32 As the body leans forward, the center of gravity goes forward and down. The other leg moves forward to catch the body.

Figure B.33 During heel strike, the downward motion of the body is transferred to forward motion.

EXERCISE B.11: TOE FLEXION EXERCISES

You can strengthen the toe and foot muscles by placing a weight on a towel (on the floor); keeping the heel on the floor, use the toes to pull the towel toward you. It is important to use a light weight on a slick floor so not to overwork these muscles. Remember, you are not trying to build muscles, you are trying to tone and condition them.

Figure B.34 Begin in the position illustrated in this figure, with the foot relaxed on top of the towel.

Figure B.35 Slowly grip the towel with the toes, and gradually pull it toward you, as shown in this figure.

Figure B.36 Return the foot to the original position, and repeat the exercise until the weight has reached you. Relax for one minute, and repeat three to five times.

EXERCISE B.12: ANKLE SUPINATION EXERCISES

To strengthen the ankle muscles, attach elastic tubing around the forefoot, and secure the other end to a chair leg by the outside of the foot. Putting weight on the heel, move the foot in and curve up toward your face (as if you are trying to see the bottom of your toes). These exercises must be performed in a slow, controlled, and continuous motion. The rubber tubing is not to challenge you too much—it is only to provide some resistance as you pull the ankle around (into supination). Continue the motion until you start to feel it (five to ten repetitions). Repeat for three to five sets.

Figure B.37 Sit in the position shown in this figure. Attach rubber tubing to the foot and the chair leg closest to it.

Figure B.38 With a slow and continuous motion, move the foot in a scooping motion, sweeping up, as shown in this figure.

Figure B.39 Return the foot to the beginning position, and repeat without stopping until you start to feel it.

EXERCISE B.13: LOWER LEG STRENGTHENING

This exercise will strengthen the muscles that bring the forefoot off of the floor—a motion that is needed when operating foot pedals in various percussion instruments (e.g., timpani, drum set, vibraphones, chimes, etc.). Walk on your heels for one-minute intervals, with a one-minute rest in between. Another option: With your shoe on and the injured leg crossed over the opposite knee, put the front of your foot under the handle of a bucket (filled with water to your weight tolerance), and lift the foot straight up as if you are trying to see the bottom of your toes.

Figure B.40 This figure shows how to do the heel walk exercise to strengthen the muscles that lift the toes and feet.

Figure B.41 This is an optional exercise. Hang a bucket from the end of your foot, with a pad for comfort.

Figure B.42 Slowly and smoothly bring the foot up toward you as if you are trying to point your toes up.

EXERCISE B.14: HEEL RAISES

Heel raises are ideal for strengthening the calf muscles (the back of the lower leg). These muscles are extremely strong—so much so that you can rarely work them too much. The reason for this is that they are always in use during the toe-off phase of walking. The exercises shown in these figures will give your foot greater strength and endurance. For a greater workout, you can jump straight up in the air without bending the knees (using only the feet), doing the same amount of sets and repetitions as indicated in the figures.

Figure B.43 Begin this exercise in the position shown in this figure, with the feet and legs relaxed.

Figure B.44 Slowly and smoothly rise up on the tips of the toes, and lower back down. Repeat continuously five to ten times for three to five sets, with one-minute rests between each set.

Figure B.45 This figure shows someone doing a straight-leg jump to build the calf muscles.

EXERCISE B.15: GENERAL STRENGTHENING OF THE HAMSTRINGS, CALF MUSCLES, AND QUADS

There are many machines that you can use to develop the strength of these muscles. However, you may notice that they all have you doing the same movement, because only that movement will strengthen that muscle. The only thing that changes is the resistance to doing that movement (the force you put into doing it). In this book, I have tried to give you stretches and exercises you can do on your own, without obtaining a lot of equipment. The exercises in these figures are simple and are effective in developing the strength of the leg muscles.

Figure B.46 The best way to work out the hamstrings is to use a curl machine, as shown in this figure. Use light weight, and do ten repetitions for three to five sets.

Figure B.47 Squat jumps are an effective exercise for strengthening the quadriceps and the calf muscles at the same time. This figure shows the beginning squat position.

Figure B.48 From the squat, jump as high as you can. Return to the squat position, and jump again—one continuous movement. Do five to ten jumps in a row for three to five sets, resting one minute after each set.

Exercises

EXERCISE B.16: STRAIGHT LEG RAISES
(ESPECIALLY FOR CHONDROMALACIA PATELLA)

This is a very simple-looking exercise, but it is excellent for strengthening the knee area without having to bend the knee. Be assured that the exercise is working even if you don't think so. Do the exercise as instructed in these figures. Do three sets of ten in the morning and in the evening. When you can do these without pain or tenderness the next day, begin to use ankle weights while doing them. When you are able to do this without soreness the next day, you may work into squats or quad extensions, or both, at a low weight, following the instructions in Exercise B.15.

Figure B.49 Begin this exercise in the position shown in this figure. Use the hands for balance.

Figure B.50 Raise the injured leg straight up, keeping the knee straight, bending only at the waist. Each motion should take two seconds. Do ten repetitions for three to five sets.

Figure B.51 Rest for thirty seconds between each set. For a harder workout, increase the resistance with ankle weights (as shown in this figure). If you aren't sore the next day, add some more weight.

EXERCISE B.17: EXERCISES FOR THE LOWER BACK

The exercises in these figures are a few of the many that will strengthen the lower back and alleviate pain. There are many books available in stores and libraries, should you want more. The movements are designed to tone and stretch the back muscles to provide support to the spine and relieve pressure from the discs. If any of these exercises produce pain, stop immediately, and see your doctor for further instructions.

Figure B.52 In the position shown in this figure, lock your elbows against the ribs, and relax the entire body from the shoulders down, allowing it to hang (ten seconds). Lie relaxed for ten seconds (do five to ten times).

Figure B.53 This exercise is a mild strengthener of the back muscles. Hold the position shown in this figure for ten seconds. Rest on all fours, and repeat five to ten times if no pain.

Figure B.54 This position will challenge the back muscles. Hold the position for ten seconds. Rest, lying flat for ten seconds, and repeat five to ten times if no pain.

EXERCISE B.18: PELVIC STRENGTHENERS

Strengthening the hamstrings, buttocks, and lower back muscles is an important step to stabilizing the pelvis and providing a firm foundation for the body. This exercise will tone those muscles. At the same time, it will stretch and loosen them, relieving stress and tension. This all acts to help relieve back pain, help with posture, and increase endurance and strength. Do these in a rocking motion—slowly and smoothly (two seconds up and two seconds back). Rest for thirty to sixty seconds between sets.

Figure B.55 Begin in a neutral position, as shown in this figure.

Figure B.56 Slowly and smoothly extend the leg while straightening the knee until you reach your maximum range.

Figure B.57 Without stopping, bring the leg slowly back while bending the back and bringing the knee to the chest. Repeat this movement ten times for three to five sets.

EXERCISE B.19: ABDOMEN EXERCISES

The abdomen is used to some degree in almost all body movements. Without a strong belly (abdomen), your posture will suffer, throwing the body movement out of whack. It will also force other muscles to be overworked and injured. Crunches are a very common exercise, but if they are not done properly, they will tighten the deep back muscles and lead to problems. Do the crunches as outlined in the figures—three to five sets of ten to twenty crunches is usually plenty.

 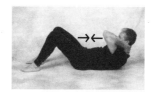 

Figure B.58 Begin in the position shown in this figure. When you do this exercise, remember to curl the belt and ribs toward each other.

Figure B.59 While doing the crunch, focus on the abdominal muscles—if the lower back tightens, you are going up too high.

Figure B.60 For those who have already developed strong abdominal muscles, a crunch with rotation adds more of a challenge.

EXERCISE B.20: UPPER BACK EXERCISES

The upper back supports the arms, neck, and head. If not strong, the upper back will fatigue early, causing pain in the arms, neck, and head. Doing pulling motions such as pull-ups and side rows with weights or using a rowing machine strengthens this area. Shoulder shrugs also help. These figures show some of the exercises that can be done at home with hand weights. Each of them works a different area of the upper back. They should all be done.

B.20.1: Pull-ups

Pull-ups work the large latissimus dorsi muscle. It is the one that shapes the upper back like a "V" and pulls the arms down from over the head.

Figure B.61 The pull-up can be done almost anywhere. The main focus is to pull the upper arm to the waist. Try not to use the arm muscles more than necessary.

Figure B.62 Pull the chin up to the bar as shown in this figure in a smooth, continuous motion, and return to the starting position the same way. Do five to ten times for three to five sets. Rest for one minute between each set.

Figure B.63 The pull-up can also be done with a wide grip, as shown in this figure. This particular grip focuses more on the latissimus dorsi muscles closer to the midback and lower back area.

B.20.2: Side Rows

This exercise works the muscles that hold the shoulder blades to the spine in the midback area, providing support for the shoulder joint.

Figure B.64 Begin in the position shown in this figure, with a light weight (ten pounds). While lifting, focus on bringing the shoulder and arm around to the back; use the arms as little as possible.

Figure B.65 Bring the arm and shoulder up and around in a smooth, continuous motion, pulling from the floor to the position shown in the figure and back. Do ten to fifteen times for three to five sets.

Figure B.66 The bent row is pictured in this figure. It is done just like the side row but with both arms pulling. It is harder on the lower back (which gives constant support during the exercise).

B.20.3: Shoulder Shrugs

This exercise builds the muscles that raise the shoulder area, which provides strength when lifting things up to the body, just as the action of the exercise shows, but it also stabilizes the shoulder when pulling on an object (opening cases, pulling straps, etc.). These muscles are relatively strong, so fairly heavy weights can be used.

Figure B.67 Begin the exercise in the position shown in this figure, with the shoulders relaxed and hanging.

Figure B.68 Moving slowly and smoothly, bring the shoulders up the front of the body. Try to make the top of the shoulders brush the jaw.

Figure B.69 Make an arc from front to back, brushing the jaw, and return to starting position. Pause slightly after each time. Do five times for three to five sets.

EXERCISE B.21: NECK-STRENGTHENING EXERCISES

These exercises strengthen the neck muscles. *If you have neck pain, you do not need these.* You must first get over the acute pain phase, then stretch the muscles. Once you are out of pain, you can begin to do these exercises.

B.21.1: Flexion/Extension Neck Exercises

These exercises work the muscles in the front and back of the neck, providing greater strength, endurance, and stability. Take three to five seconds to do the up-and-down movement. Repeat this approximately four to eight times; rest for one minute. Do three to five sets, and repeat the exercise lying on the stomach.

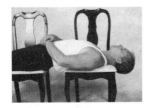  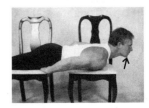

Figure B.70   The position shown in this figure is for resting. It takes pressure off of the spine and neck. Allow the bottom of the skull to sit on the edge of the chair.

Figure B.71   To exercise the front neck muscles, in a slow, smooth, and controlled motion, tuck the chin and roll the face to the chest, then go back to the original position. Do three sets of four to eight without pain.

Figure B.72   To exercise the back neck muscles, in a slow, smooth, and controlled motion, tilt the head back as far as is comfortable, and return down to resting position. Do three sets of four to eight without pain.

B.21.2: Lateral Flexion Neck Exercises

These exercises work the muscles on the sides of the neck, providing greater strength, endurance, and stability. Take three to five seconds to do the side-to-side movement. Repeat this approximately four to eight times; rest for one minute, and then repeat. Do three to five sets, and repeat the exercise lying on the other side.

Figure B.73 Lying on your side as shown in this figure, begin the exercise with the head touching the surface.

Figure B.74 In a slow, smooth, and controlled motion, raise the head to the upper shoulder as far as is comfortable.

Figure B.75 Without stopping, return the head back to the original position. Do three sets of four to eight without pain, resting one minute after each set.

EXERCISE B.22: TEMPOROMANDIBULAR JOINT EXERCISES

The temporomandibular joint is one of the most powerful joints in the body and yet is one of the most delicate. If it is not kept in good balance, severe pain can result, and the joint can get degenerative arthritis. These exercises are designed to balance out the muscles that open and close the jaw, and in doing so add stability to the temporomandibular joint. Rest the jaw in the hands with only the weight of the head pushing on the hands. When opening and closing the jaw, do so slowly and smoothly (three seconds to open and three to close). Do not do these forcefully or to fatigue, or you can do damage to the joint over time. A 30 percent effort is good.

Figure B.76 Begin with the jaw resting in the hands as shown in this figure, with the index finger on each side feeling the temporomandibular joint. Do not push the jaw against the hands—the head is heavy enough for resistance.

Figure B.77 Slowly open the jaw as far as is comfortable, with the tongue touching the roof of the mouth. If your index fingers feel the jaw moving forward, lightly push the chin in.

Figure B.78 Slowly close the jaw, monitoring the joint as indicated in the previous figure. Do not allow the jaw to jump as it closes—it should be a smooth, continuous movement. Do five to seven repetitions three to five times with a thirty-second rest after each time.

APPENDIX C

FURTHER EXPLANATIONS

THE MOST COMMON DRUM/PERCUSSION PAIN

SOFT TISSUE INJURIES

Tissues are similar cells grouped together to form a similar specific function. For this section, I refer to soft tissue as muscles, tendons, ligaments, and bursae. In my experience treating percussionist and drummers over the years, soft tissues injuries are by far the most common. This section discusses the types of soft tissue injuries that occur in drum/percussion players and how to treat them.

Once a soft tissue is injured, the best thing to do is leave it alone for a period of time and let it cool down (until the pain subsides). Most doctors will counsel the patient with a soft tissue injury to not move the area for two to four weeks.

In most cases, players cannot just stop moving for that amount of time, so they just suffer until it gets so bad that they cannot move anymore. Many times this can ruin a job for them and even affect their career. They put off seeing a doctor for fear that they will be told to stop playing—something they don't feel they can do.

In most cases of soft tissue injury, the musician can continue to play at a lower level and also have the injury heal. Not all injuries require total rest.

It is important to consult a doctor who has experience treating performers and athletes.

It is optimal if you can find a doctor who actually plays drums/percussion, because he or she understands the demands and movements of playing well enough to provide alternative ways to play without causing further injury to the area.

As a final note, it is very important to find out the movements or behaviors that caused the injury in the first place. Almost without fail, when the treatment is complete and the musician is fully healed, he or she asks, "Will this injury return?" My reply is, "If you continue to do the thing that caused the injury in the first place, it will happen again; but if you change the pattern that initially caused the injury, it will not return."

Behaviors are the main cause of injury, so we must find the behavior and change it. On the positive side, pain shows us weaknesses in our technique, and if we improve that weakness we will play better and longer.

C.1: WHAT ARE MUSCLE SPASMS?

Muscles are usually the first soft tissue to be injured, because they provide the force that moves the body. They do the work (see Figure C.1).

When the muscle works, it uses up energy. When too much energy is depleted, the muscle becomes fatigued. You know you have fatigued an area when it shakes as you try to hold it still. It will also become weaker and less coordinated.

A muscle's usual response to fatigue (overuse) or injury is to tighten up and go into spasm (constant contraction of the fibers). It does this to act as a splint: to reduce movement of the area to protect it from further damage. This process actually protects you from you.

However, this splint effect causes pressure around the blood vessels, which reduces the flow of nutrition to the injured area. Because blood is necessary to revitalize the muscle, the healing process is slowed by the reduced circulation.

Blood brings nutrients that are used to strengthen the area. This is much like the construction materials brought by vehicles. Obviously, what a person takes into his or her body is very important in this reconstruction process. Take in the good things, and refrain from the bad.

If something in the body doesn't move, the body figures it is not supposed to and develops fibrous tissue to solidify the area. In muscles, the fibrous tissue forms between the muscle fibers, preventing them from operating. So, as soon as possible, the injured site must begin movement. First, the goal is to reach normal range of motion, and then begin adding

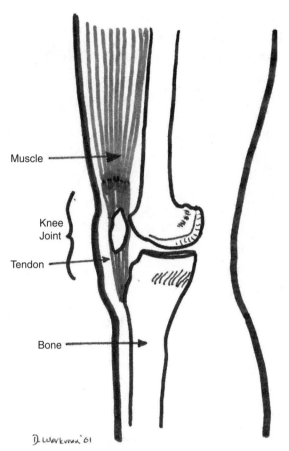

D. Workman '61

Figure C.1   Muscles attach to tendons, and tendons attach to bones. Often, when a muscle is injured, the tendon is also affected, and vice versa.

resistance and playing longer until the area reaches its normal strength and endurance.

If an injury heals without proper rehabilitation, the injury will continue to cause problems. For a chronic muscle spasm to heal properly, the fibrous tissues (adhesions) need to be broken to allow proper movement of the muscle. As you can imagine, this is usually a painful process to varying degrees (see Section A.2), but it must be done for full healing. A certified massage therapist, chiropractor, or trainer with experience working with musicians or athletes should do it.

C.2: WHAT IS BURSITIS?

Bursae are different from the soft tissues. They are various-sized sacs of lubricating fluid that are situated between moving parts within the body to reduce wear, heat, and friction that can cause injury (see Figure C.2).

They are very slick and very durable, but they can be injured from a direct hit or constant motion of the area. The chances of a bursa being irritated are increased with pressure on the bursa, speed of movement, and duration of the movement. Therefore, suddenly using heavier sticks or playing at faster speeds than you are used to can bring it on.

When shifting to a higher level of playing, it is important to do it gradually so the body can make the adjustment. The body can accomplish almost anything if conditioned properly—patience and consistency is the key.

Bursae are located between two areas that rub together. They reduce the friction. They are found around the shoulder, knee, hip, and so forth—where most movement occurs. Misuse of the area as described previously can cause irritation of the bursae, resulting in inflammation (bursitis). If you have pain in a joint during movement, bursitis is one possibility.

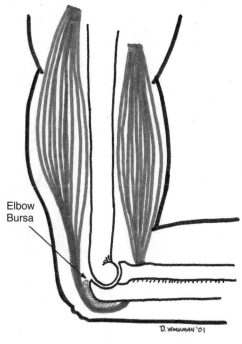

Figure C.2 This figure shows an elbow bursa. Bursae are bags filled with lubricant that are positioned between two moving objects in the body to provide smooth movement without friction.

Once a bursa is irritated, the best thing to do is leave it alone and let it cool down. The average doctor will counsel the patient with bursitis to not move the area for two to four weeks. With a little imagination, you can usually get around that. Career players cannot afford to stop a movement that makes their living.

In most cases, altering the playing situation in some way allows the musician to continue playing and at the same time lets the injury heal. A change in technique, positioning of the instrument, decreased intensity of playing by working with a sound man, and so on may be all that is needed to allow this to happen.

After the initial pain reduces in the first few weeks, you can begin moving the area. Begin with about half of the normal effort, and then play a little more each day, stopping when pain begins. With each day, you should be able to play longer and with more intensity.

Gradually, you will reach your maximum level. It is important that you do not play with pain, because it will take longer to heal, and further damage may occur. With patience, you will return to normal playing without pain.

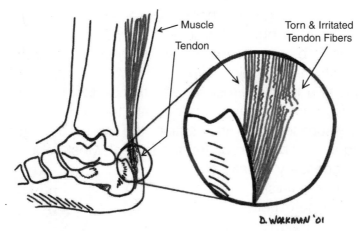

Muscle

Tendon

Torn & Irritated
Tendon Fibers

D. WORKMAN '01

Figure C.3   The muscles of the lower leg combine into one common tendon and attach to the heel. One large injury or repetitive misuse causes pain, swelling, or tearing of the tendon fibers. This is called Achilles tendonitis (circled area shows the location of pain).

C.3: WHAT IS TENDONITIS?

Tendons and ligaments are not as flexible as muscles, and they heal more slowly. Constant pressure and force on the tendon is a common cause of tendonitis. Tendonitis simply means that the constant pull on the tendons can cause them to develop small tears in the fibers. When this happens, the tendon gets irritated, swollen and painful. This can occur anywhere tendons exist in the body (see Figure C.3).

Irritation to an area leads to muscles tightening involuntarily (spasm) to protect the area. However, muscle spasm puts stress on the tendons that attach the muscle to the bone, because the tight muscle is less elastic, causing more pull on the tendon. Something has got to give, and when the muscle won't, the tendon must give more than it is designed for. This irritates the tendon.

Allow me to illustrate: If you were bungee jumping, the bungee cord would represent the muscle, and the strap that attaches the bungee to your leg would be the tendon. Imagine if you jumped off of a bridge and came to the end of the bungee, but it didn't stretch—see what I mean about pulling on the tendon?

Because we use our hands and feet so much in playing drums/percussion, the muscles that operate those areas tend to put more pressure and wear on the tendons around the wrist, hands, and feet. It is very common for players to have tendonitis that develops from overuse of an area that has chronically tight muscles.

Tendons typically take about twelve weeks to heal. During this process, the initial action should be to take the pressure off of the tendon by loosening up the attached muscle. If the injury is minor, the player can see if the injury will relieve by trying some basic massage techniques on the injured area (see Section A.2), but this is done best with moderate to deep massage of the muscle by a massage therapist, chiropractor, or trainer experienced with musician and athlete injuries.

Usually this is a painful process, and the person rendering the treatment should have the experience necessary to know where to work and how much pressure to apply. In addition, the longer the injury has been there, the longer it will need to be treated to heal. Most people do not have the patience necessary to take the process from start to finish.

Once the pressure is off of the tendons, they will need time to rest with minimal or no playing. In a severe case, after about two to four weeks of total rest you can begin playing at about 50 percent of normal intensity and time. If the injury begins to hurt during the playing, back off and try it again the next day.

With each day, you should be able to play longer and with more intensity. Gradually, you will reach your maximum level. It is important that you do not play with pain, because it will take longer to heal, and further damage may occur.

C.4: WHAT IS NERVE IMPINGEMENT?

Nerve impingement occurs when something puts pressure on any nerve, causing irritation or a decrease of its ability to function. This is called an impingement injury (see Figure C.4).

Any pressure on a nerve causes a decrease in its ability to function to some degree and is accompanied by the nerve complaining in some way (usually pain, tingle, burning

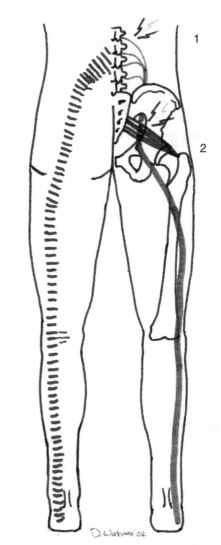

Figure C.4 This illustration demonstrates two common causes of sciatic nerve impingement (sciatica): (1) bulging or herniated lower back discs and (2) nerve pressure from muscle spasm (usually the piriformis muscle). Sciatica can be down the leg as far as the toes (nerve in solid line, and pain pattern in dashes).

feeling, numbness, etc.). A good example of nerve impingement is when you strike your funny bone (the ulnar nerve) and a tingle or shock shoots down the arm.

A longer lasting nerve impingement sensation feels like getting a dead arm when you sleep on it too long. The arm usually starts with feeling numb, then when you get off the arm you feel tingling, pins and needles, and sometimes burning or aching. With time, it slowly returns to normal. The impingement injury reacts much the same way, but on a larger scale.

A nerve can be pushed on by many things in the body, but the most common for drummer/percussion players are tight muscles, swelling of the nerve or surrounding irritated tissues (tunnels, retinacula, etc.), and even pressure on the area from inefficient playing techniques. Nerves can also be affected if their blood supply is reduced, but for this situation, it is less of a concern.

There are a number of muscles that are positioned close to a nerve. If they go into spasm, they can cause pressure to the nearby nerve. This irritates the nerve, and it cries out in one of the previously mentioned sensations. It will continue to do this until the pressure is removed, then it will gradually return back to normal. The trick is to recognize the problem and find out where the nerve is being impinged (pushed on).

The amount of time it takes to return to normal increases with the amount of pressure that was on it and the amount of time it was there. If left long enough, chances for full recovery can decrease.

It is important to consult a doctor so to remove the cause of the pressure to the nerve. After that, your ability to play will improve as the normal feeling and function comes back to the nerve. This injury is more complex and should be monitored by a doctor.

C.5: WHAT IS A STRAIN? (MUSCLE INJURIES)

A muscle belly is made of many muscle fibers grouped together to perform various movements. When a muscle tries to pull a force that is more than its ability, the fibers can (and often do) tear. Most of the time, only a small percent of them tear, while the others stay intact. However, the torn fibers usually pull away from each other, causing a gap (see Figure C.5).

The body responds by shipping in a material (scar tissue) that binds the torn ends together. The initial healing is best when (1) the fibers are closer together, (2) the swelling is reduced for greater circulation to occur, and (3) the muscle can rest to prevent the fibers from pulling apart.

Muscles are one of the fastest soft tissues to heal because they have a great amount of blood circulation. More blood circulation to an area generally means faster and better healing because there are more materials to work with. Greater amounts of damage mean a bigger repair job, and a bigger job requires more materials and time to heal.

Muscles will usually heal fully four to six weeks following a typical injury (you should begin to feel better in the first or second week). However, the amount of damage done to the area and the amount of time the injury has been there will play an important role in how fast and how well it will heal.

Fibrous tissue is shipped to the injured site and begins to patch the torn muscle fibers together. This happens best when the fibers are in close proximity and not moving. However, the fibrous tissue must be trained to act as much as muscle fibers as possible. So, after the first few weeks, the injured site must begin movement. First, the goal is to reach normal range of motion, and then begin adding resistance until the area reaches its normal strength.

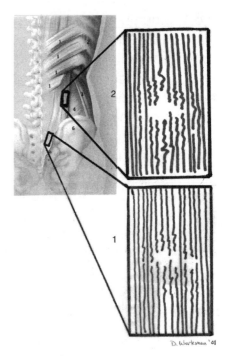

D. Workman '01

Figure C.5 (1) A sprain is a tear in the tendons or ligaments, whereas (2) a strain is a tear in the muscle fibers. Muscles typically heal more quickly than tendons or ligaments because they have greater circulation (among other reasons).

Once the scar tissue is able to hold the damaged muscle fibers together, it is important to begin putting resistance to the muscle. This means doing gentle stretching and, later, exercises. After about two to four weeks of rest, you can begin playing at about 50 percent of normal intensity and time. If the injury begins to hurt during the playing, back off and try it again the next day.

With each day, you should be able to play longer and with more intensity. Gradually, you will reach your maximum level. It is important that you do not play with pain, because it will take longer to heal, and further damage may occur.

This gradual increase in exercise conditions the muscle to once again take on forces that it was able to before being injured by training the scar tissue to form and perform much like the original muscle fibers.

The longer an injury has been there, the more difficult it is to reverse it. With time, scar tissue begins to form, and fibrous tissue develops between the muscle fibers, preventing movement, so it is important to address the injury immediately.

C.6: WHAT IS A SPRAIN? (LIGAMENT INJURIES)

Ligaments surround joints, attaching bone to bone while allowing movement. They are strong fibrous tissues that are pliable, and some believe that they are slightly elastic. They keep the joints snug in their movement rather than loose and shifting. Muscles protect the joint the most. They prevent the joint from going too far in its movement, and they tighten to secure it when moving or at rest.

The ligaments play an important role in keeping the bones lined up at the joint. When a ligament is torn or weakened to any degree, the joint is more susceptible to injury (see Figure C.6).

Generally, ligaments take longer to heal than muscles. However, because of their location and function, they are less apt to get injured from overuse or improper use than are muscles or tendons.

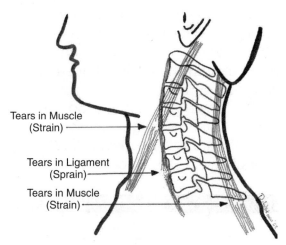

Figure C.6 A sprain typically means tears in tendons or ligaments, whereas a strain is tears in the muscle fiber. Muscles typically heal quicker than tendons or ligaments because they have greater circulation (among other reasons).

Ligaments are usually injured when a joint is moved beyond its normal range or when the muscles supporting the joint are weak and force the ligaments to do more than their share of securing the joint. By far, this happens in drummers/percussionists most when muscles are fatigued and the ligament takes the full force of the movement, causing small tears to varying degrees. You know when this happens because it hurts immediately.

Rarely does a drummer/percussionist encounter a situation that puts enough stress to a joint to force it further than its normal range. This is usually a sudden, unexpected move mostly encountered during moving equipment and marching and such.

Tearing of ligament tissues sends an alert to the brain, and the body responds by causing the muscles around the area to contract in an effort to stop movement of the joint. Further movement of the joint could cause more stress on an already damaged ligament. Every damaged fiber is one less to add stability and strength to the area, making the soft tissue more at risk for injury.

Ligaments typically take around twelve weeks to heal. During this process, the joint should be stabilized (usually with a brace of some sort) to keep the ligaments from being moved and further damaged.

It is necessary to see your doctor if you believe you have a ligament injury. You doctor should oversee all care.

The player can help increase the circulation and restore strength to the muscles that protect the joint by trying some basic massage techniques as mentioned previously (see Section A.2). Rarely is a ligament injured without a surrounding muscle also being injured.

After the ligaments begin to heal in the first week or two, you may begin using the joint (playing) at about 50 percent of normal intensity and time. If the injury begins to hurt during the playing, back off and try it again the next day. You should find that each day you can play longer and with more intensity.

It is important that you do not push the ligament to do more than it can, or further damage may occur. Gradually, you will reach your maximum level. If you push the playing when it hurts, the healing will take longer and your chances of full recovery will be greatly decreased.

C.7: WHAT IS A BLISTER?

The skin has two parts to it: the dermis (inner layer) and the epidermis (outer layer). The epidermis is made of seven layers of skin that get harder as it makes its way to the outer layers of the body as each successive layer wears off. If the outer skin is holding something, or moving excessively, the layers can loosen and rub on each other, causing friction, irritation, and swelling that forms a pocket of clear fluid or blood (see Figure C.7).

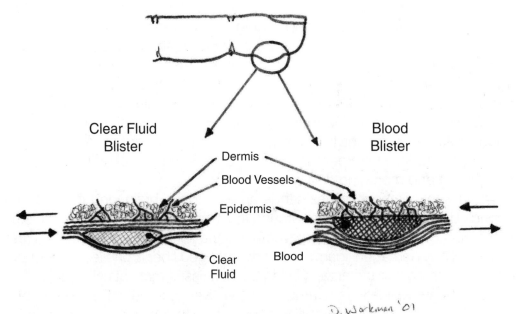

Figure C.7   This figure illustrates the differences between the clear fluid blister and blood blister. Blisters are a sign that the body is being used in ways that it shouldn't be. Corrections should be made.

If the blister goes deep enough, it can break very small blood vessels in the skin and cause blood to collect in a pocket between the skin layers (see Figure C.8). The fluid may gradually dissipate or move its way to the surface and eventually burst.

If the blister is popped prematurely, it may get infected in the deeper layers of skin. Signs of infection include swelling, redness, extreme tenderness to the touch, and possible oozing of pus or fluid from the sore. This is much more painful and takes longer to heal. They heal well on their own if the source of irritation is stopped and the sore is left alone. They usually heal in about a week—sometimes longer if the blister is larger.

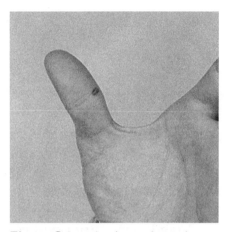

Figure C.8 This figure shows the typical appearance of a healing blood blister on the thumb.

C.8: WHAT IS A TRIGGER POINT?

The body moves in many ways (some you don't even know about), and there are muscles that perform every movement. That is a lot of muscles. Many times if something goes wrong with a muscle, it is usually caused by overuse, overload, overstretching, stress, cold weather, trauma, postexercise stiffness, or being within the pain area of another trigger point. Note that all of these causes are outside the normal function of the muscle. When something like this happens to a muscle, it causes tightness in the muscle

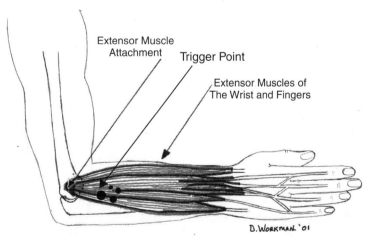

Figure C.9 This figure shows a trigger point in the belly of a muscle (large black dot). Note the lactic acid trapped within the muscle (black dots) because of the decreased flow of blood from the area through the veins.

and disrupts the flow of blood and nutrients to it and the flow of lactic acid and garbage from it.

To understand the implications of that, let me explain how the muscle functions normally. Blood is shipped into the muscle through thick, strawlike tubes called **arteries**. The blood gives the muscle food and nutrition. The muscle uses these to help it move (much like a car uses gas). When it has finished using the nutrients, there is always waste left over that must be thrown out (much like a car must throw out exhaust). Those waste products (garbage) are emptied into the **veins**—strawlike tubes that are much more flimsy than arteries but have a similar function. They return garbage-carrying blood back to the areas that empty it from the body.

So, arteries carry good blood to the muscles, and then veins pick up the garbage and return it to areas that empty it from the body. Although both are necessary, it is obviously more important that the muscles get nutrients than dispose of the garbage, because without food the muscle cannot function and may die. For this reason, arteries are the thicker and stronger of the two so they do not get damaged or compressed as easily.

Now, back to the tight muscle. Once the muscle gets damaged in any way, swelling occurs that causes pressure around the veins and arteries (vessels), which compresses them. However, because the veins are not as thick and strong as the arteries, they get squeezed, and the flow of garbage out of the area is slowed or stopped. The arteries are still able to supply the area with some nutrients but not enough to keep the muscle at its full strength. This is much like a person who hasn't eaten for some time and is weak from hunger.

The garbage that can't get out sits in a pocket within the muscle. It is called lactic acid, and it burns—especially when you press on it. This pocket of lactic acid is called a **trigger point**. The name came from the fact that when you press on it, you trigger an involuntary jump or jerk. Trigger points are very painful.

There are two types of trigger points: **active** and **latent**. The active trigger points cause obvious pain. The latent trigger points lie in the muscle without obvious pain, but they usually cause weakness and restrict movement of the area (without causing decrease in muscle size).

The latent trigger point can become active by anything causing a trigger point, being in a shortened position for extended periods of time (such as sleeping wrong), or sleeping in a position that puts pressure on a trigger point (which prevents one from getting proper restful REM sleep).

Active trigger points cause increased pain with stretches, heavy use of the muscle, and pressure on them. The pain from an active trigger point is very noticeable after a time of inactivity (sleeping) or after staying in the same position for an extended period of time. An active trigger point (even one that has moved from latent to active) will refer pain to another area, often far from it. This is called a *referred pain pattern* and is a deep, intense, stinging or burning feeling or bruised kind of pain.

In addition, *secondary trigger points* usually develop in the muscles that are neighbors, or stabilizing muscles, to the original trigger point muscle. They have to cover for it or remain tight in panic from the injury to the area. This causes other trigger points to develop.

Muscles can learn to avoid pain such as that from a trigger point. In doing this, they refuse to do the things that hurt, and they guard from doing certain movements. This

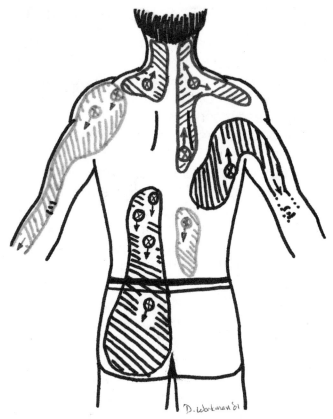

Figure C.10   Referred pain (shaded areas) from a trigger point (X) is common. This means that when the trigger point is located in one area, you may feel pain caused by that trigger point in a totally different area.

increasingly limits the movements of that muscle. In short, the body compensates for natural movements by replacing them with suboptimal substitutes. This change forces other muscles to do things that they weren't designed to do, causing more muscle damage and injury.

You can see how this can have a domino effect of injury after injury. The only way to correct it is go back and fix each and every injury, retrain the body to do things properly, and avoid the "no pain, no gain" trap.

Those most vulnerable to trigger points are females, those who are sedentary, and those in their middle years. Interestingly enough, those who use their muscles vigorously and daily have fewer problems with them. The muscles most affected are those that support the body's posture, such as the neck, shoulders, lower back, pelvis, and face and jaw areas.

Normal muscles do not have trigger points, tight knots, pain or twitching on pressure, or referred pain. If you have these symptoms, you need to get them taken care of—they are not normal. See your doctor (preferably one with sports experience or a chiropractor), and have them take care of it, or refer you to the proper person for treatment.

C.9: RHEUMATOID ARTHRITIS VERSUS DEGENERATIVE ARTHRITIS

When someone hears that he or she has arthritis, there is a sense of mild panic. As a doctor, I discuss the various types of arthritis to patients on a daily basis. Of the many types of arthritis, the type I see most is osteoarthritis—commonly called degenerative arthritis. Simply put, it is the natural aging process, perhaps accelerated. *Osteo* means bone, and *arthritis* means joint inflammation. If I had to have arthritis, this is the one I would choose.

There are many other types of arthritis, and it can be very confusing to figure out the various types and their symptoms.

The main types of arthritis are inflammatory and noninflammatory. The *noninflammatory arthritides* are few, and osteoarthritis is by far the most common in this category. The first step to take when diagnosing arthritis is to find out if it is inflammatory or noninflammatory. If it is inflammatory, it is almost sure to be osteoarthritis.

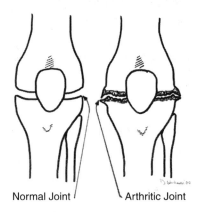

Normal Joint | Arthritic Joint

Figure C.11 This figure shows an example of a normal joint (left) and a joint with degenerative arthritis (right). Degenerative arthritis is commonly the result of wearing down of the joint from improper use (rheumatoid is hereditary).

Inflammatory arthritides are those that cause swelling, redness, and heat. The inflammatory arthritides are many and diverse. For this reason, I have selected the most widely known inflammatory arthritis, rheumatoid, and compared it to osteoarthritis, the most common noninflammatory arthritis, so you can see some of their major differences. The more you look at them, the less confusing it becomes. There are many more symptoms to compare, but Table C.1 outlines these are the most obvious to see when differentiating the two.

Table C.1 Differences between Osteoarthritis and Rheumatoid Arthritis

Findings	Osteoarthritis (Degenerative Arthritis)	Rheumatoid Arthritis
Swelling	No (noninflammatory)	Yes (inflammatory)
Pain or stiffness	Usually only one joint; fingers and large joints	Usually many joints; wrist and hands
Anti-inflammatories	Not much relief	Helps greatly
Joints hot or swollen	Rarely	Great amount
Other body symptoms	Rarely	Very common
In the blood	Not much	Yes
On both sides of the body	No	Yes
Bone changes	Bone spurs	Bone erosions

If you can see from this table that you do not have degenerative arthritis, you should consult a doctor who specializes in arthritides (rheumatologist). If you do have degenerative arthritis, follow the guidelines in previous chapters that address degenerative arthritis for your area of pain, and if you aren't getting relief, see your physician for further advice.

Figure C.12 Above is an example of the typical shoe anatomy. Although there are many special types of shoes, they all have these things in common.

C.10: PROPER SHOE SELECTION

A good shoe should protect the feet in many ways. First, it is designed to cushion you from the ground, so it should have good padding in the midsole and innersole. Next, it should hold to the foot, which enables it to function properly with support to avoid injury. A shoe must not fight the foot's natural movement, or blisters, joint problems, or even stress fractures (over a period of time) can occur.

The shoe should provide support to the foot, especially the arch and the ankle. The entire shoe contributes to the support. The heel counter supports the sides of heel (and thus the ankle) so it doesn't wobble around and cause muscle and ligament pain. The midsole provides support to the bottom of the foot to hold the arch from falling and the foot from rolling inward (flat foot). This can be very painful and cause numerous injuries, leading to serious foot problems later in life.

Figure C.13 This figure shows an example of a shoe worn by a person with pronation problems (left) and supination problems (right). Notice how the shoe rolls to the inside on pronation, and to the outside on supination. This is because the person walks on the inside of the feet on pronation and the outsides of the feet on supination. This puts the person at risk for ankle sprains.

In this day and age, there is a type of shoe to fit every activity. There are shoes that are made especially for women's feet, shoes made for people of various weight, and shoes made for various functions. The following is a brief description of the features needed in a shoe for the various drum/percussion areas. This is meant only as general advice; go to a reputable athletic shoe store for more advice. If you have a foot problem, I strongly recommend that you see your podiatrist (foot doctor) for advice on the type of shoe to buy.

SITTING MUSICIANS

No matter what kind of drums/percussion someone is involved in, great stresses are placed on the feet. Drummers who sit (such as drum set players and hand drummers) need a shoe that allows ventilation and freedom of movement. Support and cushion is not as important in this type of playing. The shoe should have a soft leather or thin nylon upper with ventilation to cool and dry the feet. The midsole should be thin and flexible, especially in the forefoot, to allow the feet to move in relation to the pedals. A good example of this type of shoe is a runner's racing flat or a kickboxing shoe.

STANDING MUSICIANS

Those who spend a lot of time standing require a shoe with good stability, ventilation, and a highly cushioned midsole. The stability is required to assist the foot in holding the body properly. A good heel counter and arch support help keep the foot in proper position without wearing out the muscles and ligaments. A good example of this type of shoe is a running or walking shoe.

MOVING MUSICIANS

In a more demanding situation such as marching, a strong stability shoe is necessary. Heel counter and arch support are essential to support the foot, keeping it from turning out. If the foot can preserve energy, the musician can march longer and have the support necessary to avoid injury. This shoe should also be well ventilated for marching in heat and be capable of keeping feet warm in cold weather. A good example of this type of shoe is a hiking boot or athletic cross trainer.

GUIDELINES FOR BUYING SHOES

1. *Prime time:* Buy in the afternoon, because the foot has been in use and is its normal size (feet swell to a larger size when they are in use).
2. *Trial run:* Try on both shoes, and wear the socks you will typically be wearing with them. Walk or run around in them while in the store.
3. *Variety:* Try several types and several brands to see what is most comfortable for your foot.
4. *Good measure:* You should be able to fit a thumb's width between the end of the shoe and your longest toe.
5. *Good fit:* Make sure that the shoe fits snugly around the heel and loosely around the toe area and flexes where your foot does. They should feel good from the very start.
6. *Quality check:* Check the quality of their construction (i.e., materials, gluing, stitching, smooth inside).
7. *In with the new:* Get a new pair of shoes every season (they lose their support ability).

GLOSSARY OF TERMS

Abdomen: That part of the body between the rib cage and the pelvis. It contains the abdominal cavity and the abdominal organs.

Abdominal: Pertaining to the abdomen.

Acetaminophen: A medicine that relieves pain and relieves or reduces fever.

Acromion: The lateral extension of the spine to the scapula, forming the highest point of the shoulder.

Acute: Sharp; having severe symptoms and a short course.

Aerobic: Living and growing in the presence of free oxygen.

Agony: Extreme suffering.

Anaerobic: Living and growing in the absence of molecular oxygen.

Aneurysm: An abnormal blood-filled dilatation of a blood vessel and especially an artery resulting from disease of the vessel wall.

Anal: Relating to the anus (the opening of the rectum on the body surface).

Antacid: An agent that counteracts acidity.

Anti-inflammatory: Counteracting or suppressing inflammation; also, an agent that so acts.

Anus: The opening of the rectum on the body surface.

Arthropathy: A disease of a joint.

Benign: Not malignant; not recurrent; favorable for recovery.

Biomechanical: Applying mechanical laws to living structures.

Biomechanics: The application of mechanical laws to living structures.

Blood: The fluid circulating through the heart, arteries, capillaries, and veins, carrying nutriment and oxygen to body cells and removing waste products and carbon dioxide.

Bowel: The intestine.

Bruise: An injury involving rupture of small blood vessels and discoloration without a break in the overlying skin.

Bulla: A blister; a circumscribed, fluid-containing, elevated lesion of the skin, usually more than five millimeters in diameter.

Bursa: A fluid-filled sac or saclike cavity situated in places in tissues where friction would otherwise occur.

Buttock(s): The back of a hip that forms one of the fleshy parts on which a person sits.

Calf (calves): The fleshy back part of the leg below the knee.

Callus: Localized hyperplasia (abnormal increase in size of normal tissue or organ) of the horny layer of the epidermis due to pressure or friction.

Cardiologist: A physician skilled in the diagnosis and treatment of heart disease.

Cervical: Pertaining to the neck or to the cervix.

Chill: A sensation of cold with convulsive shaking of the body.

Chronic: Persisting for a long time.

Coccyx: Triangular bone formed usually by fusion of the last three to five vertebrae.

Compensation: To make up for (something).

Compliance: Willingness to follow or consent to another's wishes.

Conservative: Designed to preserve health, restore function, and repair structures by nonradical methods.

Constipation: Infrequent or difficult evacuation of feces.

Constricting: A narrowing or compression of a part; a stricture.

Contraction: A drawing together; a shortening or shrinkage.

Contusion: Injury to tissue usually without laceration.

Cornified: Converted into horny (harder) tissue; keratinized.

Cortex: An outer layer, as the bark of the trunk or the rind of a fruit, or the outer layer of an organ or other structure, as distinguished from its inner substance.

Cramp: A painful spasmotic muscular contraction.

Crepitation: A dry, crackling sound or sensation, such as that produced by the grating of the ends of a fractured bone.

Cyst (cystic): Any closed, epithelium-lined cavity or sac, normal or abnormal, usually containing liquid or semisolid material.

Defecate (defecation, defecating): To evacuate fecal matter from the rectum.

Deficit: A lack or deficiency.

Deformation: Change for the worse.

Degeneration: Deterioration of a tissue or an organ in which its function is diminished or its structure is impaired.

Derangement: Disarrangement of a part or organ.

Disorder: A derangement or abnormality of function; a morbid physical or mental state.

Dysfunction: Disturbance, impairment, or abnormality of functioning of an organ.

Effusion: Escape of a fluid into a part.

Embolism: The sudden obstruction of a blood vessel by an embolus.

Engorgement: Local congestion; distention with fluids.

Epidermal: Pertaining to the epidermis.

Epidermis: The outermost and nonvascular layer of the skin.

Epithelium: The cellular covering of internal and external body surfaces, including the lining of vessels and small cavities.

Ergonomic(s): An applied science concerned with designing and arranging things people use so that the people and things interact most efficiently and safely.

Erosion: The state of being eroded.

Extensive: Covering a wide area; great in scope.

Fascia: A sheet or band of fibrous tissue such as lies deep to the skin or invests muscles and various body organs.

Femur: The thighbone.

Fissure: A break or slit in tissue usually at the junction of skin and mucous membrane.

Glossary of Terms

Fluidity: Able to flow, or likely to change.

Fracture: The breaking of a part, especially a bone.

Fray: To break threads by hard wear.

Friction: The act of rubbing.

Frostbite: To affect or injure by frost or frostbite.

Gait: A manner of walking or moving on foot.

Gastrocnemius: A muscle that plantar flexes the foot and flexes the knee joint (aka calf muscle).

Gastroenterologist: A physician specializing in the study of the stomach and intestine and their diseases.

Gastroesophageal: Of, relating to, or involving the stomach and esophagus.

Genetic: Pertaining to reproduction or to birth or origin. Inherited.

Genetics: The study of the possible genetic factors influencing the occurrence of a pathologic condition.

Genital: Pertaining to reproduction or to the reproductive organs.

Gluteal: Pertaining to the buttocks.

Hunchback: Kyphosis (increased midback curve).

Hydration: The absorption of or combination with water.

Hyperextension: Extreme or excessive extension of a limb or part.

Hyperlordosis: Increase of the lordotic curve (lower back).

Immobilization: The rendering of a part incapable of being moved.

Impingement: Encroach, infringe.

Infarct: An area of necrosis in a tissue or organ resulting from obstruction of the local circulation by a thrombus or embolus.

Infection: Invasion and multiplication of microorganisms in body tissues, especially that causing local cellular injury.

Inflammation: A protective tissue response to injury or destruction of tissues, which serves to destroy, dilute, or wall off both the injurious agent and the injured tissues.

Inguinal: Pertaining to the groin.

Instability: Lack of stability.

Intensity: The quality or state of being concentrated.

Intricate: Having many complexly interrelating parts or elements; complicated.

Involuntary: Not intended.

Isometric: Maintaining or pertaining to the same measure of length; of equal dimensions.

Isotonic: Of equal tension.

Lance (lancing): To cut or incise with a lancet.

Ligament: A band of fibrous tissue connecting bones or cartilages, serving to support and strengthen joints.

Lumbar: Pertaining to the loins (lower back area).

Macrotrauma: A lesion or injury that is larger than microscopic.

Manipulation: Skillful or dextrous treatment by the hands.

Malignant: Tending to infiltrate, metastasize, and terminate fatally.

Membrane: A thin layer of tissue that covers a surface, lines a cavity, or divides a space or organ.

Microtear: Small tears in an object or tissue.

Microtrauma: A microscopic lesion or injury.

Migraine: A condition marked by recurrent severe headache often with nausea and vomiting.

Mucinous: Resembling, or marked by formation of, mucin (chief constituent of mucus).

Nausea: An unpleasant sensation vaguely referred to the epigastrium and abdomen, with a tendency to vomit.

Nerve: A macroscopic, cordlike structure comprising a collection of nerve fibers that convey impulses between a part of the central nervous system and some other body region.

Nucleus: The central part of a whole.

Oblique: Slanting, inclined.

Onset: The beginning of something (i.e., injury or pain).

Orthosis: An orthopedic appliance or apparatus used to support, align, prevent, or correct deformities or to improve function of movable parts of the body.

Orthotics: The field of knowledge relating to orthoses and their use.

Patella: Bone that lies over the anterior knee, usually referred to as the "kneecap."

Pectoralis: Muscle overlying the chest area.

Pliable: Readily bent or influenced.

Podiatrist: A specialist in the field dealing with the study and care of the foot, including its anatomy, pathology, medical and surgical treatment, and so forth.

Proctologist: One who studies disorders of the rectum and anus.

Prognosis: A forecast of the probable course and outcome of a disorder.

Pronation: The act of assuming the face-down position in the foot, it means rotating the sole of the foot more flat to the ground.

Protrusion: Extension beyond the usual limits, or above a plane surface.

Puberty: The period during which the secondary sex characteristics begin to develop and the capability of sexual reproduction is attained.

Quadriceps: The greater extensor muscle of the front of the thigh that is divided into four parts.

Rectum: The distal portion of the large intestine.

Recur (recurrent, recurrence):   Returning after a remission; reappearing.

Reflux: A flowing back.

Rejuvenate: To give youthful vigor to.

Rheumatologist: A specialist in a variety of disorders marked by inflammation, degeneration, or metabolic derangement of the connective tissue structures, especially the joints and related structures, and attended by pain, stiffness, or limitation of motion.

Rhomboids: A set of muscles in the midback that retract and fix the scapula (shoulder blade) against the rib cage.

Rigidity: Inflexibility or stiffness.

Rotation: The process of turning around an axis.

Rudiments: A basic principle or element or a fundamental skill; usually used in plural.

Rupture: Tearing or disruption of tissue.

Sacrum: Wedged-shaped bone formed usually by fusion of five vertebrae below lumbar vertebrae, constituting posterior wall of pelvis; usually called the "tailbone."

Sciatica: Neuralgia along the course of the sciatic nerve, most often with pain radiating into the buttock and lower limb, most commonly due to herniation of a lumbar disc.

Scrotum: The pouch containing the testes and their accessory organs.

Sebaceous: Pertaining to or secreting sebum.

Serous: Pertaining to or resembling the clear portion of any liquid separated from its more solid elements.

Skeleton (skeletal):   The hard framework of the animal body, especially that of higher vertebrates; the bones of the body collectively.

Soleus: Muscle located in the posterior deep lower leg that causes plantar flexion the foot when it contracts.

Spasm (spastic):   A sudden, violent, involuntary muscular contraction.

Sphincter: A ringlike muscle that closes a natural orifice or passage.

Spur (bone):   A bony outgrowth.

Sterile: Not producing microorganisms; free from living microorganisms.

Supination: The act of turning the palm forward or upward, or of raising the medial margin of the foot.

Symptomatic: Being a symptom of a disease.

Syndrome: A group of signs and symptoms that occur together and characterize a particular abnormality.

Synovia (synovial membrane):   The transparent, viscid fluid secreted by the synovial membrane and found in joint cavities, bursae, and tendon sheaths.

Temple: The lateral region on either side of the head, above the zygomatic arch.

Tendonitis: Inflammation of tendons and of tendon–muscle attachments.

Thoracic: Pertaining to the chest.

Thorax: The chest; the part of the body between the neck and the respiratory diaphragm, encased by the ribs.

Tibia: The medial and the larger of the two bones of the lower leg.

Tinnitus: A noise in the ears, which may at times be heard by people other than the patient.

Trauma: A wound or injury, whether physical or psychic.

Trigger point: Aka myofascial trigger point. A hyperirritable spot, usually within a taut band of skeletal muscle or in the muscle's fascia, that is painful on compression and that can give rise to characteristic referred pain, tenderness, and autonomic phenomena.

Tumor: Neoplasm; a new growth of tissue in which cell multiplication is uncontrolled and progressive.

Ulcer: A local defect, or excavation of the surface of an organ or tissue, produced by sloughing of necrotic inflammatory tissue.

Vascularity: The condition of having a good blood supply.

Vessel: Any channel for carrying a fluid, such as blood or lymph.

REFERENCES

Berkow, Robert, M.D., and Andrew J. Fletcher, M.B., B.Chir. *The Merck Manual of Diagnosis and Therapy*. New Jersey: Merck Sharp and Dohme Research Laboratories, 1987.

DeGowin, Richard L., M.D., F.A.C.P. *Bedside Diagnostic Examination–Fifth Edition*. New York: Macmillan, 1987.

Dorland's Pocket Medical Dictionary–Twenty-Third Edition. Philadelphia: W.B. Saunders, 1982.

Fitzpatrick, Thomas S., Machiel K. Polano, and Dick Suurmond. *Color Atlas and Synopsis of Clinical Dermatology*. New York: McGraw-Hill.

Goroll, Allan H., M.D., Lawrence A. May, M.D., and Albert G. Mulley Jr., M.D., M.P.P. *Primary Care Medicine Office Evaluation and Management of the Adult Patient–Second Edition*. Philadelphia: J.B. Lippincott, 1987.

Guyton, Arthur C., M.D. *Textbook of Medical Physiology–Seventh Edition*. Philadelphia: W.B. Saunders, 1986.

Hoppenfeld, Stanley, M.D. *Physical Examination of the Spine and Extremities*. Norwalk: Appleton-Century-Crofts, 1976.

———. *Orthopaedic Neurology: A Diagnostic Guide to Neurologic Levels*. Philadelphia: J.B. Lippincott.

Marieb, Elaine, R.N. *Human Anatomy and Physiology—Second Edition*. Benjamin/Cummings Series in the Life Sciences. New York: Benjamin/Cummings, 1992.

Mazion, John M., Ph.B., D.C., D.A.B.C.O. *Illustrated Manual of Neurological Reflexes/Signs/Tests, Orthopedic Signs/Tests/Maneuvers for Office Procedure*. Phoenix: Imperial Litho/Graphics, 1980.

McKenzie, Robin, O.B.E., F.C.S.P., F.N.Z.S.P. (Hon) DIP. M.T. *Treat Your Own Back–Sixth Edition*. Waikanae, New Zealand: Spinal Publications, 1993.

———. *Treat Your Own Neck–Second Edition*. Waikanae, New Zealand: Spinal Publications, 1993.

McMinn, R.M.H., and R.T. Hutchings. *Color Atlas of Human Anatomy*. Chicago: Year Book Medical Publishers, 1985.

McNaught, Ann B., M.B., B.Chir., Ph.D., and Robin Callander, F.F.Ph., F.M.A.A., A.I.M.B.I. *Illustrated Physiology*. New York: Churchill Livingstone, 1983.

The New Webster's Dictionary. New York: Lexicon Publications, 1990.

Roy, Steven, M.D., and Richard Irvin, A.T., C., Ed.D. *Sports Medicine Prevention, Evaluation, Management, and Rehabilitation*. Upper Saddle River, NJ: Prentice Hall, 1983.

References

Sataloff, Robert Thayer, M.D., Alice G. Bandfonbrener, M.D., and Richard J. Lederman, M.D. *Textbook of Performing Arts Medicine.* New York: Raven Press, 1991.

Siler, Brooke. *The Pilates Body.* New York: Broadway Books, 2000.

Tkac, Deborah, and editors of Prevention Magazine Health Books. *The Doctors Book of Home Remedies: Thousands of Tips and Techniques Anyone Can Use to Heal Everyday Health Problems.* Emmaus: Rodale Press, 1990.

Travell, Janet G., M.D., and David G. Simons, M.D. *Myofascial Pain and Dysfunction: The Trigger Point Manual; The Upper Extremities Volume 1.* Baltimore: Williams and Wilkins, 1983.

Webster's Dictionary and Thesaurus. New York: Shooting Star Press, 1995.

Yochum, Terry R., and Lindsay Rowe. *Essentials of Skeletal Radiology: Volume One and Volume Two.* Baltimore: Williams and Wilkins, 1987.

INDEX

Index

Vascularity, 11; *see also* Arteries; Veins; Vessels
Veins, 10–11, 18, 285–286
 injured, 97, 164
Vertebrae, 245
 fracture, 196; *see also* Fracture, cervical;
 Fracture, sacrum
Vesicle, 41, 101
Vessels, 6, 10–11; *see also* Arteries; Veins
Virus, papilloma, 105; *see also* Warts
Vocal cords, 198, 199, 227; *see also* Voice
 coughing, 228
Voice, 197–199, 227–228
 exercises, 199, 223

W

Walking, 46, 87, 89, 99, 261
 damage, 94, 142
 program, 104, 112, 261

Warm-up, 15–17, 68
 clock, 254
 voice, 233; *see also* Exercises, voice
Warts, plantar, 105–106; *see also* Virus,
 papilloma
Waste, 10, 286
Weaver's bottom, 138–139; *see also* Bursitis,
 ischio-gluteal
Whitfield's ointment, 104
Wrist
 injuries, Sec1:vii
 problems, 31, 33, 38, 39, 60
 technique, 25, 27, 28, 34
 treatment, 26, 30, 32, 34

Y

Yoga, 76

ABOUT THE AUTHOR

Darin "Dutch" Workman is a doctor of chiropractic, practicing in Houston, Texas. He works with music-, performing-, and sports-related injuries. He has a bachelor of science degree in human biology and is a certified chiropractic sports physician.

He has authored and conducted numerous injury-prevention articles and workshops over the years and is currently finishing a book on ergonomics and prevention and treatment of drumming injuries. Dr. Workman is the chairman of the Percussive Arts Society's Health and Wellness Committee and is a member of the Performing Arts Medical Association. A drummer/ percussionist for more than thirty years, he continues to be active in performing and teaching.